Your Life After Trauma

Your Life After Trauma

Powerful Practices to Reclaim Your Identity

MICHELE ROSENTHAL

W. W. Norton & Company

NEW YORK · LONDON

Copyright ©2015 by Michele Rosenthal
All rights reserved
Printed in the United States of America
FIRST EDITION

For information about permission to reproduce selections from this book, write to
Permissions, W. W. Norton & Company, Inc., 500 Fifth Avenue, New York, NY 10110

For information about special discounts for bulk purposes, please contact
W. W. Norton Special Sales at specialsales@wwnorton.com or 800-233-4830

Manufacturing by Quad Graphics Fairfield
Book design by Kristina Kachele Design, llc
Production manager: Leeann Graham

Library of Congress Cataloging-in-Publication Data
Rosenthal, Michele, 1968–
Your life after trauma : powerful practices to reclaim your identity / Michele Rosenthal.
—First edition.
pages cm
Includes bibliographical references and index.
ISBN 978-0-393-70900-1 (hardcover)
1. Post-traumatic stress disorder. 2. Psychic trauma. 3. Stress (Psychology) I. Title.
RC552.P67R674 2015
616.85′21—dc23
2014021358

ISBN: 978-0-393-70900-1

W. W. Norton & Company, Inc., 500 Fifth Avenue, New York, N. Y. 10110
www.wwnorton.com
W. W. Norton & Company Ltd., Castle House, 75/76 Wells Street, London W1T 3QT

1 2 3 4 5 6 7 8 9 0

For you,
in honor of your courage to imagine
you can choose who you are,
love how you live, and
create a meaningful life after trauma

Contents

Acknowledgments

The contents of this book have been percolating for over thirty years. They began with the loss of my identity at the unnerving age of thirteen. A decade later I launched a quest to understand the theory of how we define ourselves—and how we might redefine ourselves when the need occurs. The urge for a synthesized program intensified as I wandered my post-trauma world repeatedly asking, "Who am I?" Finally, I discovered the delicate process of restoring my identity, which transformed the desire for answers into a calling to share these ideas with others who might find them useful.

A personal quest to do something meaningful in the world is never wholly "personal" in the individual sense—it becomes a group project. This book owes its presence to Andrea Dawson Costella, who landed on the HealMyPTSD.com website and wondered if I might like to write a book. Thank you, Andrea, for letting me think too big, reigning me in when the book needed to be smaller, giving me the most creative freedom a writer could ever hope for, and always enthusiastically embracing those unexpected phone calls when I just had to share an idea live and in person.

If Andrea's dedication to creating the best book possible was my first introduction to the quality of the W. W. Norton team it only prepared me to work with a slew of like-minded souls. Thanks to the whole W. W. Norton family (named and unnamed here) for helping me do what I most love to do: help survivors affirm life by redefining who they are and how they live. Special thanks must be mentioned to the following team members: Kevin Olsen and Rebecca Shaughnessey whose marketing approach and care are extraordinary. Sarah Peterson for patiently explaining (and re-explaining) the fine details of permissions. Katie

Moyer who deftly juggled all the moving pieces of production. Plus, Rachel Keith whose sensitive reading of the manuscript took the art of copyediting to a whole new level.

I'm not a science girl, which means that initially I was not entirely comfortable with the scientific aspect of this book. Transforming myself into a science geek happened in the hands of some wonderful colleagues who made me see that science isn't really all that scary. Great thanks is owed to cognitive neuroscientist, Dr. Andrew Hill, who not only offered hours of conversation and explanation, but also reviewed the most hard-core science passages for accuracy. Thanks also to Hysell Oviedo and Dr. Michael E. Smith for lending your editorial eye and insights and helping me better understand how the brain does what it does in response to traumatic events.

We don't heal in isolation; we heal in community. Special thanks go to the numerous online community members who have so willingly and tirelessly helped me build a positive virtual healing space. Extra appreciation must be mentioned for all of the survivors who so bravely contributed statements of personal identity restoration to this book. You rock! We are truly all in this together.

Since I can't name every colleague and expert who has collaborated with me over the years the following people represent and carry my gratitude for all who have shared perspectives and insights in conversations, meetings, connections and particularly in interviews on my radio show as we continue to illuminate the many paths to recovery: Dr. Cheryl Arutt, Martha Beck, Dr. David Berceli, Dr. Larry Dossey, Dr. Bruce Dow, Dr. Patricia Gerbarg, Dr. Tania Glenn, Dr. Mark Goulston, Dr. Rick Hanson, Tom Kavanaugh, Peter A. Levine, Belleruth Naparstek, Bill O'Hanlon, Carre Otis, Dr. Alex Pattakos, Suzanne Phillips, Dena Rosenbloom, Babette Rothschild, Dr. Robert Scaer, Cheryl Schlitz, Dr. Bernie Siegel, Dr. Dan Siegel, Dr. Ron Siegel, Dr. Francine Shapiro, Dr. Ed Tick, Priscilla Warner, Mary Beth Williams, Lee Woodruff and Dr. Rachel Yehuda.

As the saying goes, "a writer writes", which means her focus isn't exactly in the legal details of bookmaking. Luckily Sheila Levine looks out for me with terrifically strategic, kind, supportive and genuine legal counsel. So glad I have you in my corner as both lawyer and friend.

I've needed a playground to test out these concepts and tweak them when necessary. Enormous gratitude to my peeps—on air, online and offline—for allowing me to make some crazy suggestions and for trying on the ideas with a spirit of discovery and exploration. Together we have strengthened my theories and fortified the philosophies with the real experience of sound choices and deliberate actions.

I'm always telling my audience, "I believe in you!" To me, those four words are the essence of hope and possibility. If you have breathed that essence into my life in some way and I haven't mentioned you here, please know my unending appreciation and that it's only a matter of space that stops me from listing all the people who have touched me in that way.

Writing demands sacrifice, so my final and most heartfelt thanks goes to the people who bore the burden of that sacrifice and unconditionally supported and loved me through it: My parents, Eileen and Gary, thank you so much for embracing the idea of seeing me less than you would have liked to because "I'm writing!" was my frequent response to invited gatherings. My brother, Bret, our (always too short) weekly lunches have turned into fantastic sibling masterminds that make up for the reduced time we've had to spend together. Baylee, my furry boy, I owe you a lot of playtime on the beach but deeply appreciate your willingness to curl up under my desk and be near while I banged away at the keyboard. Finally, John, my beloved, you gave up so many nights of dancing without a single complaint. Muchisimas gracias, mi amor. To all of you, I plan to make up for the sacrifices now that this book is complete!

Introduction

Jeff is a very successful businessman. So successful, in fact, that he has founded his own company, the building and logo of which tower high above the skyline of a major American city. Jeff is also a survivor of post-traumatic stress disorder (PTSD) due to extreme childhood abuse at the hands of his father. Since a triggering event ten years ago, Jeff has experienced chronic PTSD. He has watched his business suffer losses due to a lack of leadership resulting from his withdrawal, isolation, and poor executive decisions. Long known as an industry icon, Jeff now recoils from just about every aspect of regular functioning. He's so anxious he can't even open email or answer his cell phone. "Something's not right," he says in our first coaching session. "I'm not the man I used to be, and I don't think I ever will be."

Kim is a social worker for the Department of Children and Families. Four years ago her husband died quickly from a shocking cancer diagnosis. Since then Kim has been unable to sleep, has had frequent nightmares, has ostracized herself at the agency, and has suffered chest pains, nausea, and frequent adrenaline rushes. By the time we begin working together, she's on medical leave. "It's that bad," she says, referring to the internal shift she has experienced since the trauma. "I'm separated from my mind and have gone one hundred percent into my body. I need something to hit me in my head to get me back to where I should be."

Saadia is a beautiful Egyptian twenty-two-year-old who was recently beaten and raped by a man who refused to let her end their romantic relationship. After a one-month stay in a psychiatric hospital and several months on a variety of medications that dulled her senses, she enters our first session with this proclamation: "I'm the Antichrist. Don't try to convince me otherwise." When I ask how she knows this is true, she explains that her parents have been telling her that since she was a small child. In our work together we uncover the original trauma of child abuse and how its impact—believing she was evil and deserved to be punished—set Saadia up for the domestic violence that followed years later.

You have your own story of trauma and its aftermath, so you already understand how Jeff, Kim, and Saadia feel. You already know, too, how profound the changes that trauma makes are. After trauma it's very natural to go with the flow of the changes; you do what you have to do to survive—even if that means embracing distorted behaviors, thoughts, feelings, and beliefs that might help you feel safe and in control. There are many ironies in the post-trauma world, and they are all connected by this system: You put in place a coping mechanism that allows you to feel more in control (an eating disorder, for example) or allows you to feel better (say, an addiction), only to find out later that the very mechanism you thought would help you be safer, be more in control, and feel better is actually putting you more *out* of control, placing you in more danger, and making you feel worse. Of course, it has to be this way. Survival mode is supposed to be a phase that helps save your life. It is not meant to be *how you live.*

Before and After

Ask a group of survivors struggling with posttraumatic symptoms if they feel different from who they were before the trauma, and you'll get a variety of responses. Some will shrug, roll their eyes, sigh, and sadly shake their head. Others will fight back tears as their eyes fill with both liquid and pain. Some will become completely animated, shout "Yes!" and launch into a full dissertation of their experience. No matter whom you ask or what the origin of the trauma, the response will always be affirmative: There is a big difference between Before and After, even when you can't remember or didn't have a chance to have a Before at all.

I bet this difference is another one of the things you already know about your life after trauma. You feel it. You sense it. Even if your trauma occurred before there was a "before," you know that the difference between *who you could have been* and who you are is the difference between a beautiful fireworks display and a smoking dud. Welcome to the world of post-trauma conundrums. In my own struggle to overcome posttraumatic stress disorder, the Before/After gap, as I came to call it, was an enormous issue. Trauma wrenched me from the safe cocoon of who and what I knew myself to be—facts I could count on about my beliefs, life, ideas, perceptions, and interpretations—and tossed me into a foggy, black, empty abyss in which I could see nothing clearly and, more importantly, could find no dependable ground to stand on. The only certainty I knew was that I was not who I had been or could be. Things that had been important and valuable before trauma seemed inconsequential afterward. I lost the ability to experience emotions and form meaningful personal connections. I lost the ability to feel relaxed or at peace. I lost the ability to sleep well, and often to focus or concentrate.

From my own PTSD recovery, plus the recoveries of my clients and those shared with me by the many survivors who contact me through my website, I've observed a universal identity crisis at the center of the post-trauma and PTSD experience and recovery process. If you are not who you used to be and are not living the life you used to live, then who are you now? Likewise, if you never had a chance to become the person you could have been, how are you to be comfortable with who you are today? Every healing survivor faces one or the other of these questions. The answers affect your ability to enter a healing relationship, feel safe, and remember and mourn. They are difficult questions and can cause you to feel enormously overwhelmed. Seeing who you are now, perhaps even many years after the trauma ended, may cause you to feel sadness, anger, despair, hopelessness, powerlessness, and a sense of complete internal disorientation. If your sense of a positive, connected identity has been snuffed out, how do you restore it? Helping you to discover your many personal and creative answers to that question is the mission of this book.

While as survivors we are all unique in the details of our trauma(s) and the evolution of our healing paths, we meet frequently in the space between. Whether you survived combat, sexual assault, domestic violence, child abuse, an accident, life-threatening illness, natural disaster, or any of the other slew of trauma and PTSD causes, there are certain elements of experience that are universal. It begins with the symptoms themselves. Many survivors encounter a variety of alterations like sleep disturbances, mood swings, intrusive thoughts, increased anxiety, and avoidant behaviors, to name a few. The similarities, however, go far below the superficial layer of diagnostic criteria. They go, in fact, all the way down to the soul. Frequently, PTSD is referred to as "a soul wound." Indeed, those of us who experience PTSD feel gashed at the very core of who we are. A comment on my blog was perfectly phrased: "A person that has PTSD, life has truly changed them, they are not the same person they were before. It is an identity problem as well as all the other things . . . We are not the same people we used to be . . . and it is haunting."

Past the initial shock of trauma and coping, deep into the exhaustion of PTSD and your safety strategy, you may be bumping up against exactly that profound sense of loss of self. Sometimes you can be fully present and still feel that something about you is amiss. Other times the loss of self presents as a form of *dissociation*, a feeling of detachment from your emotional state or body. *Depersonalization* is a form of dissociation that can make you feel separated from your identity or self. In ripping you from the familiar and dropping you back down in a completely unfamiliar landscape, trauma can make it seem as if you no longer know yourself at all. While any changes brought about by trauma can be stressful, a deep internal disconnection can be doubly so, as it cuts you off from a natural source of your resilience. Feeling connected to yourself allows you to access a sense of strength; lose that connection and you lose a source of fuel in your recovery effort.

Since trauma challenges entire belief systems—and since belief systems are the foundation of how you experience the world—a single instant can drastically alter how the world looks to you, plus how you look at yourself in the world. In consequence (and as a natural, instinctive response), you change yourself in accordance with the new beliefs you hold. You trust no one, see danger everywhere, and walk with a sense of powerlessness and worry even while at the same time you may develop an aggressiveness you don't understand. Slowly you morph into a tight, controlled, rigid, restrictive, anxious, fearful, numb, and disconnected individual. What happened to who you used to be? What happened to the person who believed in goodness, in safety, in connection, in your own confidence and self-efficacy, in your essential purpose and experience here on earth? Or, what happened to the person who would have believed in those things? Naturally, there's no time for that person in this new world order. You're too busy engaging in processes, actions, and behaviors designed to keep you safe and in control even while you feel that something is amiss. Even while you know that you have no choice . . . or do you?

True, you can't go back to being who you were or didn't get a chance to be. That person had never considered how much danger exists in the world or how to defend against it. Plus, that person hadn't experienced the trauma you did. But can you live as the person you are now? More importantly, do you *want* to live a rigid, inflexible, controlling, fearful, anxious, and exhaustingly on-edge life? The moment you fully recognize that your coping mechanisms are wrecking your world is the moment you begin healing. It's the moment, in fact, that you say (often without words), "I want to live!" Spoken, thought, or just vaguely intuited, those four immensely powerful words cause a sea change in recovery. They signify that on some level you are ready to let go of who you've become and start creating someone new.

We're All in This Together

In 1981, as a thirteen-year-old child, I was given a routine antibiotic for a routine infection—and suffered anything but a routine reaction. An undiscovered allergy to the medication turned me into a full-body burn victim almost overnight. Over a period of weeks I was cared for by a special burn-unit team in a quarantined hospital room. By the time I was released from the hospital, I had lost one hundred percent of my epidermis. Even more importantly, I had completely lost myself. For the next twenty-six years I struggled to ignore, deny, and fight against that loss. I worked hard to cope with symptoms of PTSD and still continue to build a life. At some of those things I excelled. At others I was completely unsuccessful. When my body and mind simultaneously imploded, I finally hightailed it to therapy and dove into what I affectionately call "my healing rampage." I endured many false starts and stops, triumphs and challenges. Eventually I broke through the wall and found freedom in a life completely devoid of any posttraumatic stress symptoms. Today I am entirely PTSD-symptom free and have been for several years. Along the healing journey, I returned again and again to the idea of identity: how trauma changes us; how we can change again. I have documented my struggle and victory in constructing a successful post-trauma identity in *Before the World Intruded: Conquering the Past and Creating the Future*, an award-nominated book in which I explore trauma, PTSD, identity, and healing.

All my own private efforts toward recovery centered largely around forging a reconnection to myself. Later, when my recovery was complete, my focus switched to reclaiming a connection to others and the world—hence the birth of my website, Heal My PTSD; my *Changing Direction* radio program; and my private practice, group work, and public speaking, which further expanded my personal recovery theories into a useful program that has helped many survivors. It's in the spirit of connection and reconnection, individuality, and community that this book was written.

Reconnecting to Yourself

At its core, the disconnection problem holds you in an ongoing state of powerlessness in which you never perceive yourself as the powerful being you truly are. Your identity—how you envision, define, and experience yourself—becomes stuck in the trauma loop. At this moment you may see and feel yourself as a small, powerless trauma victim still struggling to survive. Developing a post-trauma identity shifts you out of victimhood and into a persona built on strength, competence, resolve, achievement, open-ended thinking, and a truthful expression of the person you are beneath the effects of fate. That person exists. It's up to you to seek out and claim yourself.

In her seminal 1992 book *Trauma and Recovery*, Judith Herman paved the way for powerful healing with her outline of the stages of recovery: a healing relationship, safety, remembrance and mourning, reconnection, and commonality. In the chapter titled "Reconnection," she writes, "Helplessness and isolation are the core experiences of psychological trauma. Empowerment and reconnection are the core experiences of recovery." I absolutely agree and respectfully challenge the placement of empowerment and reconnection as almost the final phase of the healing process. To me, they belong in every phase.

The good news is that reconnection, and the reconstruction of your self—of your post-trauma identity—can be achieved. With a little clarity, a lot of focus, and a healthy dose of discovery and exploration, you can connect to a sense of self that allows you to feel grounded, centered, empowered, effective, confident, strong, courageous, brave, and able. More than that, it can lead you to a place where you say, "I am ___," with a sense of pride, accomplishment, and love. The journey of rediscovering who you are—and choosing who you want to be—is what can ultimately help you break that emotional weld of trauma and loose you to experience the profound process of rebirth, reconnection, and reconstruction that trauma recovery demands. It is a process that can be implemented in any phase of recovery and used to ground you in ways that enhance the work you do either on your own or with a healing professional.

Some experts assert that identity is the quality of sameness over a period of time. Part of building your post-trauma identity, then, might involve discovering what about your pre-trauma self still remains available to you today. Other identity experts postulate that identity lies in the sameness of two objects in a singular moment. So, part of your process may involve finding a way to link your Before and After selves only in the context of the present moment. If your trauma happened so early or in such a way that you do not recall a Before self, then your opportunity will be to develop who you are regardless of any past self or lack thereof, which is also entirely possible. A post-trauma identity can include elements of who you were before, but it can also be created from what you know about who you are today, who you wish you'd had a chance to be yesterday, and who you want to be tomorrow. The opportunity for creating your Now self exists regardless of your past experiences, memories, or empty spaces. As you read the chapters in this book, you'll see that the process of creating your post-trauma identity involves creativity and decision-making driven by your choices to define who you wish to be in any moment.

In essence, constructing a post-trauma identity is all about choosing who you are. It means looking at who you've become, deciding who you want to be, and planning a path to get there. This is about an experience larger than trauma. It's about the present and the future. The objective is for the past to become a very tiny part of your very large, confident, capable, and free self.

It is worth mentioning that constructing a post-trauma identity in and of itself doesn't heal decades of posttraumatic symptoms or PTSD. In my own recovery process I used several different traditional and alternative therapeutic modalities before finding complete freedom. The benefit of constructing a post-trauma identity is that it offers a solid platform from which to develop a recovery process and identify what holds you back. It gives you a dependable sense of self from which to navigate the ups and downs of healing. After your posttraumatic symptoms have been eliminated, your new identity will also aid your transition into a life of freedom.

What You Will Find in This Book

I've designed this book to assist you in your post-trauma identity development, whether you're working alone or with a trained trauma professional. For specific recovery work connected to severe trauma, you should consider seeking the advice of a professional, especially if you feel stuck in the past. This book is not a substitute for therapy work. Instead, it is intended as a self-help resource for those who are stable enough to work alone or wish to supplement therapy or other recovery-oriented practices.

With this book you will move through a process intended to help you develop a profound sense of inner connection and integration. The stories and illustrations contained in each chapter are composites drawn from the personal healing experiences of multiple clients and other survivors with whom I've been privileged to connect. All names and many identifying characteristics have been altered.

The post-trauma identity path presented here is straightforward, but like all aspects of trauma recovery, your identity path will take its time through unexpected twists and turns. Also, you may encounter resistance to ideas because they challenge your beliefs, fears, or willingness to engage with certain topics. While the phases of post-trauma identity construction flow from one to the other, you may stay in any of these phases for as long as feels necessary, appropriate, and comfortable to you. Notice your internal feedback and pace yourself accordingly.

The evolution of your post-trauma self will robustly progress through several stages, including:

- Developing your understanding of identity
- Comprehending how possible it is for you and your brain to change
- Acknowledging and grieving who you used to be (or didn't have a chance to be)
- Recognizing and accepting who you are today
- Imagining and envisioning who you want to be tomorrow
- Identifying obstacles and finding solutions

Each chapter presents a framework for the phase to be approached, offering explanation and perspective plus exercises to help you facilitate the actual tasks of that phase. I suggest setting aside a special notebook just for your activity here so that you can consolidate your work.

If you're working on your own, you may choose to do the exercises and share your insights or explore ideas with trusted friends or colleagues. I think there's great value in developing your thoughts outside your own mind. If it feels right, I hope you'll choose a safe person with whom to share your experience of this book. If not, you might consider keeping a separate journal of what you think and feel so that you can get those ideas out of your head and into the world beyond your mind. If you're working with a therapist, the ideas and exercises in this book can lead to breakthroughs, questions, or subjects that may be enormously helpful to discuss during a session. Also, as you work through the book, the emotions and memories that the process evokes can be tremendously supported and contained in the therapeutic environment or in conversations with other people you trust.

In addition to helping you construct a post-trauma identity and assess challenges to this process, the exercises and techniques in the following chapters are designed to help you take the ideas off the page and live them in your day-to-day experience. These exercises will help you (1) clarify what you know, think, believe, and feel; (2) validate why you know, think, believe, and feel that way; (3) imagine how you would like things to be different; and (4) strategize to bring about the changes you wish to make. Some of the exercises will be based in mental practices, others will involve physical techniques, and yet others will combine the two. Some exercises will be designed to help you turn inward, others to help you turn outward. Some will focus on your personal experience; others will offer you the opportunity to engage in a sense of the world at large. Your overall desire will be to stimulate both the left and right sides of your brain, plus both your conscious and subconscious minds. When you put together all of these different approaches, you will be incorporating one hundred percent of your brain, which is an enormous asset in any recovery toolbox. By engaging all the techniques provided in this book, you will also develop skills that limber up your creativity and open your perspective in ways that support your personal growth. Supplementing the material presented in this book I have developed complimentary resources related to many of the exercises for you to download at YourLifeAfterTraumaBook.com.

Special mention should be made of Chapter 6: "Ten Common Obstacles to Creating Your Post-Trauma Identity." While this material appears at the end of the book, it is relevant in this exact moment and in every chapter. The focus of Chapter 6 is helping you diagnose and overcome popular issues that frequently hijack, slow, or stall the successful development of a post-trauma identity. While Chapters 1 through 5 are meant to be read in sequence, Chapter 6 can and should be consulted in any moment to help strengthen your approach to all of the elements contained in discovering your post-trauma identity.

Throughout these pages you'll see my ideas, plus comments from healing professionals and survivors, about answering this question:

> What can help a survivor redefine or feel connected to a comfortable sense of self after trauma?

I'm always saying, "We don't heal in isolation; we heal in community." The chorus of voices contained in this book let you know that not only are you part of a large community of people who understand your experience, but you are part of a group that intimately know what it means, what it looks like, and what is required to move forward from the past into a present and future that feels good and productive—even loving and joyful.

No matter what you've experienced, thought, felt, or believed about yourself since your trauma (and even the onset of PTSD, if that's part of your experience), remember this: The changes you've noticed, whether in your behavior, beliefs, spirituality, health and wellness, relationships, or career, are all part of the normal process of learning to live in the world now that experience has demanded that you see everything differently. Often, too, they are changes that can be changed again. Never accept the negative views of others. If someone (even a highly decorated professional) says you're damaged and will be forever, change your direction and seek out others who believe in the possibility for change; it always exists regardless of how long you've struggled or how distorted your behaviors have become. Despite what has happened yesterday or what could happen tomorrow, dare to believe in yourself and who you want to be at all times.

In yoga, when we do certain poses, it's normal for the body to shake and shift as it seeks a way to balance. We're taught to find a *drishti*, a focal point that helps the body and mind find their center, strength, and position. Think of the book you hold in your hands as your new *drishti* in restoring your life. The past cannot be changed. The present challenges you to make choices and take actions. The future stretches out before you full of opportunities to design and live as the person you most wish to become. There are zero guaranteed healing prescriptions for restoring to you the mental and physical health you desire. There are only orientation points and suggestions from which you can explore, discover, and collect into a plan ideas that speak uniquely to your own healing process and needs. While the approach in this book allows you to look backward at who you were or could have been before, the overall aim of constructing a post-trauma identity is to find a comfortable and empowered way to go forward. Actually, the true purpose in helping you reconstruct who you are is to offer you the opportunity to claim what is rightfully yours: You.

Your Life After Trauma

Trauma Has Changed You

To reclaim a comfortable, connected sense of self, find a release process you feel safe with; identify how you'd like to feel when you've completed the process; and then take the journey through the process . . . [T]he "secret sauce" to full recovery is in making the decision to take control of your life!

—*Tom Kavanaugh, MA*

When an electrical fire started in the basement of Curtis's old, wood-frame house, it didn't take long for it to completely char the three-story home—and all of Curtis's life with it. Before the disaster, Curtis was a working musician living in a suburb of Chicago. The graduate of a prestigious music school, he played four instruments, had a collection of twenty-five acoustic guitars, composed music, and was finally sketching out the concepts and preliminary tracks for his first album. At forty-two, happily married to Patricia and supporting a pack of rescued canines, Curtis felt secure and confident in his profession and life. Then the house burned to the ground while Curtis and Patricia were at a show where he was performing. Gone were the dogs he lovingly brought home from the pound. Gone were the instruments he'd been collecting since adolescence. Gone was all the music he had composed. With the exception of Patricia, everything Curtis valued and everything that had defined who he was had vanished.

"It's my fault," he cries in relating the story. "I should have paid more attention to keeping up the house, making sure it was safe. I'm the one responsible for the dogs' deaths and for us losing everything."

In truth, the problem with Curtis's house was that it was old and dry. Short of remodeling the entire home, which was beyond his budget, there was nothing Curtis could have done to foresee or prevent this tragedy. Still, Curtis shoulders the blame, which has made starting a new life a long and difficult process. The guilt and grief Curtis carries prevent him from going back to music. He hasn't played since the night of the fire, nor does he hear in his head the stanzas of music that were composing themselves for his album. He doesn't even listen to music for pleasure anymore. Now, five years after the fire, Curtis and Patricia live in a small apartment in the city of Chicago. Curtis works as a security guard in a museum.

"I like the silence," he explains. "It's the complete opposite of what my job used to be, which is appropriate because I'm living a life that's the complete opposite too. I am one hundred percent a different person, whoever that is."

With the loss of both his professional and personal sense of self, Curtis describes himself as feeling "unanchored" and "unmoored" as he drifts through the days.

"The fire changed my sense of certainty. You can't depend on or trust anything. Without the things I lost, I don't even know who I am."

The sense of losing your grip on who you are is a common experience after trauma. Whether you've experienced a life-shattering event, like Curtis, or a more subtle shift, like Erik in the following story, you probably know exactly what it feels like to lose the connection to your self-definition.

After Erik's mother and father split up before his birth, Erik was raised in a city in Germany by his single Jewish mom. When he was three, she married Erik's pediatrician, Theodor Homberger, and told Erik that the doctor was his biological father. It wasn't until Erik was older that he discovered two important facts: his "father" was really his stepfather, and his real father was a man with whom his mother had had an affair outside of her previous marriage.

The news of Erik's true family of origin disturbed him, knocking out of balance factors he had used to establish his self-definition, including family dynamics, plus a moral and ethical code and culture. As a result, Erik became confused about his identity. At his Jewish day school he was an outcast because of his Nordic features: his blond hair and blue eyes. Later, at a secular school, he was rejected because of his Jewish roots. Who was Erik really, and where did he fit in?

These experiences and questions became part of the driving force that shaped Erik's identity as one of the twentieth century's foremost psychoanalysts: Erik H. Erikson. In fact, it is believed that his own ongoing effort at self-definition is the reason that, when he became an American citizen, Erik changed his last name from Homberger to Erikson (a name he devised for himself, since he didn't know his biological father's surname). Erikson's son believes the full name was Erik's attempt to define himself as a self-made man: Erik, son of Erik.

Employed by Harvard, Yale, and other top universities, Erikson broke with the accepted Freudian perspective that personalities are set by age five and instead suggested that personalities (and thus, identities) continuously grow and develop. Erikson's own identity crisis led him to develop the "identity crisis concept," a theory that suggests that a crisis of identity is an imperative phase in development that precedes the growth of a suitable identity. Erikson outlined eight stages of development that span a lifetime and suggested that successfully overcoming each one allows a person to gain a strength that assists in future growth.

Of course, there are many theories about identity and development. Erikson's is significantly applicable to trauma, as it helps to frame and reframe a common theme among trauma survivors: After trauma, you feel changed, and during that time of demoralization it can be tempting to think the changes are permanent. They are not. Erikson's theory and professional experiences proved otherwise. From a psychological perspective, you are an individual built for constant change. The same is true for you as a scientific entity. While trauma can make you *feel* as if you have been forever altered, the truth is that you have an inherent capacity to change again, and again and again.

What Is The Post-Trauma Identity Crisis? A Basic Profile and Definition

> In trauma we are disempowered from ourselves. The recovery process is about restoring our inner power. If we follow the innate wisdom of the human organism, it knows its way back to integration and wholeness.
>
> —*Dr. David Berceli*

Every trauma survivor spends a significant amount of time longing for the past. Suffering deep psychological pain and chronic digestive ailments, Gert wistfully sighs, "I didn't realize I had it so good back then. I just want to go back and start over. I want all of that innocence and perfect health." My friend Paul muses, "Who might I have been if I hadn't begun my life in trauma?" We look back searching for an escape from the pain of the present, but there isn't one. The present *is* painful, and you will have to move through it to find relief. Doing so will challenge your commitment, resilience, dedication, and beliefs. It will also make you stronger, more confident, more capable, more flexible, more creative, and more secure. When you have completed your healing process, you will shift out of this powerless feeling into a sense of being powerful, perhaps even more than ever before.

As you begin your quest for a new identity today, you belong in one of two categories. The first is for survivors who clearly see the break between their before-trauma self and their after-trauma self. If you belong in this category, this is a difficult conundrum, because you achingly remember the dynamic being you were and that you liked so much more before the trauma. While it may seem as if seeing the past versus the present so clearly can only bring pain, there is a gift: You have memories of what you loved about that self that offer clues to the terrific individual you were and the capabilities you had. All of that can be of use to you now. Knowing you have already possessed valuable things will help you to systematically recover them or develop aspects of them in new ways.

The second category pertains to those whose trauma began so early that there is no memory of a prior self. This paradox is particularly painful, because your past is full of lost promise and seemingly void of ideas that could be helpful in framing who you are today. The gift, however, is that you have an enormous freedom to create from scratch who you've always wished you'd had the chance to become. Unencumbered by "how things used to be," your process roots in the now, plus the identity desires you ultimately give yourself permission to explore.

The real post-trauma identity crisis is this: Before trauma you were one person; afterward you have become someone else. Accepting, embracing, and redirecting the changes constitute the work of constructing your post-trauma identity. Who are you now? Who will you become? You cannot go back to who you were before, or who you wish you'd had a chance to be "if only." Whether trauma occurred in utero or in life, your past self hasn't had your experiences or learned what you did from them. To go back to your old identity, you'd have to transform into someone lacking your memory on both the psychological and biological levels. Of course, this can't be done. As of this moment, stop trying. Instead, focus on what has always been true: You are a dynamic being. Trauma has only highlighted the fact of change, plus your need to expand and deliberately engage your capacity for it.

TRAUMA CHANGES BELIEFS

[What has helped me feel more connected to my identity after trauma is]. . . [a]ccepting my scars by looking at them and reminding myself [that] it is what it is and to be thankful I am even here.

—*Gina Quarles*

A belief is a statement or concept you hold to be true based on ideas you willingly accept. Your whole life you've been forming beliefs about many things, from simple concepts like the color of the grass to more complex ideas like religion. Some of your beliefs have developed through a sort of osmosis because of the people you've been around. It's very common for children, for example, to embrace the religious beliefs their parents model. Likewise, there have been things you've witnessed and experienced that have formed and even altered your beliefs.

You are who and what you believe, because perceptions create your experience of yourself and of your world. For example, consider how Craig's trauma-related belief shows up in daily life:

Raised in a horrible situation of child abuse, in a home in which any kindness was merely a setup for pain, Craig developed the belief that "kindness is dangerous." As an adult, anytime someone was kind, Craig immediately became suspicious of her or his motive and feared future destructive action. One day in the coffee shop Craig frequented, the waitress added a free piece of pie to his meal. Even when he tried to pay for it, she insisted it was on the house because he was such a great customer. Disturbed by this act of kindness, Craig never visited the coffee shop again.

To be sure, trauma introduces questions and concepts that are difficult to integrate into a functional life. In doing so, it challenges and can even alter beliefs about your sense of self. You are faced with inevitable questions like:

- Why me?
- How do I live knowing I am vulnerable?
- How do I accept the fact that I can be victimized?
- How will I protect myself in the future?

Your responses ultimately redefine how you perceive yourself, others, and the world. In doing so, they change your identity by shifting your belief systems, which in turn shifts your choices, changes your actions, and alters the experiences you bring into your life.

Change Your Core Beliefs

What has helped me . . . has been the incredibly rare time spent with a
friend who talked with me as an equal, morally and intellectually. He
didn't try to "fix" me, cheer me up, or interrogate me. We actually shared
a few laughs, the first I've managed with another human in months.

—*Russell Stueber*

At the center of all of your perceptions lie core beliefs. Identifying them
is as easy as expanding your awareness and as action oriented as deliberately making a change.

Step One

To identify a core belief, notice your behaviors and follow your emotions. Whenever you have a feeling or behavior you don't like, ask
yourself either (1) "What thought created that emotion?" or (2) "What
thought made me take that action?"

Then, notice how much you believe the thought behind the feeling
or action. Rate it on a scale of 1 to 10 (10 being strongest). If the belief is
in the 8 to 10 range, then it operates as a core belief.

Step Two

To begin shifting your beliefs, question them. Consider each belief individually and ask:

- How do I know this is true?
- How possible is it that the opposite is true?
- What evidence is there that it is true?
- What belief would I prefer to hold?
- What evidence is there that this new belief is true?
- If I hold this new truth, what action does that invite me to
  take?

TRAUMA ALTERS MEANING

> . . . I was never going to go "back" to who or what I had been
> before the trauma—you can't go "back." I found someone willing
> to walk with me to make meaning out of the meaninglessness
> of my trauma, and together we found the new me.
>
> —*Anna D.*

When we talk about beliefs, we have to also take into account the presence of meaning, which is the significance you give to an idea, fact, or event. After a trauma occurs, identifying what is significant becomes incredibly important. This is partly an automatic process your brain employs to learn new survival techniques. Partly, too, the process of making meaning derives from consciously examining an idea, determining what you believe is true, and then living in alignment with, honoring, and respecting the significance of that belief.

The key to meaning lies in the roles of perception and interpretation. Perception is your ability to become aware of something through your five senses. When you perceive something, you become consciously aware of a realization or understanding of it. Interpretation happens when you explain the meaning of something. This process is tremendously pliable according to the decisions you yourself make. For example, let's say yesterday you went to the store:

You left home, followed the familiar route, entered the store, purchased what you needed, and reversed your path to reach your home again. Nothing odd happened; no surprising incidents occurred. Today, how do you feel about that little outing? Pretty calm, probably. You understood it all. You felt the familiarity of the neighborhood, the layout of the store, and even the anonymous people you passed. It was just another mundane errand. Everything felt okay, so you went on with your daily schedule without calling anyone and reporting, "I just went to the store!" You didn't sit down afterward and reimagine the outing from the moment you exited your front door to the second you entered the store, all the way to the moment you relaxed once again in your living room or kitchen. The trip was too unremarkable for you to share or reexamine once it had ended.

Now imagine this alternative scenario: When you reached the store, tornado sirens suddenly began to sound, everyone in the store panicked, people screamed and dove for cover, and a fellow shopper knocked you to the ground in a spastic effort to beat you to a place of safety. Then you found yourself locked in a dark storage closet with four strangers, two of whom were so terrified they were physically ill. When the all-clear sounded, how would you feel if the five of you emerged from the closet to find death and destruction strewn about the remnants of the store? What if the five of you were the only survivors? How possible would it be for you to just retrace your steps home and go about your normal day?

The answer is, you wouldn't experience the rest of your day as if it were any other hour. You're human, so you have a keenly functioning sense of logic, analysis, and reason. You would review the memories to see what you could learn, should have known, and would do differently the next time. You would also probably feel an urge to tell people what you had survived, and perhaps to connect with others who had survived similar experiences. During and after trauma, part of the survival response is to "tend and befriend"; when your brain is stressed, its response is to release chemicals that drive you to bond. It would be natural for you to want to connect with others. It would be natural, too, for you to interpret this unexpected and frightening event as a meaningful experience in your life. After all, your life was threatened; that's very meaningful indeed.

Now let's consider this scenario from a different perspective. A professional tornado chaser, for example, would have a completely different reaction. His job is to witness and participate in tornado events. His livelihood depends on it. His blood races with excitement when the sirens sound, and his mind calculates the opportunities this storm will bring. While you consider the tornado to be "dangerous" and "scary," a professional scientist ascribes to it completely different meanings, including "anticipation," "great video footage," "success," and "money." The different perspectives and interpretations of the event create different experiences of its meaning.

WHAT'S YOUR STORY?

I was watching the sun set in Tucson, Arizona. When its orange glow reached me, I knew the only way "out" of the turmoil I was in was to stop, take a deep breath, and start over. I needed to be brave enough to dare to not know and go with that. I needed to dare to start a new adventure, and I was the adventure.

—*Monique H. Greven*

A story is the narrative you construct about everything you experience, both related to trauma and otherwise. It's informed by your beliefs and meanings, perceptions, and interpretations and shapes how you understand and interact with yourself and the world around you. You either say, "I went to the store and the most frightening tornado hit and I had an awful experience!" or "I was at the scene of the most extraordinary tornado today; you should have felt the energy in the air!"

The same happens with your personal trauma narrative. Curtis, whom you met earlier, says, "I lost my house and with it my entire life, and now I can't get back any of it." The story that Curtis tells is one of pain, sorrow, grief, culpability, loss, and hopelessness. To be sure, anyone could find those elements in the objective facts of what happened. However, the more Curtis repeats this story to himself, the more he solidifies that as his experience. Likewise, the more you tell yourself a negative and distressing trauma story, the more you create that experience for yourself.

There's another reason your story has power: It fills in the blanks that trauma creates. Maybe there's a gap in your memory, or perhaps you feel the break between your past and your present. Living with discontinuity causes feelings of great disorientation and disconnection. Crafting your story and the details of it can facilitate a sense of control, connection, or reorientation—if you craft a healthy story.

Unlike me.

After my trauma, it didn't take long for it to seem as if the real me had been so decimated that I had become someone else. When I looked in the mirror, I saw a new person. The story I told myself was that I was a new girl now. And that my original self, the one who had not suffered, was dead. The new survivor identity became very much alive and lived according to a story that celebrated not my survival of the trauma, but the fact of the trauma and my survival of every moment afterward. I no longer saw myself as a regular person, but as a "special" person, separated from everyone else because I alone had suffered and faced death. In her book *Faith,* Sharon Salzberg writes that "sometimes . . . I secretly build a monument to [my distress], as though I am really very special in [it]." That was me. In fact, the more I suffered further traumas, the more connected to myself I felt. My story became, "I'm incredibly special in how unsafe I am in every moment and everywhere. Horrible things can happen to me and no one will be able to help. I could die at any moment much more quickly and severely than most people." Year after year this story kept me chained to expecting the worst and finding myself in experiences that corroborated my story.

What negative trauma story do you tell yourself? Jot down a few sentences here:

CHANGE YOUR STORY

After . . . dozens of healing modalities [and] years of therapy—my healing was instant. I . . . realized I had spent my whole life trying to rescue or protect my inner child . . . [W]hen I realized that I am loveable and acceptable just as I am, the child in me is safe with ME, that day, 99% of the symptoms disappeared completely.

—*Caryl Wyatt*

Every event contains the seeds for multiple stories. While the story Curtis tells is accurate, at any time he can change the story. For example, an equally true story would be, "I'm being challenged to recreate my life and it's hard as heck, but I'm going to do it." I could have changed my story, too. A much healthier story would have been, "I was strong enough to survive, which means I'm special and ready to do great things in the world." The story you choose is the story that defines you. Even when you don't wholly embrace or feel comfortable with a new story, learning to tell it can help you learn how to live it, which can introduce you to its truth.

Of course, there are major challenges to changing your story. By now, your story has become comfortable, familiar, and offers a sense of unique individuality. However, you want your story to do that in a supportive, life-affirming way. You may notice that your current story offers many benefits that make you feel as if you should hold on to it. Some of those benefits may include:

- *A sense of safety.* When you feel disconnected from yourself, the emotions evoked in your story (e.g., futility, depression, victimhood, anxieties) can make you feel as if somehow you really are connected to yourself, even if in a negative way.
- *An identity.* Your old self is gone. Who are you now? Defining yourself wholly and solely as a trauma survivor gives you an immediate frame of reference for your existence.
- *A dependable worldview.* The world will always serve up bad things; expecting and then experiencing them helps the world seem trustworthy and reliable.

Take a look at the story you jotted on the previous page. What benefits does your story seem to offer you?

While your current story has been appropriate and even necessary in getting you where you are today, constructing your post-trauma identity will require you to relinquish it. Now you have the opportunity to create a new story, one that is even more powerful, beneficial, and useful in helping you feel better.

Changing your story can begin with just slight adjustments. For example, look at this tiny change in my story that actually makes a big change in the long run:

> I'm incredibly special in how unsafe I am in every moment and everywhere. Horrible things can happen to me and no one will be able to help. I could die at any moment.

changes to

> **Like many other people** I am unsafe in every moment and everywhere. Horrible things can happen to me and no one will be able to help. I could die at any moment.

The story hasn't dramatically changed from negative to positive, but it has changed from a feeling of isolation to a feeling of being part of a larger group. I am not so uniquely special; there are many others just like me. That one small change alters a lot in the feeling of the story.

Another small change could be:

> **Like many other people** I am unsafe in every moment and everywhere. Horrible things can happen to me and no one will be able to help, **but I've learned a lot about my ability to survive even disastrous moments.**

Again, I'm keeping in line with the truth of the danger, while also teasing out another truth in the form of my personal strength and fortitude.

You, too, can change small parts of your story, revising one element at a time as you work up to changing the whole story itself.

If you were going to change your story, even slightly, what might you change it to?

_____

_____

_____

_____

Play with this concept more fully over a period of time in your notebook until you have a complete revision.

TRAUMA SHIFTS YOUR SELF-CONCEPT

> I have repeatedly done what I thought I couldn't, or what other people thought I shouldn't, to prove to myself I'm strong.
>
> —*Jana M.*

Helen Keller is a great example of a survivor who elevated change and success to an art form. Born a completely healthy baby, she contracted an illness at the age of nineteen months that left her deaf and blind. Since she had never had the chance to learn to speak, Keller's illness left her a wholly disabled invalid, mute and unable to communicate in a mature manner. Surely, Keller's experience of losing her ability to see and hear was traumatic and dramatically altered her perception of herself and the world before she had a chance to make any positive choices. Yet, "a trauma victim" is not how we remember her. We remember Helen Keller as a groundbreaking, highly accomplished author, political activist, pacifist, suffragist, lecturer, and recipient of the Medal of Freedom. We remember Keller the way she created herself: as a woman who burst out of the confines of what she experienced and decided not only who she would be but how she would live and what she would accomplish. With the help of her teacher, Ann Sullivan, she built herself from scratch.

If self-definition is determined by you, then trauma cannot change your identity. Any change in how you experience who you are is caused by *your response to the trauma.* As you'll see from the science in Chapter 2, you are, in fact, more in control than you feel or think. Your body and mind possess huge potential to physiologically change and adapt in both positive and negative ways. The psychological process by which you create your identity is filled with similar opportunities for change.

How you understand, experience, express, and visualize who you are, think you are, or would like to be is your true source of identity. Do you describe yourself (to yourself or others) as a survivor? How does that make you feel? When you describe yourself, do you like the image of the person who emerges, or do you feel uncomfortable with it? When you describe yourself, do you feel you're being honest or misleading? Do you feel you're telling the truth or fabricating? Your answers to these questions let you know whether you've designed a healthy identity or one that needs to be updated.

Building a concept of who you are demands that you look at all the things that define you—not just the facts in relation to the trauma. Other elements include physical, social, economic, emotional, intellectual, professional, experiential, and relational aspects, plus the beliefs and meanings you ascribe to them. From these and other accumulated assortments of details, you choose the descriptors you want to represent what it feels like to be you and facilitate the development of that identity. While the outside world can label you, only you have the power to choose your identity. It is a self-referential process based on what you see, think, and feel about your presence in the world.

The decisions you make about which elements define your essence come from two acts:

1. Stepping into making choices about what defines you.
2. Stepping out of allowing distorted thoughts, beliefs, feelings, and the opinion of others to make choices for you.

Which of these options do you feel ready to attempt?

If you feel prepared to step into making choices about what defines you, a simple place to begin is with descriptive words that either are true or you want to be true about you. Take a moment to write down some of those now.

_____

_____

_____

If you feel ready to stop allowing trauma's myths or others' opinions to define you, take a moment to clearly imagine what that means. Write down some specific, negatively defining ideas that you're willing to step away from:

_____

_____

_____

What Does a Post-Trauma Identity Look and Feel Like?

I am connecting to my new identity. It will never be what it was before,
but perhaps [in it] I can help [others] to find themselves again.

—JennJones

Right now you're inhabiting a *trauma identity*. Or, as I often call it, a survivor identity: a way of seeing yourself and your world through the perspective of victimhood, threat, danger, symptoms, and the need to keep yourself safe. This type of identity means that you can experience:

- *Intrusive thoughts and/or memories.* Unwelcome ideas, facts, snippets, and full recollections repeatedly pop into your mind. Nightmares and flashbacks are also included in this category.
- *Avoidant tendencies.* You stay as far away as possible from anything that reminds you of your trauma, including sights, smells, tastes, sounds, people, places, thoughts, and feelings.
- *Acute stress.* Within one month after a traumatic event, you find yourself feeling extreme anxiety, a decrease in emotional responsiveness, a decrease in your desire to participate in

previously pleasurable activities, difficulty concentrating, disturbed sleep (insomnia), and behavioral disturbances.

- *Increased arousal.* You experience "hypervigilance," that is, the need to be on the lookout for danger. Your senses are particularly sensitive and your approach to threat-detecting and safety-oriented behaviors becomes exaggerated.
- *Dissociation.* You live with a feeling of detachment from yourself, others, the world, and the present moment.

Given the way trauma changes your brain (as you'll see in Chapter 2), plus how a traumatic experience changes your perceptions, for a long time afterward it seems as if remaining in your survivor identity is the smartest thing to do because you believe you are safe and in control. Unfortunately, that rigid, high-stress way of living actually causes enormous harm. You'll be more flexible and adaptable when you shift out of your survivor identity and into something more life sustaining: a *post-trauma identity*.

As I'm specifying it, a post-trauma identity is how you perceive, define, and understand who you are in relation to yourself, others, and your place in the world when you are cognizant that you have survived a trauma but have released the need to be driven or motivated by unhealthy actions, beliefs, or behaviors related to the past. It is the person you feel most alive and comfortable being according to the messages coming from your innermost core self, and who you are when you carry out thoughtful decisions and empowered choices derived from a sense of what is most important for your happy, healthy, successful, productive, and meaningful life.

Your trauma identity is the state you're in right now: seeing yourself most clearly in the role of a survivor dealing with symptoms, uncertainty, and a visceral feeling of powerlessness. Evolving into a post-trauma identity occurs when you release a trauma-centric perspective and replace it with a perceptual shift that allows you to see, connect with, and act from the whole person you in fact are—that is, a person who contains traumatic memories of the past but operates from a place of strength and courage in the present. The success of achieving a post-trauma identity means your trauma self functions as a small part of the overall healthy, stable, and in-charge post-trauma self. The success of this process does not mean your future life will be devoid of fears, worries, challenges, and apprehensions. Rather, you will be equipped to manage them from a powerful versus powerless position.

The transformation from a trauma to a post-trauma identity can happen in a variety of ways. Rick and Angelique show two different but equally successful processes:

Rick, a man in his early fifties, was one of the most beloved and successful account executives at an advertising agency in Los Angeles. Then one summer he and his wife, Angelique, were bound, gagged, beaten, and burglarized in their bedroom in the middle of the night while their kids were away on a camping trip. After the event, Angelique, who had been a shy stay-at-home mom, found it hard to be in the house alone during the day. Despite the newly installed state-of-the-art alarm system, she constantly imagined hearing windows rattled and locks picked. She began experiencing anxiety attacks and developed a rash that no prescribed medication eliminated. To get out of the house, Angelique found a part-time job at the local green market. With a place to go every day and a team to work with, Angelique found herself making new friends, developing a safe network in the community, and shedding her shyness in the warmth of connection. The more she blossomed in her role outside the house, the more confident she felt inside it. Gradually the anxiety attacks subsided, the rash cleared, and Angelique found herself able to be at home without thinking of potential danger.

While the trauma ultimately led Angelique through posttraumatic growth that led her to become more of herself, Rick was having an opposite reaction: He found it hard to exit the house and go to work each day. Afraid to leave his family in a vulnerable position, he bought a gun and took lessons at a local range.

"The minute I drive away from the house, I break into a cold sweat," Rick explained. "My heart starts to race and my mind just keeps flashing back to that night: what the two men looked like, what their sweat smelled like, the sound of the ropes being tightened and the tape being unrolled. Sometimes it all seems so real I have to pull off to the side of the road."

Eventually Rick began to dread the time every morning when he would leave for work. He developed morning migraines and an upset stomach. He was awake most of the night anticipating having to leave the house. Sleepless, irritable, and feeling out of control, Rick found his performance at work faltering. He missed deadlines and client meetings and was unable to properly manage his team. When the launch of a new client's advertising campaign was bungled by Rick's lack of attention, the client withdrew the account, costing the firm substantial profits.

"I knew then that I had to take a leave of absence and find some way to deal with all of this," Rick said. "I've never destroyed a campaign or lost a client. That guy is not who I am. I'm the guy who gets it done, wins awards, and has new clients beating down his door. At least, that's the guy I *was*. I'm not sure I can ever be him again. That guy seems gone."

Until the trauma, Rick had had no reason to consciously assess who he was, or why. He hadn't paid attention to how he made decisions, what beliefs and meanings drove his behavior, or which specific details shaped the type of man he wanted to be every day. Like most people, he had simply lived from day to day without much thought. In his quest for recovery Rick made a serious effort, for the first time, to discover his whole, core self—the part of him that was bigger than any experience, tapped into his deepest wishes and most innate strengths, and lived with a sense of purpose.

Rick began this process of self-discovery by imagining that his small survivor self was held in the lap of his much larger core self. From there, he imagined what type of larger self would hold something as emotionally fragile as his survivor self. Together we made a list of attributes as he thought more and more broadly about what kind of man would shelter a wounded individual. During his daily meditation, Rick began visualizing his core self and engaging in conversation with it. One day, at a deep point of meditation, Rick felt himself expand into the body of the core self he'd been imagining. This marked a major shift in his recovery.

From that day forward Rick embraced and embodied the idea of living from his core self: a man of strength, power, and vision. As he became comfortable with this new role, the morning migraines disappeared and Rick began sleeping restfully through the night. Eventually, he went back to work. Over the following years Rick became so much more successful and productive than he had been previously that he was asked to assume the role of CEO of the advertising firm.

To feel safe, you may have attempted to shrink the world and yourself to a tiny size to make them easy to manipulate and control. Actually, however, the opposite is true. Being able to see more of the world in its context can save you. Imagine this: You've been walking in a maze, bumping into walls and leading yourself down dead ends because you can't see where you should be going or the quickest way to find the exit. Now, imagine this: How would things change if a part of you were so tall it could see above the maze and view it in its entirety? That part would easily see how to navigate with efficiency and could effectively guide you to freedom. You would actually be safer because a part of you had a metaview versus the microview to which you'd become accustomed.

In coping after trauma, you have learned to live from the small amount of information collected by your small survivor self versus the information of your big core self. Balancing your perspective so that you can see the microview but with the added information of the metaview is a major purpose in constructing your post-trauma identity.

DEFINING IDENTITY

Higher education self-empowers me . . . , provides me with a community of seekers, thinkers and support . . . and . . . awakens my authentic voice.

—*Courtney H.*

To imagine how you can create a post-trauma identity, it helps to understand the characteristics of identity in general. As I'm using it in this book, *identity* relates to the conceptual idea of who you are and what defines you as a person in the world. It's how you describe yourself and choose the specific characteristics that make you the unique person that you are. The identity development process ebbs and flows in response to experience and provides the lens through which you view not only yourself but also others and the world at large. In the spirit of continued identity formation, your only choice now is to progress your identity development by going forward, making new choices about who you wish to be and creating a post-trauma self that restores and combines all of the best of who you were before (even if you can't fully remember) or who you had the potential to be (if trauma occurred before you had the chance for any self-expression) with the best of who you are now and the vision of who you wish to become in the future.

A main factor in how you define yourself is the context in which you understand where and how you belong. Naturally, your identity has changed since your trauma(s), because your understanding of who you are and the world in which you live has dramatically altered. Losing a sense of safety, control, and certainty shifts you into a *less than* feeling. Perhaps today you see yourself as someone robbed of innocence, trust, love, well-being, and the feeling of being able to protect yourself. You may imagine and even deeply feel that you are physically damaged, emotionally or psychologically disfigured, or undesirable. This new self-definition impacts how you see the world, think about yourself and others, and make choices and take actions.

Though your new identity seems bleak, another part of you sees the bigger picture. That's the part that inspires and motivates you to move toward (re)claiming a more positive, solid, stable, and proactive sense of self. While your *less than* self may dominate who you are today, your *more than* self gains ground in every moment you work toward restoring yourself. It is your *more than* self that forms the basis of who you will become when you (re)construct your identity.

Though the process may feel uncomfortable, the forward-only prescription works to your benefit. Consider this: *What if who you are is a function of what you decide and has zero to do with what you have experienced?*

Your personal identity develops according to *your perception of experience.* You are an individual and your perspective of the world is unique to you; what feels traumatizing to you may not feel that way to someone else. Likewise, what feels traumatic to someone else may seem unimportant to you. If perception plays a key role in trauma, then it can also play a key role after trauma. While it doesn't feel this way at first, how you perceive yourself becomes an element of choice. Who you are is . . . who you decide you are.

THE BUILDING BLOCKS OF IDENTITY

[M]usic healed me . . . [S]oothing sounds . . . helped me feel understood and reconnected to my body and soul . . . [and] able to actually feel again. The sounds were deep and meaningful in a world that I found shallow and unmeaningful.

—*Teresa Weber*

When we talk about identity, we focus on how you define yourself, including:

- *Featured characteristics.* Which dominant, distinctive qualities most describe your beliefs and perspective, social status, professional direction, personal dreams, and family associations? These details lay the foundation of your personality.
- *Context.* If you were asked to describe yourself to a friend in the comfort of your own home, you would answer differently than if you were asked to describe yourself to a new colleague in the conference room at work. Environment influences your self-perception, which leads to differing definitions of your position in the world.
- *Narrative.* Since the day you were born, you've experienced a million moments, all of which have contributed to forming your character and personality; none of them defines your identity. How you arrange the details of those experiences

into an account that tells the story of your history builds a picture of who you are.

- *Values.* Your focus and attention will always be pulled to what you define and hold as important. This focused attention will result in behavior motivated to honor those things, which will define you as a person who places respect in those areas.

These four categories provide a basic framework for sketching out your identity. You can expand this list to include other factors that you find applicable to how you explain and express who you are.

Get Reacquainted With Who You Are

One thing that helped me reconnect to my identity was taking the time to do yoga and meditate. Both helped me to look inside and see that what was really there inside had not really changed. My character was the same.

—*Jennifer*

Unlike other losses in life, when you lose your old self, you don't *completely* lose your old self. While it's impossible to actually be that specific person again, elements of who that was or could have been still exist in you. Pause for a moment and experiment with this.

Note: Many of the exercises in this book suggest closing your eyes so that you can more easily focus. If closing your eyes does not feel comfortable to you, the exercises can be done with your eyes open. In that case, find a focal point on which to train your sight for the duration of the exercise. Later, when you feel more comfortable with the material and your process you may revisit the exercises and experience them with your eyes closed. If at any time an exercise causes you to feel intolerably uncomfortable open your eyes, pay attention to your breath, and use your senses (sight, sound, smell, taste, touch) to ground yourself in the truth of the present moment.

1. Sit in a quiet, safe space.
2. Close your eyes and breathe in deeply and slowly.
3. Go inside and imagine you are sitting in a serene and beautiful room. Take some time to use all five of your senses to become acquainted with the room.
4. Take a deep breath in and let it go, slowly. Again.
5. Notice what in the room makes you feel safe and secure. Bring it closer to you, so close you can touch it.
6. Now, think of one thing you love or value about who you used to be or could have been. Name it. "What I love/value is _____."
7. Bring into your mind that aspect; remember or envision as much about it as you can.
8. Feel the feeling of that quality now as you recall it.
9. Imagine you can see and feel that quality as clearly as you can feel the intake of your breath.
10. How would it make you feel to embody that quality right now?
11. Pretend that quality has a wonderful scent; inhale it as easily as you just inhaled your last breath. Follow the scent as it enters your nostrils and goes down into your lungs.
12. Sit with the feeling that quality creates for ten to thirty seconds; breathe it in again and even more deeply as if it were oxygen.
13. What object represents that element? Imagine it appears. Hold it in your hand and feel its weight, temperature, texture, and other details.
14. Imagine there is a shelf in your mind; place the object prominently where you can see it.
15. Imagine there's a movie screen in your mind; see yourself going through the rest of the day with this quality resting there on the shelf inside your mind. How does having that element affect how you feel inside yourself? How you behave toward the outside world?
16. When you're ready, take one final deep breath in, sealing in every good feeling you've just seen, thought, and felt, and exhale out any disturbances.

17. Gently begin to shift your awareness from inside yourself to the details of your body in the position it's in. When you feel fully ready and reconnected to the present moment, open your eyes.

To make this and all following exercises easier, consider speaking the prompts into your computer or cell phone recorder so that during the exercise you can listen to the replay without distraction. Or, visit YourLifeAfterTraumaBook.com to download the complimentary audio of this and other exercises throughout the book.

With this exercise, as with all the exercises in this book, you may experience resistance or other feedback that causes you not to achieve the results you wish the first time you follow the prompts. Whatever you can do (even if that's just thinking about but not even attempting the exercise) is perfectly fine. With each subsequent approach, you will develop your unique process for success in carrying out the full sequence.

Rate this experience in terms of intensity on a scale of 1 to 10 (10 being "I felt the aspect that I love/value very intensely.")

You are able to feel something only when it's inside you. Whether you would rate that feeling a 1 or a 10, feeling it even faintly proves how much you do contain that quality. As a matter of fact, you proved its presence in your willingness to read about and even do the exercise. The moment you imagine something, you already own the seeds for having and experiencing it completely.

Note: Even if you didn't feel or experience anything, that doesn't necessarily mean you don't possess the quality. It can mean that (1) you don't yet feel safe enough to experience it, (2) you haven't given yourself permission to own it, or (3) you are still so emotionally numb that such a feeling cannot yet come through. Rather than seeing such a situation as an obstacle, see it as a challenge. Your desire for this feeling indicates that somewhere in you, it already exists. Proceed into the book and circle back here at a later date.

Resolving the Post-Trauma Identity Crisis

Identity . . . is a sense, a new feeling of presence, a connection to yourself and others . . . that is unalterable yet transformative when cherished and set free.

—*Ronan*

When you're mired in posttraumatic stress and symptoms, it can seem as if your life will always be this exhausting, frustrating, limiting, out of control, damaged, and memory oriented. You may wonder if healing the parts of you that feel broken is even possible. Can a post-trauma identity crisis be resolved?

The answer is, absolutely. The process contained in this book offers a way to update how you define and perceive yourself so that your sense of who you are is more relevant to your present and future than to your past. What I've learned from my own recovery, plus years of work with clients and as the leader of a large trauma community, is that while we are all individual in our traumas, we are universal in our posttraumatic experience, and then individual again in our healing journeys. What you do in your healing and identity work will be unique to you. For some survivors (including me), resolution means an identity that is symptom-free and offers you the liberty to create who you are in the world in any way you choose. For others, resolution means a persona that manages symptoms and allows you to be functional socially and professionally. Your process will be guided and based on what definitions make sense to you. Later chapters will walk you through exactly how to define and work through a post-trauma identity transformation. Let's look at some preliminary examples, concepts, and exercises to get you in the mindset before we delve in further.

Clarice grew up in a happy home. Her parents were full of love and thought everything she did was marvelous. They encouraged her to take risks, supported her dreams, helped her overcome obstacles, cheered her successes, and soothed her failures. Her younger sister was her best friend and confidant. While every childhood has its bumps and scrapes, Clarice grew up believing the world was basically fair, that she was safe, that her parents could protect her, and that she was capable of making judgments and forecasting outcomes for herself.

It was within those beliefs that Clarice defined who she was. "I was the girl who was confident," she said in one of our first meetings. "I could figure out how to achieve pretty much anything I set my mind to. Whether it was becoming an honor student, getting into the college I wanted, or landing a job, I knew I could do it. And then my trauma occurred, and all that changed. I went from seeing myself as someone who *could* to someone who *can't*. It wasn't a logical progression. It was just a slow and subtle shift that came from feeling completely disconnected from my can-do self."

Survivor of a severe accident in which her car was hit by a drunk driver, nineteen-year-old Clarice sustained major injuries that included a broken pelvis, dislocated shoulder, and concussion. By the time she emerged into regular life after being hospitalized for weeks, she knew she would eventually make a full recovery. Although her physical wounds were healing, however, emotionally she still felt shattered. More than that, she felt like a different person.

"When I look into the mirror, I can see the same face I've always seen, but it's not the same *person* looking back. This is someone else, a girl who looks hollow, skittish, and afraid. A girl who is closed, uncertain, and without joy. I don't look forward to anything. I don't enjoy the things I used to like doing. I used to be very social, but now I'd rather be alone." Clarice sighed. "I'm just so different from who I used to be."

Maybe you, like Clarice, have experienced a single defining event at a time in your life that you can look back to to clearly see the difference between who you are and who you used to be. Or maybe you're more like Terrence, who can't remember a time before trauma. He explains:

"My trauma started before birth. Pop didn't want me, so he beat up Ma while she was pregnant hoping she would have a miscarriage. She lived in total fear of him every day. Eventually, she moved out and went to live with her parents, who were very strict and religious. They told her she would burn in hell for the sin of having a baby out of wedlock. She had nowhere else to go. A few times she tried to reconcile with my father, but the meetings always ended in beatings. When I was finally born, my ma was a real mess emotionally. By then she didn't want me either. I don't have a Before self. I never got to have a self that was pure. From the very beginning my life has been marked by trauma. Who I am has always been based on that little baby who survived the beatings and then came into a world where he was unwanted and neglected."

Regardless of which scenario resonates with you, trauma can cause mutations in who you are and often leads to profound "dis-ease" when it comes to assessing your identity. The question I hear most from clients and others in the survivor community is, "Who am I now?" Coping with posttraumatic symptoms, plus your response to (and interpretation of) the meaning of the experience, throws into question all of what you knew or ever suspected about yourself. The "Who am I now?" question sums up the biggest part of the post-trauma identity crisis and is the question that will be answered by the end of your successful transformation.

Until then, it's important to remember that no matter what your trauma was or how long you've lived with the aftereffects, change is always possible—especially change in who you are, how you live, the way you see yourself, and the way you present yourself to others. The process of identity change is subtle and happens gradually over time, either by isolating particular details you wish to change or working toward an overall concept. In keeping with the nature of healing, these choices are unique to you and guided by what feels right, comfortable, and good in your process. They can be large or small, involving others or only yourself. The key to change is undertaking and executing plans you feel ready for.

Take my client Margaret, for example. Her family had called her Maggie her whole life. To her, that name had come to symbolize a child sexual abuse survivor whose family did not protect or support her (even after they discovered the source of her trauma), and a girl who had accepted herself as being *less than,* damaged, and undeserving. Through our work together she developed a different self-view, one of a woman beginning to make strong and deliberate choices about profession, relationships, romance, and geographic location. With all of the changes she was experiencing and the empowerment they instigated, she evolved from a child to a fully mature woman; "Maggie" no longer seemed like an appropriate name. That was the name of the abused child, the silent adolescent, and the young adult who accepted being devalued. As she moved into a newly empowered state, Maggie decided she wanted to be known by her full name. Today, she goes by Margaret.

While changing your name may seem like a small shift, as you saw earlier with Erik Erikson it's an action deeply tied to your self-creation. Your name is how you're known. Choosing how you are known deeply impacts your sense of who you are and also how others relate to you. Another of my clients, Vick, was molested between the ages of seven and twelve by his father and the priest his father invited to join him. When Vick told his mother what was happening, his mother refused to believe him. Instead, Vick's mother and father began telling everyone in the community that Vick was prone to lying. Accomplishing his healing two decades later, Vick married and decided to legally change his name to his wife's last name so that his original name was no longer attached to him at all. "Part of what feels right to me for my new identity," he explains, "is being completely free from my family of origin. That means not speaking to or seeing any of them, and legally severing all connections." The process of changing his name presented new challenges for Vick. He had to fill out forms, go to the courthouse, and even have a lengthy meeting with the judge. Every step of the process introduced Vick to uncomfortable fears, anxieties, feelings, and thoughts. As he shared with me later, these challenges proved to be terrific experiences. "They ultimately helped me step even more solidly into my new identity because they made me consciously confirm and validate my choices and fully consider each action prior to taking it," he confided.

The large effect a name change creates points to how much impact choice, plus seemingly inconsequential details, have on self-perception. By thinking of herself as Margaret, one survivor began turning herself into a thriver. Now when she introduces herself, she says her full name and feels the weight of what it means: a woman creating a life undefined by the past. Margaret smiles more, stands up straight, and looks people squarely in the eye. By legally changing his name, another survivor took responsibility for redefining his past, present, and future. Vick freed himself from ties to his trauma and in doing so discovered how able he was to protect himself.

Your post-trauma identity development process will seem exciting, invigorating, challenging, and sometimes uncomfortable. Because you are emotionally invested in the outcome, you will naturally ebb and flow through the changes. Those around you, however, may not. To this day, Margaret's family refuses to adapt to her decision. To them, she always has been, and always will be, Maggie. They decline to recognize the changes she is making to her whole self. They pretend not to notice that she has reduced her oversized breast implants, uses less garish makeup, and wears more modest clothing. Instead, they say she has "lost weight," looks pale, and needs to go shopping. For a while Margaret patiently reminded and corrected her mother, father, sisters, aunts, uncles, and cousins about her full name. For a while she chafed and was hurt and disappointed that no one would honor her request. When it became clear that her family simply would not engage in her personal development, Margaret had a choice to make: Give up or go on. Margaret chose to go on, keeping the contact but letting go of the need for her family to support her actions. She identified friends, work colleagues, and new acquaintances who complied with her request. She gathered from nonfamily sources the support and response her family refused to provide. What remained most important to Margaret was being true to her vision of who she wanted to be.

Until today, you may have sat back and allowed your identity to create itself in all the chaos of a swirling winter snowstorm. Today, however, you are beginning to consciously create changes in your identity—changes intimately tied to your image of, and feelings about, who you truly want to be and can be.

Embrace Yourself

You may feel all alone, but the truth is that your larger, calm, confident, and omnipresent self remains with you in every moment. You have an opportunity now to make contact and experience what it feels like to be safe inside yourself:

1. Sit in a quiet, safe space.
2. Close your eyes and breathe in deeply and slowly.
3. Go inside yourself and imagine you are sitting in a serene and beautiful room. Take some time to use all five of your senses to become acquainted with the room.
4. Take a deep breath in and let it go, slowly. Again.
5. Notice what in the room makes you feel safe and secure. Bring it closer to you, so close you can touch it.
6. Notice that while at first you may have thought you were sitting on a conventional piece of furniture, you are actually sitting in someone's lap. This person is much bigger than you, breathes quietly and rhythmically, and feels familiar and safe.
7. Imagine that the support against your back, which up until this moment you may have assumed was a piece of furniture, is actually the torso of this larger person. Notice how it provides a comfortable and firm brace behind you.
8. Bring your focus to your breath and notice how it times itself to the gentle rise and fall of the body behind you.
9. Notice the arms that encircle you and rest comfortably around you. Notice the feeling of comfort and security this presence introduces. Recognize it's another version of you.
10. Focus fully on the details of this person who embraces you. Notice any scents, sounds, feelings, or other sensory details you can discern.
11. Allow yourself to quietly sit in the presence of this self for as long as feels comfortable.
12. When you feel ready to return to your day, thank this part of you

for spending this time with you. Agree you will return to deepen the connection whenever you wish.

13. Slowly withdraw yourself from the serene room and bring yourself back to an awareness of the present moment and the physical space you are in. Focus on the sounds you hear in your environment, even if they are silence. When you are ready, open your eyes.

14. In your notebook, write down everything you remember about what you saw, felt, heard, and experienced.

When you look at the following picture, what do you see? Where is it, what is the railing for, and what kind of purpose does the structure serve?

Photo credit: Bret Rosenthal

Since you are able to view only this one small part of what is surely a larger picture, it's impossible to have any idea about the location, use, or safety of the structure. It looks alone, fortified, and disconnected from any greater whole that would define it or offer a clue to the meaning of its existence in the world.

Now, look at this picture:

Photo credit: Bret Rosenthal

This is a picture of the fishing pier on Juno Beach, Florida. It's a partial view from one of my favorite spots on the sand, where I spent many difficult hours of inner work during my PTSD healing journey. It's also the spot where I now spend many luxurious hours basking in the sun and my psychological freedom. Looking at the photo from this perspective, suddenly you understand that the structure—with an incredibly fortified and reinforced foundation—is the anchor for the entire pier: a place from which the view of the sky and horizon are naturally beautiful.

How much of your whole self do you see in this moment? To construct the identity you want, it will help to see the larger parts that make up the entirety of who you are. Like Rick, when you see your full self in context, you will be able to identify distorted beliefs, thoughts, feelings, and actions that create your experience in any day. Choosing how to shift, release, and change these elements infuses you with power in determining who you are and how you live, plus gives you a road map to alterations over a period of time. When you successfully construct a post-trauma identity, you call forth the selves you most want to influence your life and integrate them into one functional overall self. This is part of what leads to posttraumatic growth. You have within you a part that can stand up and see the big picture above the height of the trauma maze. If you let it guide you, this part can play a big role in moving you forward.

Let Yourself Grow

The part that can see the big picture is your strength, your courage, and your bravery. It's also the part of you that wants you to feel better. It can assess situations, see opportunities, figure out alternatives, and problem-solve in healthy ways that keep you safe; it is present in every moment. You have an opportunity now to make contact and begin experiencing what it feels like to have this inner guide and mentor:

1. Sit in a quiet, safe space.
2. Close your eyes and breathe in deeply and slowly.
3. Go inside yourself and imagine you are sitting in a serene and beautiful room. Take some time to use all five of your senses to become acquainted with the room.
4. Take a deep breath in and let it go, slowly. Again.
5. Notice what in the room makes you feel safe and secure. Bring it closer to you, so close you can touch it.
6. Notice now that another presence has entered the room. You remain calm and curious. You recognize this person; it is a part of you. In fact, it is the part that wants you to overcome the past. It is strong, proactive, determined, brave, courageous, and committed.
7. Look at that self: How is it dressed? What does its voice sound like? How does it move, walk, and gesture?
8. Imagine you stand face to face with this self; look into its eyes. Put up a hand; notice it mirrors what you do. Practice lead and follow. Notice how easy it is to connect with this self. Feel its secure energy. Notice that being near it you feel safer, as if someone is protecting you.
9. Now, notice that self begin to grow one foot taller, and then another, and then even another foot taller still. It continues grow-

ing a full story as you feel its energy increase and as you witness the ease with which it grows. As you stand below looking up at it, watch as it continues to grow another story and then even another story taller while a new energy emanates from it like the glint of the sun, until it stops growing at just the perfect height.

10. See how easy it is to grow bigger in your form and energy and body. Now it is your turn: Bring your attention to feeling yourself grow, slowly at first as you get used to the feeling of growth. Feel yourself grow to the height of one extra story while you become more and more comfortable with change, so that it becomes easier and easier to feel yourself grow. The more easily you feel yourself grow, the more quickly it happens, and the more quickly it happens, the more easily you feel yourself grow, so that you grow as tall as the part of yourself that stands before you.

11. Take a look at the other part of you now that you are face to face again. Then take a look around you and observe how different everything seems from up here. See how different your whole life looks from this height, with all the things in the past so small below you. Notice how different your body feels in this shape. Even how different things sound from this height.

12. As you bring your focus back to that strong self that stands in front of you, notice that it wants something from you. What does it want?

13. It has a message for you. Listen to it; what does it say? What is your response?

14. If you have a question for this part of yourself, ask it now. What advice do you wish it would give you?

15. You can connect to this stronger part of you in an even deeper way: Move around to stand behind it. As you stand behind, notice the feeling of energy that emanates from this part of you. Allow yourself to soak it in. Then, take a step forward, and then another and another, as many as it takes to get right up close to this part, as if you could breathe right onto its neck.

16. Count to three and then step right into this part. Feel your feet slip into its feet. Feel your shins inside; your thighs, your hips, and your waist settling; your belly and chest and your arms all the way down to your fingertips settling into this self and your fingers wiggling; your neck and your head settling into place with a small snap. Now you are connected to a Super You, with new ways of accessing all you need to accomplish what you want in moving forward. Stay with this feeling as long as you like. Imagine what it would be like to move through the day as this self.

17. When you feel ready to return to the present moment, thank this part of yourself for spending time with you. Agree you will return to deepen the connection any time you wish.

18. Slowly withdraw yourself from the serene room and bring yourself back to an awareness of the present moment and the physical space you are in. Focus on the sounds you hear in your environment, even if they are silence. When you are ready, open your eyes.

19. In your notebook, write down everything you remember about what you saw, felt, heard, and experienced.

What to Expect From Your Post-Trauma Identity (and the Exercises in This Book!)

I surround myself with good people, including fellow trauma survivors who share an understanding of human suffering and have personal insights into healing. Their compassionate souls and empathetic hearts help reestablish my connection to the world and restore my belief in humanity.

—*Lisa Victoria*

During an interview on my radio show a few years ago, Dr. Rachel Yehuda, a renowned trauma expert and professor of psychiatry and neuroscience, answered a question by saying, "Michele, there's a reason we don't have eyes in the back of our heads!" She meant we're not supposed to keep looking behind. Understandably, after trauma you may have become a bit compulsive and even obsessed with that perspective. Since you don't have eyes in the back of your head, however, you have to turn and face that direction in order to look that way. When you do that, you can't see what's happening in front of you, which means you miss opportunities to grow, heal, and move forward. Because your attention may feel pulled by and compelled to turn to the past, it's imperative that you develop a process for, and commitment to, forcibly turning yourself to the future. Constructing your post-trauma identity helps you do this in three important ways:

1. ***Shift from powerless to powerful.*** If you're struggling after trauma, you're experiencing a sense of powerlessness, guaranteed. In this state you feel disconnected from abilities, talents, and skills that would allow you a feeling of being able to protect yourself. Experiencing disempowerment means you lack confidence, a key ingredient in ably making decisions. Paradoxically, making choices is one of the quickest ways to feel empowered. Choosing your identity offers a process for very firmly taking back control, both over who you are and also how you live.

   When you choose, gain control, and shift into a state of identity efficacy, you transition out of powerlessness into an ever-growing sensation of power*ful*ness that alters how you reconstruct and experience your entire life. Incorporated in these results will be a *reclaiming* of aspects of yourself that constitute the person you most wish to be. Sometimes that will mean going far back into the past and bringing qualities forward. Other times it will mean looking to the recent past for valuable elements you've mistakenly released. Or, it may mean imagining what you wish you had a chance to possess long ago, and finally possessing it today. Last, it may include looking at characteristics you've accepted that you wish to eliminate. In developing your ability to make decisions and self-regulate, you will *recalibrate* the experience of what it means to be you. Transforming yourself from a state of discomfort to a state of comfort shifts you into a place of feeling calm, settled, confident, and in control. All of these changes *reorder* your self-sensations from chaos to equanimity.

2. ***Transform loss into connection.*** After trauma, many things can vanish. In addition to your sense of self and safety, you can lose loved ones, a career, financial security, relationships, and spirituality, to name a few. If you loved what's been lost, then you will feel sadness and even prolonged grief. One of the ways we overcome these feelings is to create new experiences that restore good feelings in the areas in which loss has occurred. In terms of your sense of self, that means bridging the loss of self in the past with a deep and meaningful connection in the present that lays a foundation for creating your future. It means finding new meaning, purpose, gifts, lessons, rewards, and value in yourself and in your life.

   Connection requires you to *reintegrate* your self-definition with your internal experience while educating others to recognize the new you. Teaching your fragmented selves to *relate* to each other in more dynamic and trusting relationships (which creates a sense of internal stability) becomes a key element in this process. When you feel stable, you can begin to *redefine* your thoughts, feelings, actions, behaviors, perceptions, and desires so that your entire perspective shifts to a new experience of the world and new ideas about your place in it. With this combination of changes, you *relocate* the locus of control (which trauma has placed outside of your intention) inside your deliberate choices. This moves you directly into a present full of possibilities, opportunities, and dreams.

3. ***Replace confusion with clarity.*** Chaos (emotionally and physically) reigns in the post-trauma experience. The lines blur between past, present, and future; safety and danger; real and unreal; good and bad; meaningful and not meaningful. The world looks even messier when your internal space is cluttered and overwhelmed by erroneous, flooded, overreactive, and disjointed input. Letting outside sources—people, experiences, symptoms—define your

internal landscape places perspectives that are not yours at the center of who you are. Slowing down your emotions, responses, and actions, and making deliberate decisions about what you want yourself and your world to look like, helps bring the world back into focus. Being detailed in identifying who you want to be and how you want to live creates good feelings and clear images that can be used to navigate your movement through both recovery and the world. The result: reduced anxiety, a deeper shift to powerfulness, and a sense of safety and control that rests within you the way a pearl rests within an oyster.

The launch of the clarification process begins with how you *reinstitute* meaning, purpose, direction, and focus. What is your mission in life? What do you feel you have to offer the world that would help someone or something? The process of introducing yourself back as a member of society forces you to *release* any remaining inner rigidity. To collaborate in the world means you must enter the flow of the world at large. Doing so *refreshes* your connection with both the world outside trauma and also the larger world in which you exist. When you achieve this, you *reenergize* as the flow of energy from others to you, and from you to others, creates a source of creativity, emotional sustenance, intellectual stimulation, motivation, and inspiration that comes from the larger natural forces operating throughout the world in every moment.

WORKING WITH YOUR MANY DIFFERENT SELVES

I knew that the only part of my identity that felt like it had a part of me left was my relationship with my daughter. I packed the precious few pieces I could fit into my car and left the States to . . . restart my life close to [her] . . .

—Jennifer

For weeks in my work with twenty-seven-year-old Augusta, she entered every session with a peppy, cheerful attitude wanting to discuss her bouncy two-year-old baby boy, or her distant husband, or her all-consuming job. She wanted to talk about friends, her love of poetry, her irritation with her mother. To sum it up, Augusta wanted to focus on everything except the reason she'd sought me out: to overcome post-trauma issues related to childhood sexual abuse.

"What happened in the past doesn't really bother me," she said, waving away the topic with her hand.

"Then why are you here?"

"Well," Augusta paused, thinking. Then her eyes filled with tears. "It bothers . . . her." Blinking hard and forcing a laugh, Augusta settled back in her seat, her shoulders slumping forward slightly.

After a moment, I gently asked, "Who does it bother, Augusta?"

Another silence. Then, "The five-year-old." Augusta sniffed, and with that one sentence—plus all the tears that suddenly spilled from her surprised eyes—she finally stepped into her post-trauma identity and recovery work.

While she cried, Augusta described her five-year-old self: pigtails, blue eyes with long blond lashes, favorite polka-dot dress and favorite doll carried everywhere. Augusta described the girl's innocence and purity; her trust, faith, and belief; her sense of comfort and ease in the world.

"I can sense her pain. I feel so badly for what happened to her," Augusta sobbed. "But she's so far away from me I don't know how to make her feel better."

I asked Augusta if it would be all right to try an exercise; she agreed. I asked her to close her eyes and take some deep breaths. She complied, and after focusing on her breathing for a few moments, Augusta reported that she felt calmer, at which point I asked her to imagine the little girl, however far away she might seem. When Augusta accomplished this, I asked her to invite the little girl to move closer. What happened next surprised Augusta: The little girl very willingly moved closer and closer until she was so close she crawled into Augusta's lap! This made Augusta laugh. She began rocking in the chair as if holding a small child. She soothed the little girl, and a happy smile spread across Augusta's face.

"I had no idea I could do this," she whispered.

I guided Augusta in a conversation with this past self. Then, before letting the little girl go, I asked Augusta where the little girl would feel most safe, loved, and secure. Augusta chose a small chair at a tiny table in the bedroom of her little boy. She took the girl there, letting her explore the room and come to a place of rest in the chair. Augusta promised to visit, and then she came back to the present moment and we ended the exercise.

When Augusta opened her eyes, they were filled with amazement, plus a new tranquility. The pain and the little girl had always seemed so out of reach, while in fact they were very accessible. More than that, they were very willing to come forward, be assuaged, and then integrated into the present moment. Augusta learned she could handle their nearness, and also discovered the value of being willing to step forward and engage. Especially in matters of healing, Augusta had avoided this kind of proactive action. Inspired by her younger self, however, she adopted an attitude of more open willingness in fixing the problems in her life. The little girl became a guide and a role model; by developing in herself some of the little girl's attitude, Augusta became stronger, more decisive, and more action oriented.

While Augusta's process was extremely fluid, Jake's, though similar, was more complex. Having grown up in a religious cult, Jake had experienced extreme emotional, physical, and verbal abuse at the hands of the cult leader when he was seven. At the age of twenty-three he left the cult and went on to become a successful entrepreneur. A year prior to our meeting he had sold his business after a trigger rendered him agoraphobic. Now fifty-two, Jake lived alone in a large house with all the shades drawn. We worked via phone, and almost immediately Jake mentioned that his seven-year-old self (Little Man) was crouched in a corner and would neither turn around to face him nor step away from the wall. Little Man, Jake reported, was furious with him. Why? Because Jake, having shut down his life, wasn't doing anything to help either himself or Little Man.

Coaxing Little Man to engage took a couple of weeks. First Jake and I strategized to come up with ways to move Jake into a more proactive, empowered perspective and state. As Jake began following through on some of the exercises I designed (at first, just simple things like going outside to sit on the porch or take a walk around the house), Little Man became more attentive and eventually came out of the corner to sit on the bed in Jake's bedroom. This was a landmark event, connecting Jake to an important source of his disturbing emotions. During his years in the cult, he had learned it was safer to suffer silently and not show any emotion. Little Man, however, was completely the opposite. He was loud and aggressive and tearful and bossy—he held a self-protective power Jake longed to have. Over subsequent weeks, Jake's dialogue with Little Man expanded. He found himself joining in with the little boy's passionate responses. The more he mimicked the little boy, the better Jake felt and the more the little boy trusted him. Releasing the pent-up anger allowed Jake to replace it with an internal compassion and connection: He developed a buddy feeling with Little Man that reduced his sense of loneliness and disconnection while allowing him to become more expressive of his emotions.

The whole of who you are is made up of parts, all encompassed in one personality. You can think of these parts the way you think of parts of a car: They each have an individual function and combine to make an operable vehicle. For every age you've ever been, there's a part. For every kind of person you want to be, there's a part. For every kind of person you already are, there's a part.

Normally, all of your parts collaborate the way the bees in a hive arrange their lives and work around one central member, the queen. Ideally, all the parts inside you arrange around your core authentic self, contributing to your being or becoming the person you most wish to be. Trauma, however, is like splitting a hive wide open—with a demolished structure, none of the parts have a central focus; the whole becomes fractured and splintered into many selves (still within one personality) that no longer work together. Each disconnected part buzzes around on its own, a situation that can make you feel unhinged, distracted, and even crazy. This is especially true when the trauma parts buzz more loudly than the rest.

Your selves (both past and present), however, contain enormous value and can act as guides in constructing your post-trauma identity. They contain knowledge you may have forgotten. In the post-trauma lockdown you may not remember how to love, connect, hope, and anticipate, but your inner six- (or two-, or ten-, or one-) year-old does, or at least, can imagine how. Plus, these selves can teach what you need to (re)learn to become the strong and vibrant person you wish to be. The purpose of these selves, in their fleeting or constant existence, is to remind you of your options and opportunities, plus the capabilities, interests, passions, gifts, and skills you possess. Gleaning and combining the knowledge of many selves educates and informs your overall core identity in ways that allow you to develop strength, clarity, and productivity.

A major aspect of constructing your post-trauma identity will be recreating a sense of order and integration among all of your selves. This begins by pulling your past selves into contact with your present self. The purpose here is to identify what elements of your past selves you want to have present in who you are today. This process has three phases: *connecting* to that past self or selves in ways that are gentle and declarative; *borrowing* qualities to exhibit in your daily life; and *choosing* to consciously employ these facets of your past self in your present self in the way you approach, perceive, and behave.

In their quest to develop one self with core control of their identity, many of my clients discover that the self they choose needs to develop additional skills before it is truly ready to take control. Kate's story is a great example of what happens when you combine the power of your past and present selves.

Kate married her college sweetheart. Supporting them while her husband followed his dream to become a surgeon Kate deferred her desire for a family until Hal was securely on the fast track to success. Eventually, they had twin daughters. This should have been a happy time for Kate, except for the fact that Hal had changed since their college romance. Success had made him demanding, controlling, ego-driven and often mean. When she tried to speak to him about these things he derided and snarled at her, then slammed out of the house, often disappearing for several unaccountable hours. When Kate discovered Hal was cheating she finally decided to leave. With that decision she entered a battle for her freedom. Hal's financial and social power in the community massively overshadowed any resources Kate had been able to develop. Twenty years later the wounds of her divorce were still fresh.

"I didn't gain my freedom," she says sadly. "I lived in a prison of Hal's control. Because he could afford better lawers than I could the terms of the divorce were in his favor. I had no job and two little girls to raise. Hal threatened me constantly with phone calls and letters and emails that claimed he was going to take the girls from me and leave me homeless and penniless. On a couple of occasions he got so angry he shoved me up against the wall and made his threats verbally. I lived in constant fear." Feeling helpless and powerless Kate developed a large distrust of men and her own ability to choose a man who could maintain a healthy relationship. By the time she reached her mid-fifties she'd been alone for over twenty years. She was a single woman desperately wanting to be in a loving relationship with a man but too traumatized by her divorce to imagine finding a partner. Reclusive, Kate rarely went out socially, preferring her animals (three dogs, a cat, and a parrot) to interacting with people. When our work together brought her to a sense of healing that allowed her to trust herself again and consider being more social Kate decided it was time to open herself to finding love.

Her first forays into her community did not go well. Out of practice with just the basics of being social, Kate found herself at a loss for words, uncomfortable meeting new people, and lacking confidence that any man would want to speak with her.

"I just don't have that social ease I used to have," Kate commented one day. "You should have seen me when I was twenty—I was a hell-raiser!" She continued to describe the free spirit she had been in college: dancing in bars, inviting other students to join her table of friends, and having a reputation as the most cheerful person on campus. When I asked Kate to describe to me the qualities of that twenty-year-old self—what made her the strong, vibrant woman Kate remembered—she readily listed many.

Healing from trauma requires focus, dedication, and commitment. To help support my clients in developing these traits, at the end of every meeting I give them an assignment for the upcoming week. On this day, my assignment for Kate was to identify three qualities that she most loved about her twenty-year-old self and find ways to embody them in her present-day life. The purpose was to connect Kate with a part of her identity that she valued and from which she could deliberately draw strength, inspiration, and action. She did this and returned the next week, breathlessly exclaiming, "That was fun!"

Having established a comfortable connection with this self, Kate expanded her work to include getting to know and then inhabit every aspect of who that twenty-year-old had been. She listened to her music, ate her favorite foods, adopted her hairstyle, dressed in her updated fashions, and even spoke with her energy. With constant connection to her younger self, Kate's present self relearned how to enjoy, be bold, lean in, and stand out. She joined a new church, through which she developed a vast and active social network. She also joined a dating website, through which she is currently exploring group get-togethers and individual dates as she seeks The One.

Establishing your connection to and focusing on your past and present selves sets you up to create your vision and then a strategy for becoming the future self you most desire. As you construct your post-trauma identity, you'll notice that one self naturally leads to another and another and another, with an authentic core connection that continues to strengthen. My grandmother collected elephant figurines with their trunks up for good luck. As a world traveler, she'd picked up different depictions of elephants from places as close to home as California (she lived in San Diego) and as far away as Spain, Portugal, and India. When I was a child, what I loved about her collection was how it spread around her apartment like several herds. Of all the individual figurines, my favorite part of the collection was the elephants walking in a line holding each other's tails. I liked the connection of the many individuals through just one simple gesture. Your selves can create this same kind of connection, holding on to each other loosely to form one long line of traits, qualities, and characteristics that make up the overall you from past to present and on into your future.

The Take-Aways

Trauma is defined by the corruption of the present moment by false conditioned procedural memories from traumatic events, perceived as physical symptoms that intrude on the present moment, and therefore shatter our sense of self. Restoration of that sense of self requires therapies that extinguish these false, somatically based perceptions through techniques that enlist the body in the healing process.

—*Robert Scaer, MD*

- While trauma can make you *feel* as if you have been forever altered, the truth is that you have an inherent capacity to change again, and again and again.
- Accepting, embracing, and redirecting the changes constitute the work of constructing your post-trauma identity.
- You are who and what you believe you are, because perceptions create your experience of yourself and your world.
- Any change in how you experience who you are is caused by *your response to the trauma*. That response can change, and so can your identity.
- When you successfully construct a post-trauma identity, you call forth the selves that you most want to influence your life and integrate them into one functional entity.

A Brief Look at the Science of Trauma

RECOVERY STARTS HERE

> Abandon your past and quiet your mind. Create a mind that is similar
> to a still pond. This can be done with meditation, mantras, fantasizing,
> visualizations, and more. When one realizes only you create your thoughts,
> you can release the past and not let it continue to rob you of your life's time.
>
> —*Bernie Siegel, MD*

Brain science now tells us that while our traumatized selves feel stuck and scared, a post-trauma identity—and healing—is indeed possible; this chapter will run through some brain science essentials to explain why this is the case. We begin with Dorothy's story.

When Dorothy was three, she witnessed her mother shake her infant brother to death. Throughout her childhood and adolescence, Dorothy was subjected to such severe physical abuse that she was in a body cast by the age of twelve. At the age of fifty-five, when Dorothy came to work with me, she was completely withdrawn, suicidal, and overwhelmed by posttraumatic symptoms that triggered panic and anxiety attacks, sleep deprivation, frequent nightmares, emotional mood swings, extreme weight gain, fibromyalgia, and migraines. The effects of all of this rendered Dorothy unable to work, estranged from her friends, at odds with her extended family, and feeling disconnected from her husband and children.

Dorothy's biggest complaint in our first session was how she lacked control over her body. "My body isn't really my own," she explained. "It does what it wants, and I'm just a prisoner trapped inside it. It's like my mind is in the present moment while my body feels the same fears I felt as a five-year-old child."

During and even after trauma, perhaps you, like Dorothy, have experienced moments in which your body and mind have behaved in ways that don't seem good to you and you don't understand. Maybe you blacked out or froze, or maybe you can't remember the details. Perhaps you have flashbacks, anxiety or panic attacks, or trouble sleeping. Or maybe you feel jumpy, are oversensitive to sounds, don't like to be touched, endure frequent nightmares, or feel disconnected from yourself and those around you. All of those experiences are typical for life after trauma when the stress has not been fully processed and released.

Your response to any of these brain-instigated actions can often be one of frustration, irritation, and even self-blame. When things feel out of control, it's natural to find fault with yourself, experience guilt and shame, or even feel victimized by normal and heroic body and mind functions. Many of your trauma responses (both psychological and physical) occur without your specifically choosing how they manifest, or where or when. Recognizing why this happens and how to stop it have much to do with understanding the science involved in how your mind and body process trauma, plus what they both need in order to be reset and freed from the past. Construction of your post-trauma identity gains strength from understanding why you feel the way you do and appreciating how possible it is to create change in your mental, physical, and emotional function.

What Is Trauma? Defining PTSD and "Little Ts" vs. "Big Ts"

> I . . . dug in and did research. I got my hands on every healing
> resource I could . . . [K]nowledge has been power. I found that
> what I was going through wasn't just "normal"; it was natural.
>
> —*Teresa Weber*

An experience is defined as "traumatic" when it overwhelms your capacity to cope and adapt psychically and physically. Some experts go so far as to say that trauma is any experience that is less than nurturing and alters your perception of yourself and your place in the world. From this perspective, trauma can be as immediately life-threatening as a car accident or more subtle, like neglect.

When you survive trauma, your body encodes that event in memories all the way down to each tiny cell. Afterward, your brain interprets what happened in ways meant to extract meaning and also to learn ideas and concepts to be applied in future moments. Simultaneously, your neurobiology shifts to incorporate this experience into how your body processes information. All of this is done through a filter system unique to you and dependent on your past experiences from the time you were born up until your trauma. In fact, all of those unique elements cause you to develop a highly individualized brain, both in structure and in how the various parts function and communicate.

You can imagine the world of trauma as dividing into two categories: "little t" trauma and "big t" trauma. The "little t" trauma category applies to those everyday moments that unexpectedly go awry. While these incidents challenge coping and response skills, lead to disappointments and stressors, and introduce outcomes that leave you feeling altered in minor ways, they never threaten to disable your ability to remain alive, adapt, and move forward. In other words, they operate within the realm of manageable stress without shifting your body or mind into classic survival mode.

The category of "big t" trauma contains those life-threatening moments that require an enormous output of survival energy that involves complex physiological and neurological changes. After this type of traumatic event, it would be normal for you to move through a short period of acute stress in which your mind and body seek to organize the chaos of experience into an integrated memory. During that time it's typical to feel emotional distress, muscular and digestive problems, and sleep and mood disturbances, plus physical responses like increased blood pressure, rapid heartbeat, sweaty palms, palpitations, and dizziness. In a perfect scenario, acute stress resolves itself in a few weeks and all its symptoms disappear.

For some people, like me, the stress response never ends and turns into posttraumatic stress disorder (PTSD). You might be struggling with symptoms of PTSD if you have experienced an event that threatened death, injury, or violence to you or someone else and you now experience:

- ***Recurrent intrusive memories or thoughts*** (including nightmares and flashbacks) that make it seem as if the event is occurring again in real time, plus distress from things that remind you of the trauma
- ***Avoidant tendencies*** toward anything that reminds you of the trauma, including inside your own mind and outside in the world
- ***Changes in mood*** or your ability to mentally process information and stimuli
- ***Increased arousal*** in terms of vigilance, anger, sleep disturbances, concentration difficulties, and exaggerated startle response

While many PTSD symptoms present in a period relatively close to the trauma, some people experience *delayed onset* in which symptoms appear more than six months following trauma. In addition to the symptoms outlined above, many survivors also experience dissociative symptoms, which include *depersonalization* (feeling detached from your mind and/or body) and *derealization* (feeling that the world and your surroundings are unreal). If you recognize elements of your experience or symptoms here, it is possible that you are struggling with PTSD, which is a very treatable condition. Receiving a professional diagnosis would be your next step and can be accomplished by meeting with a mental health professional trained in trauma and the diagnostic criteria. A PTSD diagnosis is made when symptoms have persisted for more than four weeks and cause disruption in how you function in life. A PTSD self-test (like the one found at www.HealMyPTSD.com/education) can help you gain greater clarity in how your present-day experience relates to PTSD and is a useful tool to present to any practitioner.

If you've been struggling for a long time, you might question whether or not shifting out of who you've become to who you would rather be is even possible. I had the same thoughts. My healing process began after twenty-four years of living with posttraumatic stress disorder. I wasn't sure I could achieve the transformation I desired, and then I did, one hundred percent. You can borrow hope and use my story as a precedent for what might be possible for you. Plus, consider this:

You already possess a long history of your identity changing and expanding. Since you were a tiny person, who you are and how you define yourself have morphed depending on what you have thought, how you have felt, and what you have experienced. The tendency after trauma is to *forget* that you are a malleable being. In fact, trauma can produce such a deeply buried, frozen response that you believe the changes you've experienced in yourself are static and that who you are today is how you will live and who you will be for the rest of your life.

If you subscribe to that false belief, then you will be repeating the same mistake scientists made about the brain years ago: For centuries they believed that by a certain young age, your brain had developed as much as possible and that it would remain that way forever. Today, we know they were wrong. The brain can change all the way up until the day your heart ceases to beat. Your identity has that same potential. Indeed, as an organism, you are designed to flex and adapt in the world. That's how evolution happens; much like cavemen learned to run from a tiger, you respond to experiences in ways that make it more likely that you will survive. When you first developed your trauma response, it was an intelligent reaction designed to help you survive in the new post-trauma world. But like the caveman's response of running from the tiger, the trauma response isn't supposed to last forever. Eventually, the caveman must stop running or he'll collapse. So, too, you must change your response to a pattern more conducive to long-term survival now that the threat has passed.

Power Position

Since the body-mind connection produces a terrific feedback loop, you can develop it in many ways to add to your sense of control. Your body takes cues from your mind. Your mind takes cues from your body. A nifty trick to send a message of safety and security from your body to your mind can be found by sitting in this simple posture:

- Sit on the edge of your seat with only about a quarter of each thigh supported by the chair.
- Place your feet flat on the floor parallel to each other, hip-width (about 6 to 8 inches) apart.
- Place your palms, face down, flat on your thighs.
- Roll your hips forward so that you are seated on your tailbone.
- Allow your spine to extend in straight alignment.
- Imagine a string gently pulling your head up toward the ceiling.
- Roll your shoulders up beneath your ears, then roll them back as if your shoulder blades are trying to reach each other, then roll them down and back.

Tip: Combine this posture with breathwork and/or meditation (described later in the chapter) for an added bonus of calm.

How Does Trauma Affect the Brain?

[G]etting rid of recurrent posttraumatic nightmares is the most important intervention for healing. Dreaming may play a key role in the development and maintenance of our sense of self. Restoring normal dreaming helps traumatized people reclaim their sense of self.

—*Bruce M. Dow, MD*

Your brain is a constantly evolving, ever-changing organ. In response to information flowing through it consciously and unconsciously, your brain alters its structure and performance. In fact, it shapes itself according to whatever your mind rests on. Every experience becomes encoded in neural pathways that inform how you interpret and interact with your world. This fact might be the single most useful tip because it puts you back in the driver's seat: If your brain changes in response to experience, then you have the opportunity to deliberately help your brain change again based on *new experiences you create*.

To move forward in recovery, you will need to actively choose where you allow your brain to focus and also offer it positive and supportive experiences. When you spend all day looking for threat or danger, allowing your mind to concentrate on how "I could be victimized in any moment," your brain morphs itself to help you perceive that danger better, faster, and more effectively. To accomplish this, your brain develops neural pathways (connections between different parts of your brain and nervous system) that constitute the imprint of those thoughts, as well as the beliefs and feelings they connect, so that you can access the thought process and response more quickly the next time. Over a series of days, weeks, months, and even years, you can actually program your brain around the idea of being in danger.

Dorothy is a good example of how trauma can leave an enormous and unending imprint. Unable to surmount her symptoms or live a normal life because of them, her world shrank to the perimeter of her bedroom. Overwhelmed by PTSD symptoms, Dorothy spent her days in bed watching the same movie over and over. She never answered the phone, saw friends, cooked dinner, or kept house for her husband. Under the care of both a psychologist and psychiatrist who placed her on multiple medications and told her to "learn to live this way because you can't heal PTSD," she spent ten years struggling to follow their advice. Finally she gave up hope. She was continuing to have nightmares and her emotions were out of control, including a rage that scared her. She was deeply depressed, slept about one hour a day, and could barely think straight.

The Sedona Method

This easy-to-use process can be a very simple and yet incredibly effective way to engage the focus of your brain and pair it with the reduction of disturbing feelings. The next time you feel uncomfortable, try this:

Become very present with and aware of the disturbing feeling. Then ask yourself the following questions. Pause for each question until you can genuinely offer a positive answer (this may take a few seconds or a few moments):

1. *Can I welcome this feeling as best I can?*
2. *Could I let this feeling go?*
3. *Would I let this feeling go?*
4. *When?* (Wait until you can say *"Now."*)

Repeat as many times as necessary to feel emptied of the feeling. Completing this exercise may take ten or more repetitions of all the steps; that's absolutely okay—you're training your brain the whole time!

When she reached out to me for help, she said, "I can't bear to live this way any longer. I'm going to commit suicide."

No wonder Dorothy had lost her desire to live; despite all those years of medications and therapy, she wasn't really living at all. Instead, her body and mind had taken over with visceral responses to both real and imagined threats that kept her in constant fight/flight and arousal mode. The trauma had ended long ago, but Dorothy's brain continued to react with survival instincts.

"Every five minutes I feel as if I'm in absolute and total danger. And

I feel like a freak because anyone can see I'm home alone and safe in my house. It doesn't make any sense," she complained.

What Dorothy was experiencing was an inability to regulate her physical and emotional states, a hallmark of PTSD and even lesser post-trauma issues. As you'll see in the next section, in a healthy and whole brain, the higher-level, executive functions inhibit lower-level, reflex-oriented, hypersensitive functions. Innately you have the mental equipment necessary to choose how and when and in what way you respond to stimuli. Trauma, however, often upends brain function, allowing the more primitive levels of the brain to take control. Regaining that control and element of choice lies at the core of the healing process.

YOUR BRAIN BEFORE TRAUMA

Over the millennia your brain has evolved into a terrifically complex and yet wonderfully simple structure, generally divided into three parts:

1. *Reptilian (brain stem).* Responsible for instincts, vegetative functions, arousal, body processing (including digestion and breathing). Predominant motivator: Desire to *avoid* harm.
2. *Mammalian (limbic, midbrain).* Responsible for emotional processing and sensory relays. Predominant motivator: Desire to *approach* rewards.
3. *Neomammalian (cortex, forebrain).* Responsible for cognitive processing, executive (decision-making) function, learning, memory, emotions, motor control, cognitive functions. Predominant motivator: Desire to *attach* to others.

The diagram above offers a simple and generalized illustration of the three parts. The reptilian and mammalian structures are your older lower, inner, and midbrain regions. They actively perceive danger and intensely feel and record emotion. Your newer neomammalian layer exists in higher, exterior brain regions. It alone operates through a state of logic and reason. It is also the part of your brain that understands the pain of traumatic experience.

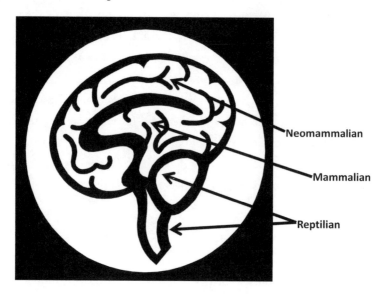

In this model, your brain works most effectively when your cortex remains in control. Due to the way each layer is built, the higher you go in this triune model (from reptilian to mammalian to human), the quicker your brain learns and the more plastic, or changeable, it becomes. This is because the cortex has many more neurons (specialized cells that transmit nerve impulses and are the building blocks of change) than the lower regions.

One of the biggest problems with trauma is that it embeds in the lowest, most instinctual parts of the brain. Because these parts possess fewer neuronal connections and less executive function, they require more time, more focus, and an enormous amount of repetition to manifest alterations. When trauma trains your brain so that you can't trust that your basic safety is secure, it interrupts your ability to evolve in terms of self-actualization and other "higher" skills.

Body Scan and Progressive Relaxation

Quelling emotions and feelings in the body can be a function of how you allow your brain and body to work together. Take yourself to a safe, quiet, undisturbed place and try this:

Part One: Sitting in power position, do five cycles of whatever breathwork you prefer.

Part Two: Imagine that in your body the places you feel fear and anxiety glow with a red light. Imagine that you can scan your body, starting with the top of your head, and at each point of redness focus the white light of your attention (for however long it takes) to soothingly shift the red glow into a cool blue sensation. Scan your whole body with this purpose. Imagine that all negative, uncomfortable, painful, or disruptive energy exits your body through the fingers and toes.

Part Three: Imagine that just by bringing your focus to the top of your head, all the muscles in your scalp easily and automatically relax. As this happens, any lingering uncomfortable feeling is steadily smoothed away by the white light and replaced by a cool blue sensation. Now move to the muscles in your face, and then in your neck, shoulders, and arms. Shift your focus slowly and gently; don't move on to the next muscle group until the muscles you are focusing on have relaxed and the red color (if any) has shifted. Continue focusing through your whole body, piece by piece, until you have relaxed even your smallest toe. Allow yourself to be present and experience this new state for as long as feels appropriate.

YOUR BRAIN DURING TRAUMA

The lower regions of your brain constantly scan the environment, reading stimuli and determining whether or not you need to rev up or dampen a response. Originating in your lower brain structure, instincts and trauma responses are subcortical; they occur below the logical cortex and conscious awareness. The information they gather instructs your body when to arouse and when to relax. When it's necessary to arouse, here's what happens:

Taking its cues from the sensory information delivered by your brain stem at the back of your brain (the oldest part of your brain and the one that receives information from all of your body's sensory outlets), your *sympathetic nervous system* shifts your body into fight/flight mode, shutting down all systems unnecessary for survival (e.g., cognitive thought, digestion, reproduction, immunity, repair). Your thinking processes slow or even stop and your ability to express emotion decreases. All systems necessary for survival engage, including breathing, circulation, and stress hormones. Your heart beats more quickly, adrenaline pumps, cortisol rises, and your breath becomes more shallow, all of which prepare you to physically respond to threat.

There are three main brain structures that collaborate to keep you safe and in a state of balance:

- *Amygdala.* An almond-shaped mass located deep within your brain, the amygdala is responsible for emotions and actions motivated by survival needs. Tuning in to the most dominant experiences, the amygdala amps up your arousal and autonomic responses associated with fear, activates the release of stress hormones, and engages your emotional response. Involved in the processing of intense emotions, the amygdala is also responsible for deciding what memories are stored and where they should be placed around the cortex. The amygdala applies feeling, tone, and emotional charge to memory. This can create a "flashbulb memory" whose strong emotional content remains connected to a visceral experience of fear and threat.
- *Hippocampus.* Horseshoe shaped and adjacent to the amygdala, the hippocampus forms, organizes, and stores memories as it converts them from short-term to long-term. This process is called *consolidating* memories, and the consolidated memo-

ries are then sent to the appropriate parts of your outer brain for storage. When necessary, the hippocampus also retrieves these remembrances.

- *Prefrontal cortex.* Located in the front, outermost layer of your brain, the prefrontal cortex contributes to movement, decision-making, problem-solving, and planning. The prefrontal cortex is responsible for both your personality expression and also the planning of complex cognitive behaviors.

Typically, the high-functioning strength of your cortex allows it to inhibit the instinctual and emotional responses of lower brain structures. During trauma, however, the survival mechanisms of the lower and midbrain structures override the cortex in order to sustain your ability to live.

YOUR BRAIN AFTER TRAUMA

By design, your body fluctuates between activation and repair. In a perfect world, your reactive (aroused) and responsive (relaxed) modes easily balance out each other. In the reactive mode, you burn resources faster and deplete your body's store of them. Later, when all of your avoidance, approach, and attachment needs from the three brain layers are met, your body shifts into responsive mode, where it can repair, refuel, and heal from a burst of stress and activity.

When danger passes, your *parasympathetic nervous system* kicks in to reverse the stress response. It slows breathing, lowers blood pressure, returns appetite, reduces stress hormones, and increases all of the other processes that support rest and repair. On a day when this process operates successfully, you naturally shift between the sympathetic and parasympathetic systems according to what your environment and situation demand. When the threat ends but the shift doesn't naturally occur, you stay in an aroused state despite the safe and relaxed atmosphere around you. Remaining in an aroused state for an extended period of time increases the likelihood that you will experience chronic stress, depression, rage, memory loss, intrusive thoughts, nightmares and flashbacks, language deficiency, learning issues, hypervigilance, arousal, issues with attention, reduced planning ability, and decreased ability to inhibit threat responses, plus impairment of many systems, including digestion, immunity, and regulatory drives that control feeding, fighting, fleeing, and sex.

Several factors may inhibit your shift into responsive mode, including the following:

- **Caught in a constant reactive state, your amygdala becomes overstimulated and hypersensitive.** When this happens, your amygdala continues to behave as if threat is present *even in the face of zero stimulation*. When scientists have measured brain activity in subjects who are chronically aroused, they have found that reactive parts of the brain continue to fire despite a lack of threatening sensory information. Scientists have also discovered that during moments of intense reliving of the traumatic event (e.g., a flashback, uncontrollable emotions), the prefrontal lobes actually experience decreased blood flow, meaning they are less active. When this happens, the cortex cannot behave in its inhibitory role to reduce your instinctive stress responses. In this chronic state, your amygdala works overtime and can actually enlarge as it continues to signal your body to respond to threat. One way to think about hypervigilance is to understand that chronic overreaction of the amygdala heightens sensory processes, which is why the visual cortex becomes overactive even when the eyes are closed and even when there is no reason to scan for input.
- **An increase in the stress hormone glucocorticoid kills cells in your hippocampus.** This disrupts the ability of the hippocampus to make synaptic connections necessary to pro-

cess explicit (individual event) long-term memory. The consolidation of memory is an action that signals the end of an experience as the information shifts out of short-term space. An interruption in this process can cause your body never to receive the message to relax. The memory hangs caught in an activated loop, which leaves your brain constantly reacting in the activated fight/flight mode. When the hippocampus operates less heartily than it should, it can shrink, and hippocampal atrophy is one of the precursors to depression. (The most successful strategies for treating depression seem to work via a common mechanism for upregulating growth factors in the hippocampus.)

- **The variability of fluctuating processes decreases.** It's hard for your body to regulate itself when your amygdala constantly activates and pegs your *cortisol* (a major stress hormone) at the high end of its range. A signaling molecule, cortisol acts in a fluctuating range to expand and contract your arousal response. When cortisol continually goes up and comes down, your body knows that when the level increases or decreases, it is required to respond in ways that prepare the body to either take an action or refuel and repair. When variability decreases, your body's ability to read the cues also decreases, and so the stress response level remains high.

It may sound as if these changes are permanent, but often they are not. For example, the hippocampus can create new neurons from stem cells, so the damage there, if addressed in a reasonable amount of time, can be reversed. Studies have also shown that while your amygdala can increase in size from extensive hyperuse, it can shrink back to its original dimensions when trauma is adequately treated. Likewise, the hippocampus, which can shrink during symptoms of PTSD, has been found to enlarge back to its original size with successful trauma treatment.

Change Your Physiology in Two Minutes

One of the quickest ways to bring about physiological change that allows you to experience more calm and shift into responsive mode is to use your breath. When you do this, the secretion of an inhibitory neuropeptide calms the amygdala. It's fast, facile, and free.

In just two minutes of practicing this simple breathing technique, you can change the relationship between your prefrontal cortex and your amygdala in a way that increases activity in your prefrontal cortex, builds resilience, and convinces your amygdala to pipe down. Follow these steps:

1. **Inhale** slowly through your mouth or nose.
2. **Exhale** slowly by shaping your lips as though you were breathing out through a straw.

Another option: Slow your breathing to about five breaths per minute. You can do this by using a 4-4-6-2 count: Breathe in for four counts, hold for four, exhale for six, hold for two.

How Does the Brain Heal? Four Key Traits

> Getting . . . information had an instant effect on me. From that day,
> the voice telling me there was something wrong with me went away. I
> became aware that I had a challenge but was not damaged goods.
>
> —*Judy A. Clemmer*

When Dorothy and I first began working together, her body was full of pain and her mind was stuck in "I-don't-feel-like-it" mode. While she wanted to heal, she didn't want the discomfort she expected the process of recovery to bring. Plus, Dorothy had serious doubts about what we could accomplish. Feeling she'd been enormously damaged for too long, she was afraid our work would leave her "banging on a wall and I can't get out." Fear of failure and disappointment introduced into Dorothy's recovery process some very real, and also some imagined, roadblocks.

I hear similar resistance from most survivors when they enter the substantial work of healing. It's a challenging time rife with self-doubt: The most important asset in recovery is yourself, and that self doesn't feel very dependable. Luckily, you don't need to be super-dependable in order to feel better. Forward motion has much to do with the daily choices you make and the actions you take, which means you don't have to sustain enthusiasm or energy consistently over a long period of time. You can make a difference in your progress by working at it in any way you can on any particular day. Some days you may make just a small effort, whereas other days you may make big gestures.

When you feel powerless, depressed, and out of control, it can be difficult to believe that you contain the ability to overcome the patterns and habits that hold you back. Knowing the *how* and *why* behind your innate healing capability can decrease resistance and increase motivation. It all begins with understanding that your brain is hardwired to evolve.

NEUROPLASTICITY

Your brain alters itself when it makes new internal connections. "Neuro" refers to the nerve cells and systems your brain uses to transmit electrical impulses. *Neurons* send messages to excite or inhibit parts of your brain and form connections through *synapses*. "Plasticity" is the technical word for your brain's adaptable reflexes. Creating change in your brain depends on the idea that *neurons that fire together wire together*. Meaning, neurons form new connections throughout the brain based on the frequency with which they simultaneously send signals. The more often neurons fire together, the more entrenched that *neural pathway* becomes, leading to long-lasting effects. So, while initial connections between neurons can occur in the brain (through a process of learning) within minutes to hours, repeated activity between those circuits over time (what scientists label "practice") wires them more and more tightly. While this is a terrifically promising fact for positive changes in recovery, on the flip side, this is also why reexperiencing trauma can be retraumatizing.

The space your brain gives to any specific pathway is governed by the rule "Use it or lose it." When you build and repeatedly use neural connections, they become stronger, outmuscling less used neural pathways and eventually taking over that space. Through a process of *pruning*, your brain constantly changes itself by eliminating unnecessary pathways in favor of expanding more efficient and immediately useful connections.

Due to advances in brain imaging technology, we know that your brain, very much like every other muscle in your body, develops with use and has the innate ability to grow, change, or diminish. We also know that such plastic change travels deep into your brain. When one brain system changes, it affects all other systems attached to or affected by it. Even your innermost brain structures that regulate your instincts maintain a level of plasticity.

USE YOUR IMAGINATION

Einstein famously said, "Imagination is more important than knowledge. For knowledge is limited to all we now know and understand, while imagination embraces the entire world, and all there ever will be to know and understand." It turns out Einstein was more right than he could ever have imagined, especially when it comes to neuroplasticity. A thought produces a physical reaction (the release of chemicals) that creates a feeling (a physical sensation). Recent studies illustrate how powerfully every thought you have alters the physical expression of your brain synapses all the way down to the microscopic level. Brain scans today prove that whether you're physically engaged in an activity *or just imagining engaging in it*, many of the necessary motor and sensory parts of your brain activate. Consider this:

A study by Erin M. Shackell and Lionel G. Standing at Bishop's University revealed how powerfully imagination informs your body. The study measured the development of muscle strength in three groups of participants. The first group continued with their usual life routines. The second group engaged in two weeks of extremely concentrated strength training for one specific muscle, three times a week. The third group sat on their couches at home while being guided by an audio CD to imagine going through the same workout as the second group, three times a week. The results were provocative: The control group, who didn't work out, saw zero muscle strength changes. The exercise group, who trained three times a week, saw a 28-percent gain in strength. And the group who sat on the couch and merely imagined exercising saw almost the same gains in strength as the exercise group: 24 percent. The group that actually worked out and the group that only imagined working out saw nearly the same benefit in physical change.

How does this apply to your healing? The more you imagine doing something, the more you train your brain and the more quickly you will be able to do what you imagine. When you're exhausted by symptoms, it's easy to say that your brain just doesn't work properly. However, your imagination works any time you decide to utilize it. In fact, it works even when you don't decide: Every time you worry, you are, in effect, imagining the future. Putting your imagination to positive use through frequent practice (e.g., by imagining how you would like to manage your emotions or handle stress) can strengthen, support, and even create new neural pathways and connections that lead to changes in how your brain regulates itself.

Imagine the Future

Choose an emotional post-trauma response that feels out of your control. Maybe you're quick to get angry, or to cry. Maybe you dissociate or lack focus. Right now, spend a few minutes imagining how you *would like* to behave in those moments:

- Close your eyes and let your mind wander to what that experience would look like, sound like, and feel like.
- See the whole scene from just before its beginning all the way through to the end.
- Imagine you behave exactly as you wish. Imagine you stay levelheaded, dry eyed, present, and completely focused.
- Repeat this exercise for two to three minutes twice daily. (Hint: It takes thirty *consecutive* days for your brain to completely solidify a new neural pathway.)

LEARN

Learning prompts individual neurons to change their structure and strengthen new connections. The more motivated you are to learn something, the more your brain responds plastically by linking neurons in new ways. This process turns on when the brain experiences something novel, surprising, or important, or when it's paying close attention. As a matter of fact, novelty and newness keep your plastic regulatory system from atrophying and may even trigger *neurogenesis*, the production of new neurons. Neurogenesis is a process begun in childhood that extends even through adulthood (albeit at a lower rate). Young cells survive when they make connections with other cells, which they do substantially through learning processes. You can activate neurogenesis at any time by engaging your brain in something that requires it to assimilate new information. That can be word games, math puzzles, or learning a new language or skill. Virtually anything will offer the desired benefit as long as it challenges your brain to step out of its expected patterns or intensely focus your attention.

The key to success in any educational process is that of *spaced practice*. Your brain learns by repetition: The more you do something, the more the neurons that fire together to perform the action wire together, and the stronger the connection becomes. If you want your brain to

The Ninety-Second Rule

A thought creates a physical reaction. Any emotion you experience comes from a thought, which releases chemicals in your brain that create a feeling in your body. Here's what's important to know: That chemical reaction lasts only ninety seconds. After ninety seconds the chemical naturally subsides and disappears. If you can ride it out for ninety seconds and *shift your thoughts and focus elsewhere*, you can absolutely impact and lessen your experience of fear.

Hint: If you keep thinking stressful thoughts, you will keep producing stress chemicals that freshen the feeling of stress; the chemical will keep being released. At the same time as you focus on your preferred grounding technique, it will also help to change the thought you're having to something that is positive, calming, confident, and supportive. Some ways you can do this are:

- Counting to ninety, or watching the time go by on a clock
- Any kind of breathwork
- Singing your favorite song
- Reciting a poem
- Picturing a movie screen in your mind and running through a scene from your favorite movie
- Using your five senses to imagine you are in your favorite location
- Looking at a picture of a person, place, or thing you love

Another thing that can help you self-soothe and redirect your attention is hearing (in your head or from someone else) a thought or idea that makes you feel secure, stable, and grounded. In those moments of fear, what do you wish someone would tell you that would make you feel so much safer? Write the statement here:

_____

_____

Going forward, you can use this statement as part of your grounding technique to help you refocus your mind. Remember: The statement must be positively phrased and as specific as possible.

learn how to interrupt a flashback or regulate your emotions, you'll have to spend time learning (and then practicing) how to do that so that your brain can create the neural pathways necessary to produce the results you seek.

Flex Your Learning Muscle

There are two immediate ways to use learning to your neuroplastic advantage:

1. **What have you always wanted to learn how to do but never made time for?** Investigate what it would take to begin learning it, then commit to a daily or weekly schedule and follow through. This doesn't mean you have to learn an entire new language overnight. It can mean that you commit to a frequent schedule of small experiences, like learning ten new vocabulary words per day.

2. **Building on your imagination exercise on page 65, write out every one of the steps it would take for you to achieve your vision.** Learn the process by breaking it down into its smallest increments. Then focus your attention on practicing that process repeatedly. Ideally, this practice will be done in moments of low stress so that your brain imprints the patterned process and begins to build a neural structure it can quickly and easily access in moments of high stress.

THE ROLE OF HORMONES

Your body relies on the activity of hormones to function properly. Produced by cells and glands, hormones are the messengers that deliver information to organs and cells within your body. During a trauma, for example, the stress hormones adrenaline and cortisol help your body shift into reactive/survival mode. In healing, it helps to increase your feel-good hormones for the beneficial effects they have on both your body and your mind.

Dopamine

The hormone dopamine is your brain's primary pleasure neurotransmitter. As part of your brain's reward system, it is often released when you're doing something that feels exciting and adventurous (as learning can be). Benefits of increased dopamine include:

- An increase in good feelings, which offers your brain the opportunity to become sensitive to pleasurable experiences.
- The stimulation and motivation of your cortex, which helps it regain its powerful inhibitory function.
- The inhibition of pain and aversion centers that accompanies the firing of pleasure neural pathways.
- The strengthening of neural networks and consolidation of plastic changes.

Oxytocin

Oxytocin is often called the "bonding" hormone, as it promotes trust and connection. This can mean bonding between you and others, or even bonding with yourself; hugging yourself for a moment or two can significantly increase your oxytocin level, which provides important benefits:

- When you feel positive connection, your brain actually facilitates neuroplastic change; those positive bonds trigger unlearning and dissolve old neural networks, thereby paving the way to create new ones constructed on the present focus of your attention.
- Research suggests that oxytocin may activate the "tend-mend" response, your body's natural antidote to the fight/flight stress reaction.
- Oxytocin contains anti-inflammatory healing properties that can help relieve physical pain.

- Oxytocin reduces stress, blood pressure, and cortisol.

The take-away here is the importance of using your brain. Whether it's through imagination, learning, or processes that encourage the production of hormones that trigger neuroplasticity, it's important to keep your brain active in recovery. Letting your brain stagnate and atrophy through underuse and monotony allows crucial aspects to weaken, which makes healing even more challenging. Monotony actually undermines your dopamine production as well as the engagement of your attentional systems (where and how you place your brain's focus), both of which are critical to facilitating neuroplastic change.

Admittedly, when you feel discouraged by depression and overwhelmed by active post-trauma effects, it can be tempting to just let your brain be idle. We've all spent our fair share of hours zoned out in front of the television. Bogged down by symptoms, it can also be difficult to *want* to take any actions, but that only underscores how vital this process is to your recovery. In the beginning of this journey you don't do what you want; you do what you need. The exciting news is that your experience of any of these things doesn't have to be huge in order to have beneficial effects. Taking just the smallest actions in the areas listed above, over a consistent period of time, can produce significant changes.

FOCUSED ATTENTION

Noisy thought hid my recognition to the many amazing accomplishments
I was making. It was then that I learned the key to re-connecting to my
true identity was to pay attention to what is directly right in front of me.
—*Cheryl Schiltz*

Dorothy escaped her family of origin in her junior year of high school when she became pregnant and moved out of her house to live with the baby's father. They married, then divorced a few years later. Soon Dorothy became pregnant for a second time and moved in with her new boyfriend, the expected baby's father. Three years after the birth, the pair split up and Dorothy accepted the proposal of a longtime friend. She and her two children moved into the home that would shelter them for the next several decades.

Away from her family and in a stable and loving relationship, Dorothy expected that her anxiety, frequent nightmares, and hypervigilance would subside. In fact, the opposite was true. With every passing year she felt increasingly distressed. Early in our work Dorothy and I began to discuss what it would mean for her to be back in control of both herself and her life.

Immediately Dorothy shook her head. "My mind is so out of control. All the crazy thoughts turn me into a crazy person. I try to stop thinking about what was done to me or how unfair it was or about what someone has said or how I've been hurt, but I just can't stop!"

Dorothy's experience illustrates one of the most common issues and most difficult challenges of the trauma recovery process: Your mind can become a little obsessive-compulsive and resist your desire to shift focus. Whether or not this is a familiar problem to you, the following information about attention and how you can lasso it will offer solutions for how to better train your brain.

The arousal self is a survival pattern into which you shift, and out of which you can also shift. Your objective in trauma recovery is to constantly increase the flow of information to your cortex (specifically your frontal lobes and particularly the left hemisphere) so that it can more actively and effectively organize and regulate the processes that occur in your deeper brain regions. One of the main ways your brain achieves change is through *focused attention*, an activity regulated by your prefrontal cortex.

There are many ways to redevelop your ability to control your attention. Mindfulness training (including mindfulness-based stress reduction) and traditional meditation practices (vipassana, samatha, metta, transcendental meditation) have proven to be among the best. By understanding and exploring these accessible methods, you can deepen your process of deliberately encouraging your brain to change.

Relabel and Redirect

With your reptilian brain highly sensitized to threat and your attention not working as optimally as it could, you might find yourself having subtle obsessive-compulsive tendencies or even full-blown obsessive-compulsive disorder (OCD). The two-step process described below will help you begin training your brain to unlock itself whenever you feel it becoming stuck:

1. *Relabel.* Observe your stuck behavior and identify it as an OCD-type habit. Say to yourself, "This compulsion is just my brain getting caught in a loop."

2. *Refocus.* Immediately engage yourself (for thirty minutes if you can) in an activity that brings a good and pleasant experience.

The practice of *relabeling* shifts you out of a mode of self-blame and recrimination and opens up space inside of you between your thoughts and who you are. *Refocusing* helps restrain the old behavior in favor of the new one while simultaneously developing new neural circuits.

Training your attention requires only a small effort on your part. (As you become more and more comfortable, you can build up the amount of time you devote to engaging in these activities.) Naturally, you will want to see immediate results. Set aside that desire. Instead, focus on your intention to create a habit rather than a specific and single outcome. Like most things in recovery, results take time and practice. In the case of mindfulness and meditation, it takes one to two full months of daily practice to see extensive benefits. You may, however, experience and notice small achievements along the way.

Learning to employ mindfulness and meditation requires you to take actions that reduce stress, which can at first feel awkward, unfamiliar, and even threatening. Practicing these techniques in conjunction with the sidebar exercises throughout this chapter (especially by employing the breathing technique prior to any practice) can help quiet your fear response so that you move into a gentle process of learning.

MINDFULNESS

[What has helped me connect to myself is] ensuring I have safe space to
work through the recognition process. [Also,] start[ing to] understand
those connections, plus building a strong support network who know me
to be the accomplished, active, vivacious person I am today is so helpful.

—S. S.

Your mind's ability to expand its capacity for clarity and calm is limit-
less. A process that naturally increases empathy (a fantastic quality to
apply to how you treat yourself), mindfulness allows you to develop the
skill to notice what you feel in any moment while also noticing that the
being that is you is separate from the neurobiological responses creating
the sensations you experience. In my radio interview with mindfulness
expert Ronald D. Siegel, PsyD, he put it this way:

Mindfulness is actually an attitude toward your experience . . . . It's
a way to relate to whatever arises in the heart, the mind, and the
body . . . . This attitude toward experience . . . involves awareness
of present experience with acceptance. Things arise and pass unless
we think and resist. When people take up mindfulness, they notice
it's very hard to accept the distasteful things that come up in the
mind. It's either frightening or a little bit painful, so there's a lot of
resistance. We have to remember that mindfulness is about training the mind to accept what comes up, to have a kind of loving and
warm attitude, even toward the uncomfortable thoughts and feelings that arise. Thoughts take us out of the present moment; mindfulness takes us out of the thought stream and back into the present
moment. We train the mind to bring attention away from the constant stream of words flowing through our heads and more toward
our senses. This helps us to have some perspective on our thoughts,
which helps us to take those thoughts less seriously.

While meditation changes the physical structure of your brain
through consistent focus, mindfulness trains your brain for ongoing
consciousness. Specifically, mindfulness entails observation of your

experience in the present moment through a view of suspended judgment. You can thus think of mindfulness as these two processes:

- Self-regulating your attention by directing it toward the observable facts of the present moment as portrayed through your thoughts, feelings, emotions, and physical responses.
- Adopting a perspective toward the "now" experience that is curious, open, and accepting; whatever emotions or thoughts come up in response to what you notice is okay. In this action, you accept the thoughts and feelings even while you may reject the situation that causes them.

The purpose of using mindfulness is to create an ongoing inner state of consciousness and equanimity. In this state your experience becomes one of being in tune with yourself and responding in appropriate ways. You will notice an increase in emotional regulation, strength, and flexibility. When you observe what's happening inside of you (an action that engages your frontal lobes and keeps them online), you delineate the difference between your experience and reaction. You also allow yourself to learn about your responses versus being controlled by them, which is an action-oriented experience that puts space between what you feel, how you think, and what you do. In that space, you reclaim control through your ability to make choices about how you react in any moment.

When it comes to developing a mindfulness practice, Siegel suggests an approach that considers anything fair game. As long as it helps your mind become more aware of experience "with acceptance," it qualifies as a mindfulness practice. He says,

> Informal mindfulness involves just making some shifts in how you do normal daily activities so that you do them in ways that make you more mindful. This can be done even in the midst of a busy day. For example, you can go out for a walk and simply bring attention to the sensation of your feet touching the ground. You walk normally but notice the contact of your feet, and then the lack of contact. Or,

you can notice the details of what is around you: the colors, sounds, and smells. Decide each time you walk you're going to make that an opportunity for mindfulness practice. Or taking a shower, which is a very rich, sensual experience in terms of the feeling of the water, the fragrance of the soap, etc. You can decide that every time you go into the shower, you're going to pay attention to how it feels. There are many opportunities in the day that you can commit to paying more attention to your experience while you continue about your normal routine. On the other hand, formal mindfulness practice involves setting time aside and being with some object of aware-ness -- engaging in an activity exclusively to develop mindfulness. For example, you might close your eyes and bring your attention to the sensation of the breath, or to the sounds around you. It's like tak-ing time out of your busy day to train your mind at the mental gym.

It takes only five to twenty minutes per day to develop a constructive mindfulness practice, and those minutes can be either sequential or dis-connected. Plus, mindfulness can be done anywhere, anytime, without anyone noticing. This means you have zero excuses for not doing it! The next time you're on the bus, stuck in traffic, in a crowded restaurant, or walking alone down the street, you can employ some simple steps to train your brain in a matter of seconds.

Mindfulness Made Simple

1. Pause what you're doing.
2. In your mind, take a step back from the moment.
3. Notice your breathing.
4. Notice the situation you're in through all five of your senses.
5. Notice your thoughts.
6. Notice what you're feeling.
7. Acknowledge your thoughts and feelings as representing the moment you're in.

8. Release and suspend judgment about your thoughts, feelings, or behavior.
9. Focus on the facts of your environment.
10. Observe more deeply the information coming from your senses.
11. Place and hold your focus somewhere (internal or external) pleasant (e.g., on a feel-good memory, image, or song).

Start yourself off easy. In the beginning, try this process only once a day if that's all that feels comfortable. After a week, double that. After another week, double that again, and so forth until you continue to build up enough of a stable practice that your brain automatically, and daily, falls into the practice of mindfulness in moments you least expect.

MEDITATION

I certainly do feel a sense of loss of self, which leaves me feeling insecure, inferior, frightened, and vulnerable. My key to healing is meditation, which helps me spiritually, physically, mentally, and emotionally.

—*Denise Stokell, South Africa*

When you routinely practice relaxation, you can improve the expression of genes that control your stress response. One of the most powerful ways to train yourself to relax is through meditation. With a practice that requires only five minutes per day, you can actually lower your blood pressure, improve your breathing, lower your resting heart rate, and dramatically reduce your stress hormones. You can also start to beat insomnia: Serotonin modulates your sleep cycle. Low levels of this neurotransmitter are a cause of insomnia. Meditation, however, increases serotonin and so can enhance sleep. Plus, during meditation your brain produces theta brain waves, the waves present during light sleep and the REM dream state.While the myth of meditation is that you need to clear your mind, that's absolutely the wrong way to approach meditating. There's more than one way to meditate; some require mind-clearing exercises while others don't, which means *you can choose what feels right to you* and still reap the benefits.

One final thing to remember: The aim is to train your mind to refocus your attention. For meditation to work, your mind *needs* to wander.

Meditation processes fall into three categories:

- *Focused attention.* Techniques in this category require concentration and activate brainwaves related to focusing on a single object for a period of time. They build your ability to choose your focus and stop distractions. Examples: Staring at a candle or a spot on the wall, or paying close attention to a consistent sound (including your breath).
- *Open monitoring.* Techniques in this category require mindfulness and being present to the most extreme degree possible. They activate brainwaves related to internal mental processing through noticing your internal experience. This increases your ability to be in touch with your internal state and more evenly distribute your attention. Example: Being aware of your thoughts and feelings through simple observation.
- *Automatic self-transcending.* Techniques in this category go beyond the limits of self or the moment. They activate brainwaves associated with executive and overall integrated functioning of the brain that promote a relaxed inner wakefulness. In this practice, you simply "be" versus deliberately trying to control your attention. This is the most effortless form of meditation as it requires zero cognitive processing. Example: Repetition of a phrase or sound.

Choosing which type of meditation best supports your primary objective depends on what type of response you wish to facilitate in your brain, plus what you feel you're prepared to do. Through the course of your recovery, there may be times that you use one method and then times you switch to another depending on the desired result and your level of competency.

Meditation was one of the first practices that Dorothy and I discussed implementing. Because she existed in such an anxious state, I suggested she begin with an automatic self-transcendent practice that would help reduce her overall stress level. Transcendental meditation (TM) has a terrific track record in this area. The purpose of TM is to detach yourself from anxiety by developing harmony and self-realization through the private practice of repeating a mantra.

Like many people, Dorothy balked at first at the idea of sitting still, closing her eyes, and going inward. When I explained that this practice simply asked her to exist and told her that however she did it would be right, Dorothy agreed to set aside fifteen minutes every day to sit in a quiet spot, close her eyes, and repeat a word. I asked her to choose a word that made her feel good and that had good memories associated with it; she chose *love*. To underscore the special significance of her commitment to meditate, Dorothy developed a special meditation space in her home office. She set up a chair with a comfortable cushion and a light quilt. She placed lavender incense on a small table along with some smooth stones that helped her feel the presence of peace.

At first Dorothy complained that fifteen minutes felt too long; her mind wandered away from the word and she felt antsy. There was too much to think about that interfered with her making sure she was meditating properly. To help relieve her mind's busyness, I made a recording that began with a slow body relaxation and then shifted into a fifteen-minute repetition of the word *love* before gently bringing her back to the present moment. Taking the pressure off Dorothy's learning curve did the trick. Within a few weeks, she was shocked to discover that she had become much less anxious. Plus, she was more able to handle stressful moments. She found herself wanting to get out of bed, shower, wash her hair, and get dressed. Six weeks into the practice, its effects, along with our weekly sessions, brought Dorothy the desire to map out a manageable schedule to begin cleaning her house. From there, she started planning meals and sending her husband to the grocery store with detailed lists of ingredients. Eventually Dorothy herself ventured out of the house to accompany her husband on these errands.

Choose Your Meditation

Do you feel uncomfortable with the idea of meditation? The following are some examples of how you can get started by personalizing the process. To discover what feels like the best practice, set aside time to try each process and choose the one that most resonates with you. If you feel most comfortable meditating with your eyes open, choose to develop your practice that way using any of these methods. In that case, you will combine the idea of a visual focal point with other aspects of the technique.

- *Quiet mind.* Go inside yourself and focus your attention on turning down the volume in your mind until there is a sense of quiet stillness. Imagine that in your mind there is a volume knob and you can tune it down at a pace that feels comfortable until you have muted out all sound.
- *Breathe.* Focus your attention on your breath. Simply follow the rise and fall of your breathing with your full attention. When you notice your mind wandering, gently bring it back to your breath.
- *Repeat.* Choose a word that means something to you, or that you would like to feel (e.g., *peace*). Hold that word in your mind. See an image of it if you can, or simply repeat the word with the voice in your head. When your mind wanders, gently bring it back to the word.
- *Look.* Choose a focal point on which to train your attention. This can be anything—a candle, a flower, a patch of grass, a spot on the wall. Focus on noticing your experience of seeing it. When your attention wanders, bring it back to really looking at the object.
- *Listen.* Music can be a great source of focused meditation. For this, choose a slow, relaxing, spalike track or album. While the music plays, deliberately focus your mind on uniquely hearing each individual note.

- *Observe.* Meditation is all about focusing your attention and keeping it where you place it. This means you can literally sit back in your mind and choose to focus your attention on observing your thoughts. For this, create an active shift in your mind so that you deliberately detach from your thoughts and then focus your attention on noticing each individual one.

Take a Time Out

Every negative behavior or reaction begins with a positive intention. By this, I mean that even the wildest fit of rage commences from a desire to bring yourself something good. You might scream at someone to make him or her back off, thereby establishing your boundary. Or, you might become angry to mobilize your own energy in order to respond to a threat. While the behavior may be over-the-top and destructive, its initial purpose is to help you.

When you feel yourself swing into a negative behavior, try implementing the following steps:

1. *Pause.* Stop all action.
2. *Step back.* Become mindful of the situation and your behavior in it.
3. *Ask.* Question what it is that you need in that moment.
4. *Assess.* Identify healthy options for achieving that outcome.
5. *Act.* Take the steps necessary to accomplish the outcome.

In the beginning, it will be challenging to implement these steps. That's okay. The more you learn, think about, imagine, and practice them, the more confidently you'll employ them in moments of need.

THE VALUE OF POSITIVE EXPERIENCE

Just to hug [my kids] and interact with them helped define the old me.
—*Marian Callahan, RN*

Through her recovery process, Dorothy built on her successes by continuing to expand her engagement with herself. While meditation brought her into a space of more relaxed, less stressed daily experience (especially because the deep rest provided by TM can be more profound and restorative than sleep), she began adding in two activities that brought her good feelings. From childhood Dorothy had been a writer. At the age of sixteen she had published her first piece in a local newspaper. Now that she was feeling more conscious and aware in her recovery, she felt the familiar tug of writing. Although she hadn't been in her home office to work in quite some time, she discovered herself going into it more and more often to read or even scrawl in a journal. Then one day she heard a story form in her head, just the way she had as a child. She sat down at the computer and began to write. What poured out was a story that became the basis for a novel she worked on over the next several months.

At the same time, Dorothy also got back in touch with her love of gardening. Before the effects of trauma rendered her homebound, Dorothy had loved to cultivate a fairy garden behind her home. Originally built for the magical delight of her children and then grandchildren, the fairy garden contained all kinds of beautiful plants and blooms, many of which had become overgrown or were suffering from lack of attention. After morning sessions of writing, Dorothy spent many afternoons recultivating the garden, putting in new plants and redesigning the landscape.

Both writing and gardening became activities Dorothy looked forward to every day. They made her feel good about herself and life in general. The more she engaged in these feelings, the better she felt about the possible future of herself and life and the more she developed an attitude of strength, hope, determination, and further commitment to the recovery process.

Dorothy's not alone in reaping the benefits of feeling good. Studies suggest that people's lives radically improve and move toward success when they have a 3:1 ratio of positive to negative experiences. Even after a trauma ends, the effects of it—and how those effects change you—heavily tip the ratio toward the negative. With a negativity bias (your brain's natural inclination to find the bad/threat), increased fears, restrictive and isolating behaviors, and a decrease in self-confidence and efficacy, it's natural that your daily experience probably includes more stressful than good experiences. Feeling good, however, has enormous impact on promoting plasticity in your brain. Learning to create and engage in positive experiences—both those that occur in connection with others and those that occur inside you—has an important place in healing.

Taking in the Good

Feeling a sense of inner connection, confidence, and security makes integration in the world at large much easier to accomplish. You learned earlier that a major glitch after trauma is the body's failure to switch out of reactive mode and into responsive mode. Positive experiences promote relaxation, safety, and a sense of connection that help the body make that shift. "Taking in the good," as it is called, refers to mindfully absorbing a positive moment into the deepest part of who you are. Because creating brain change requires both spaced practice and sustained attention, it's not enough to breeze through a positive moment every once in a while; your mind and body need a chance to record its occurrence. Plus, this needs to happen often enough that the effects build up, allowing you to ground yourself in a sense of calm expectation that good things are around and will happen to you.

Opportunities for taking in the good come from a variety of sources, including sensations, thoughts, desires, emotions, actions, interactions, and behaviors that arise during pleasurable moments, giving you a chance to notice the pleasant side of what it's like to be you. Repeated focused attention on these positive experiences tunes your amygdala to seek and expect these types of instances and make them dominant. They focus your amygdala's attention on a habit of learned optimism, which distracts it from its previous quest to find all of the (potential) bad.

If you're worried that taking in the good sounds like a lot of work and will require more energy than you possess, relax: It takes only ten to twenty seconds of mindfully holding on to a good experience for your brain to encode it in a neural pathway. Plus, every positive experience doesn't need to score a perfect 10 on a pleasure scale; scoring just a 1 or 2 can be equally effective. The point is less to be earth-shattering in scale than consistent so that the repetition of the good experiences begins to take effect in your brain.

Take in the Good Daily

In his book, *Hardwiring Happiness,* neuropsychologist, Dr. Rick Hanson, presents a full explanation and detailed summary of a taking-in-the-good practice. You can begin counteracting your negativity bias through the following adaptation of his ideas. Remember that taking in the good can happen in any instance from pulling fresh laundry out of the dryer and pausing to enjoy the scent, or deliberately catching the sunset and pausing to appreciate its beauty.

- Create and/or notice and engage in a good experience.
- Pause to notice that the experience is occurring.
- Slow down time as much as possible and allow the experience to continue.
- While the experience is ongoing, take time to consciously label what it is and how it feels (You might say to yourself, "Petting this puppy feels really good", or "Drinking this hot chocolate is very comforting", or "Walking in the park on this beautiful day is so relaxing.").
- Enrich your experience by bringing your awareness and the

experience into your body. Imagine where in your body you feel the good feeling the most and how that part absorbs the feeling like a sponge.

Deepen your experience by continuing with these steps I've added to help you develop basic imagination and learning skills to further enhance your experience:

1. Imagine that the good feeling is a ball that has a color and a size.
2. All feelings spin: They tumble forward or backward, clockwise or counterclockwise. Identify which way the feeling spins. Then, if it feels right, make it spin more quickly in that direction. (Note: If this feels uncomfortable, try reversing the direction. While for most people the original direction is optimized when the speed is increased, for a small percentage the process will work in reverse. The purpose is to increase the good feeling by spinning the emotion more quickly in the direction that feels good.)
3. Deliberately focus your attention on feeling the experience come more deeply into you. Imagine that your body holds wounds (both physical and emotional) that the experience enters with an intense healing intention, perhaps even a white light. Imagine that those wounds are red and that as the good feeling spreads into those areas, the red turns to a cool, soothing blue.
4. Spin the feeling ball faster and, while doing so, imagine that the faster it spins, the more the good feeling is powered to extend throughout your entire body. Imagine that the good feeling extends from the original source all the way to the top of your head and all the way to the soles of your feet. Take a long, slow, deep breath. Be aware of any sounds and smells and sights in the moment. The more real you make the experience by noticing all of your senses, plus imagining the sensation of goodness coming into you and spreading, the more strongly your brain will encode the experience.

The objective with this process is to be uniquely present, entirely aware that you are the one experiencing the good feeling (that you own it; it is yours), and to focus on it intently so that you feel you have this goodness *inside of you.*

If you practice taking in the good enough (Dr. Hanson suggests six or more times a day, usually in the flow of everyday life) the eventual payoff will be that the positive mental state you experience in those moments ultimately converts to underlying neural traits; you'll build new positive neural pathways and connections that become faster, more efficient and edge out older negative processes. Your brain will begin seeking out those good feelings all by itself. Plus, you will develop your ability to be your own best friend, deepen your dedication to self-care, and increase your capacity for building internal resources. When you first begin practicing taking in the good, you may notice that you resist either the actual good experience or the process of interacting with it. That's completely normal. It can seem awkward, unfamiliar, uncomfortable, and even unsafe to turn your attention to something pleasurable. You may also feel that you don't deserve to feel good or that doing so is selfish or betrays others. If this happens, simply turn the moment into an opportunity for mindfulness practice: Allow those feelings to come up, acknowledge them with suspended judgment, and then set them aside the way you would a cup of coffee. (If the thoughts are very persistent, set them aside while offering to pick them back up at a later time.) Since taking in the good requires only ten to twenty seconds of your time (or longer if you feel like deepening the benefits), there's plenty of time to go back to your regular uncomfortable feelings. After you have practiced taking in the good over a period of time, you may discover that you hold on to the good feeling more and more and feel less and less prone to reclaiming those old, bad feelings you'd like to release.

Practice Gratitude

"Taking in the good" requires you to open up space within yourself. If you're carrying a lot of negative and uncomfortable feelings, where will you place the good ones? Another simple practice to create spaciousness in how you think and how you feel is the practice of gratitude. You can do this in three easy steps:

1. *Seek*. Become a goodness sleuth by looking for things (both tiny and enormous) for which to be grateful; keep a running log throughout the day.

2. *Absorb*. At night before you go to bed, take a moment or two to reflect on and embrace the things for which you are grateful that day.

3. *Appreciate:* Notice what about you (personal qualities, choices, actions) allowed you to connect with those things for which you feel grateful.

INTEGRATION

Through understanding psychology and utilizing visualization of my fragmented parts becoming familiar with each other, then comfortable around one another and finally merging each part of myself back together, I now have a very strong sense of who I am and what I am.

—*Heidi (Dr. Sousse)*

One day Dorothy began our session by explaining, "I feel like I've been divided into five separate women and they're all in my head. There's my terrified survivor self, my hero I'm-going-to-survive self, my warrior I-can-withstand-the-pain self, my professional we-need-to-get-a-grip-on-life-self, and my sad I-think-I'm-going-to-cry-forever self."

I immediately knew what Dorothy meant; I'd felt that same sense of divided parts (not separate personalities) in my own recovery. While you may not experience this exact type of internal categorization, many survivors feel a sense of fragmentation either within themselves or in their lives. Some of the most common metaphors to describe the post-trauma world come from the idea of destruction. I often hear survivors describe life and even themselves as "shattered," "fractured," "fragmented," "shredded," "broken," or "torn." As if a bomb blew up, trauma can leave you experiencing the chaos of pieces scattered in every direction, plus the sensation that what was once whole now has many different parts. Healing these rifts is a major component of reclaiming who you are.

Putting back together your fragmented parts happens through a process of *integration*. This means incorporating the trauma (often a memory that is held apart) into the overall view of your life, plus bringing into one whole persona the different fragments of who you have become.

Dorothy went on to say, "I don't know which part is supposed to be in control. Each one has a different agenda, and it feels like they're all trying to be in control at once."

A huge objective for Dorothy became integrating the parts and consolidating their agendas. She accomplished this by focusing on two parts that seemed to contain the most intense energy: her professional self and her sad self. By interacting with them, she discovered that they represented her grief about the past versus her desire to claim control over the direction of her life. At times, Dorothy felt as if those two parts were at war inside her mind and body.

To help resolve the battle and promote the outcome she wanted (her professional self claiming the ultimate control), Dorothy worked hard to integrate the needs of both parts in ways that were manageable. In some moments that meant finding ways to allow her sad self to explore what it loved so much in the past. In other moments that meant slowly and reasonably expanding her interaction in the world in ways that allowed her professional self to reengage with the (fun) process of living. By the end of her recovery, Dorothy had effectively negotiated an integration of all the parts so that the sad self gently moved into the background, allowing her professional self to become the part that guided her daily living choices. It was on this self that Dorothy formed the foundation of her post-trauma identity.

Nine Areas of Integration

After trauma, many survivors swing on a pendulum between rigidity and chaos. As you seek safety and control, you either place a tight, manipulated grip on your world, making it small, routinized, and predictable, or you give in to a hands-off-the-wheel approach in which you get tossed along in a sea of unpredictability. Ideally, integration allows you to experience neither rigidity nor chaos but a sense of well-being that rests in a balanced-living approach supported by internal and external connections that deliver feelings of safety and control.

Psychiatrist Dr. Dan Siegel focuses on the purpose of integration creating connections, both internally and externally, while honoring and sustaining the differences between the items being linked. For example, the limbic system sends emotional information up to the cortex, which sends back down regulation of reflexes and emotions. Or, the left and right parts of your brain exchange information about thoughts and feelings. Integrating different systems sustains the importance of both while linking them in beneficial ways. The more connections you create in your mind, body and interactions the more sense of well-being you will develop. Also, the more integrated your neural pathways and processes become the better your brain functions.

Knowing the nine possible areas of integration and developing a plan for enhancing the ones you feel would support your recovery can give you clear ideas for moving forward. The nine areas as defined by Dr. Siegel, in his book *Mindsight*, include:

Consciousness—Awareness of your body, your mental/emotional state, your relationship with the outside world, and a sense of openness to things as they are in this moment.

Bilateral—Synchronizing the left (logical, linear, analytical) and right (non-verbal, bodily-based, metaphoric) hemispheres.

Vertical—Synchronizing all three parts of the brain from the lower (reptilian and old mammalian) to higher (cortex).

Memory—Linking implicit (memories you don't know are from the past) with explicit (memories you consciously work to retrieve) memories. (When traumatic memories remain only implicit they gain control. A part of healing trauma can mean making implicit memories explicit so that you are no longer involuntarily stuck in the past.)

Narrative—Being able to not only tell your autobiographical story because you know it but go beyond that to make sense of it. In this way you link the past, present and future.

State—In the brain there are different states of firing that create different states of mind. *Within-state* means honoring the different impulses you have to experience different things, i.e. being social versus being alone. *Across-state* refers to honoring the different needs of each state and making time for each.

Interpersonal—Developing the ability to honor and support the differences between you and others, plus maintaining your own state even while you link in healthy ways to other people.

Temporal—Connecting time in a mapping process where you know there's a future and even though it contains a lot of uncertainty you feel comfortable with it.

Transpirational—Connecting the experience of your body and external relationships with your sense of self; your place, purpose and meaning in the world; your identity.

Over the course of eighteen months, Dorothy and I worked together every single week. Sometimes she felt elated with success, and other times she felt the pain of slow progress. Regardless of the pace, Dorothy showed up, engaged, followed through, resisted and embraced perceived setbacks, and devised strategies to move ahead. Using a combination of self-applied and professionally administered processes designed to sever

---

The nine areas of integration are used with permission of Mind Your Brain, Inc., for the services of Dr. Daniel J. Siegel.

old neural pathways and put new ones in place, plus her own diligent application of exercises and tools, Dorothy and I retrained and rewired her brain so that today she is free of PTSD symptoms and off all medications. She sleeps through the night and has reengaged with the world. She has gone on vacation (her first in a decade), participated in her grandson's high school graduation, and lost sixty pounds, and she is working on completing her third novel. Periodically I receive emails from her, full of jubilation and glee. "I am FREE!" she writes, and then brings me up to date on her latest adventure.

Wheel of Awareness

This concept, developed by Dr. Dan Siegel, offers a terrific way to place some distance between who you are and what you feel. It also engages your cortex while integrating both your felt sense and your cognitive sense, leading to vertical integration.

- **Imagine an old wagon wheel or a bicycle wheel.** At the center lies a hub from which spokes lead out to the rim. You are the center of the wheel, the hub of awareness.

- **As the hub, you are the peaceful felt sense** at the center of who you are. Even when you don't feel like a peacefully centered person, this is still who you are at the core. Your aim with this exercise is to identify the existence of that core self while at the same time noticing how other parts of you feel.

- **The spokes leading to the outer rim attend to your thoughts, feelings, and perceptions.** Your focus here is to train yourself to notice the difference between the hub and the spokes. For example, say to yourself, "That fear is a temporary feeling. It's what a part of me is feeling, but it is not the totality of who I truly am. I am awareness at the hub of the wheel."

The Take-Aways

Learn specific breathing and movement practices that balance your stress response systems and activate your body's innate self-healing systems. Use Coherent Breathing to reconnect with your sense of self and to restore your ability to bond with others.

—*Patricia L. Gerbarg, MD*

- Many of your trauma responses (both psychological and physical) occur without your specifically choosing how they manifest, or where or when.
- When you survive trauma, your body encodes that event in memories all the way down to each tiny cell.
- Your brain is a constantly evolving, ever-changing organ that alters its structure and performance based on the information it receives.
- If your brain changes in response to experience, then you have the opportunity to deliberately help your brain change again based on *new experiences you create.*
- Whether it's through imagination, learning, or processes that encourage the production of hormones that trigger neuroplasticity, it's important to keep your brain active in recovery.

Who Were You Before Trauma?

ACKNOWLEDGE YOUR LOST SELF

> Gratitude is a healthy sensation . . . [Y]ou do need to find something
> meaningful to acknowledge, something that came your way, that brought
> you hope or a sense of meaning or a feeling of connection beyond yourself.
>
> —*Frank Ochberg, MD*

Just two weeks after her high school graduation, Phyllis joined the army. She was seventeen years old and excited at the prospect of serving her country. A sheltered girl from a small midwestern town, Phyllis expected to find camaraderie, discipline, distinction, and the fulfillment of a patriotic dream. What she got instead were several instances of military sexual trauma on two separate bases that included verbal, emotional, and physical abuse. She explains:

"The harassment begins the moment you enlist. Male or female, the protocol is to strip your identity. For women this becomes incredibly expansive, as we are also expected to eliminate our femininity. We're told not to cross our legs, tilt our head to the side, or excessively blink our eyes. There's an intense focus on harassment related to female parts until you find yourself despising the fact that you're a woman. There's pressure to be unattractive and unseductive and not to be 'whores' who get the guys in trouble. But those are all secondary issues to the instances of physical abuse I experienced. For example, in the middle of a class I was bit by an airman in what was termed a sexual assault. The individual teeth marks left bruises that covered one-third of my bicep. He threatened to further hurt me if I reported the incident, so I didn't. But class members who witnessed the attack did report it. Afterward, the airman was slightly reprimanded and then came after me for a second attack in retaliation. When I sought help from my female platoon leader, she didn't want to get involved for fear it would hurt her career."

After another incident extensively tarnished Phyllis's reputation, she ended her army career. Today, she is in school and on her way to becoming a social worker, but the effects of the trauma linger. She shares, "The cost of all of this is a complete and total loss of self—both the identity I was building as a late adolescent, and also the healthy sexual identity I should have had the opportunity to develop but as a consequence never did. Instead, I stopped being who I was and became someone else. I overly obsessed about my reputation and appearance. I was always on guard. I lost connection to that girl I was before. She was carefree and innocent and confident. She was hopeful and forthright. She didn't hide. She was all the things I wish I could be today. I miss her so much, even now."

If it weren't for what happened, you could have been someone else. It isn't fair that forces outside of you decided how your life would change and be redirected; what would be taken from you, or not given. The pain of lost chances, withheld choices, and a life that would have felt good can bring up intense, constant, and palpable regret. On your odyssey toward freedom, it's going to be necessary to acknowledge all that has been lost about who you are, whether that's who you were before or who you could have been. As long as that self feels disconnected, lost, and abused, you will continue to feel those things. Moving forward necessitates reconnecting that self to who you are today—in fact, absorbing it inside of who you are right this minute.

Of all the choices that have been withheld from you, there are many that still exist. Motivational speaker Al Foxx is a traumatic brain injury survivor. Semiparalyzed on the left (a condition that affects both his speech and mobility), he achieved the impossible: When doctors said he'd never walk, talk, work, or drive again after a horrific motorcycle crash, Foxx decided he had other plans. Today, he is an author and humorist who speaks for companies as big as Boeing, Costco, and John Deere, plus universities and government and healthcare agencies. Foxx's ready-to-wear motto fits every type of trauma survivor: "Winners focus on what they have, not what they don't have." For example, you have options for where you place your focus, and the decisions you make. You have options for how you will create your life from this day forward. In the past, perhaps you had zero options; today you have many, and they all relate to how you choose to create your future.

Up until this point, you have probably focused on the negative elements associated with your past self: what you miss, what you long for, what you feel angry about having had to give up. It's time now to look back for two different reasons: compassion and exploration. Your past holds the seeds and clues to who you are today. Feeling disconnected from or disturbed by your lost self withholds positive, strong, and supportive elements from who you are in the present. Restoring that connection and access to what seems most important about who you were or could have been can add value and purpose to who you are and will become.

Perhaps this is the first time you're considering your past self or selves. As you prepare to fully recognize and document who you were or could have been "before"—and all the changes since—your sensation of loss may become more acute, focused, and palpable. Now is a time to support yourself even more avidly than ever before. Refer to Appendix A for a go-to stress reduction cheat sheet summarizing the tools from Chapter 2. Then commit to a schedule of daily practices to more deeply ground and center yourself for the work ahead.

Build a Picture of the Past

[M]y role being a Child of God has not changed . . .
[T]here is at least one unbroken thread running through my
life and identity before and after trauma, and this has helped
me to feel safer and more able to redefine my identity . . .

—*Anonymous*

When she was nine, Ashley got into a typical childhood fight with Jess, her seven-year-old sister. Jess punched her, and Ashley smacked her back so hard she knocked the wind out of Jess, who collapsed on the floor. Ashley's parents were furious and punished her. They needn't have: Ashley was shocked by the impact of her unexpected strength. Looking at her sister gasping for breath, Ashley promised herself she would never, ever hurt another soul. Not only that, she would make sure *she* was always hurt before anyone else suffered. Through the rest of her childhood and into adulthood, Ashley kept her promise.

Then, at the age of twenty-three, she was raped. Soon afterward Ashley began struggling with PTSD. In our work together, as we examined the picture of her nine-year-old Before self, Ashley, now thirty-six, found the origin of her most troubling After feeling:

"I'm at the last stage of recovery," she explained, "and I have this one lingering issue: I don't believe that if I needed to I'd be able to defend myself. The idea of putting others ahead of myself is so engrained that it's become my first response to everything. I had totally forgotten about this memory, but in examining it now I can remember how strong the emotion was that day, and the promise I made. I see how it's impacted me for the rest of my life . . . even on the day I was raped. I didn't fight back. He wasn't armed and we were about the same size; if I had fought back, could I have escaped?"

Developing a full picture of the past, from the incident at age nine to the trauma at twenty-three, allowed Ashley to recognize, embrace, and appreciate how deep-seated had become her belief that she shouldn't stand up for herself. Seeing that truth so clearly, Ashley revised her experience of both the childhood memory and her critical assessments of herself on the day of the rape. First, she viewed the original memory more maturely: As a young child she made a promise to herself in the midst of a traumatic learning experience. That nine-year-old girl, however, had no way to know that the world might sometimes require her to negate the promise in order to ensure her personal safety. Second, she forgave herself for what she felt had been an inappropriate response to her attacker. While she had been extremely critical of herself for not fighting back, Ashley could now see how years of conditioning to eschew her physical strength might well have prevented her from mobilizing a more empowered response.

In addition to the belief shift, Ashley also discovered an important aspect of her younger self: She had enormously strong beliefs and capabilities when it came to protecting herself. This information showed Ashley direct proof that she did indeed have (however buried inside her) the impulse and wherewithal to self-protect. Bringing that instinct from her past into her present became a major act of healing and created an enormous shift not only in how Ashley viewed dangers in the outside world but also in how she viewed herself.

Like Ashley, the beliefs you developed as a child have become a part of your philosophy today. Yet those beliefs are not always appropriate. As an adult, Ashley still values protecting others, but she understands she must not sacrifice herself to do so. Looking back as part of her healing process led Ashley to look forward with a new perspective. For you, too, the intention in recovery is less to excise the past than to integrate it, folding it into yourself and your brain so that it becomes a small part of the larger you.

Reduce Discomfort

There may be aspects of the exercises in this chapter that are uncomfortable, or that you resist altogether. This will be completely normal. You are about to challenge coping skills that have organized and labeled uncomfortable things as dangerous so that you avoid discomfort. If you feel ready for this work, proceed ahead. When you experience any uncomfortable responses, try the following steps:

- Let those emotions come up.
- Practice mindfulness.
- Respect and honor the information your mind and body supply. Remind yourself, "These feelings are my body and mind sending me necessary information."
- Share what you are feeling, thinking, and experiencing with a trusted source (your journal, therapist, family member, friend).
- The information contains a message about something important to you. What is it? Take some time to reflect and then write down the ideas that occur to you.
- Activate your self-care and support mechanisms.
- Take a break from the work.
- Engage help to process the exercise.
- When you feel ready, slowly focus on your next step.
- Proceed with caution and respect for your reactions.

WHO WERE YOU BEFORE? (OR, WHO DID YOU NOT HAVE THE CHANCE TO BE?)

Creating your picture of the past begins by asking yourself a leading question.

If you have a clear vision of who you were before trauma, the question is, "Who did I used to be?"

If you do not have a clear Before self, the question becomes, "Who could I have been?"

Finding a full and complete answer starts with memory (in response to the first question) or imagination (in response to the second). It continues with a detailed examination of your perspective about yourself, others, and the world.

These exercises are meant to be freely associative. Every answer is right. Some questions may spark a plethora of immediate ideas, while others may plant a seed for further exploration over a period of time. The objective is to begin mining the superficial, off-the-top-of-your head, easily available information and then allow your thoughts to ramble to a deeper level of feeling and knowing. Resist any response that says, "I don't know!" You do know. Or, a part of you knows. Your job is to access that part. Sometimes this will happen immediately; at other times you may have to put down this book, allow the ideas to percolate, and then come back to the exercise. In other words, "I don't know!" is an unacceptable answer. When those words come to mind, say, "Cancel that!" and then create an attitude and environment in your mind that allow new ideas to formulate. Suspend judgment. Lose the impulse to criticize or assess the answers. Just let the answers be what they are. With an attitude of discovery, allow the ideas to lead you down an unexpected trail of thought.

Work through the following exercises if you have a clear Before/After shift. (If you don't have a distinct before and after self, skip down to the next section.)

Record your answers to the following exercises in your notebook. If you don't have a specific answer for any of the questions, use your imagination. Reframe the question from one that asks for concrete details about your past self to one that invites you to *imagine* what that self used to do or be like.

- Describe your Before self. How did the person you used to be walk, talk, dress, play, love, explore, work, plan, hope, dream?
- When you were that self, what did you think was true about who you were? List all positive and negative thoughts.

- When you were that self, how did you feel about yourself? List all positive and negative emotions.
- When you were that self, what kind of actions did you take to care for or harm yourself?
- What fears about yourself did you possess? Include both major and minor fears.
- In what ways are you similar to this past self? In what ways are you different?

Describe your Before self in relation to others:

- What did you used to think about other people? List all positive and negative thoughts.
- How did you feel about other people? List all positive and negative emotions.
- What kinds of actions did you take to reach out or recoil?
- What fears about others did you possess?

Describe your Before self in relation to the world at large:

- What did you used to think about the world beyond your immediate home? List all positive and negative thoughts.
- How did you used to feel about the world? List all positive and negative emotions.
- What kinds of actions did you take to reach out or recoil?
- What fears about the world did you possess?

If you do not have a clear Before/After shift, follow these exercises:
Describe who you might have been if your early childhood had been trauma free:

- What kinds of thoughts about yourself do you imagine you might have had or wish you had? List all positive and negative thoughts.

- What kinds of feelings do you imagine you might have had or wish you had? List all positive and negative feelings.
- What kinds of actions might you have taken to care for yourself?
- What fears about yourself might you have had? Include both major and minor fears.

Describe what your relationship to others might have been if trauma had been absent from your early childhood:

- What kinds of thoughts about other people do you imagine you might have had or wish you had? List all positive and negative thoughts.
- What kinds of feelings about other people do you imagine you might have had or wish you had? List all positive and negative feelings.
- What kinds of actions might you have taken to reach out?
- What fears about other people might you have had? Include both major and minor fears.

Describe what your relationship to the world might have been if your early childhood had been devoid of trauma:

- What kinds of thoughts about the world do you imagine you might have had or wish you had? List all positive and negative thoughts.
- What kinds of feelings about the world do you imagine you might have had? List all positive and negative feelings.
- What kinds of actions might you have taken to reach out or recoil?
- What fears about the world might you have had? Include both major and minor fears.

WHAT IS VALUABLE ABOUT YOUR PAST SELF?

Delving into your former self is a task equal to sorting through a departed loved one's closet, with one advantage: While this action solidifies the loss, it also begins the process of resurrecting it. What you will find is that while you can grieve the life and person you used to be or could have been, you can also simultaneously begin incorporating elements of that other life into who you are today. In short, you can resuscitate what you miss about that past self (regardless of whether or not it actually existed) so that it lives again in the present.

One dark, rainy night in Nevada, forty-three-year-old Milo, an architect, was driving down the highway when a man coming toward him in the opposite lane suffered a heart attack at the wheel and hit his car. Milo's car flipped multiple times before coming to rest in a ditch. While Milo survived he sustained a mild traumatic brain injury. After months of rehab and recovery, his speech and cognition recovered. He was told he could return to part-time work at the firm that had been holding his job. There was just one problem. Tensely, he explained, "I used to be an international traveler. I used to make trips to Europe and Asia at the drop of a hat. I was totally comfortable in all modes of transportation and felt completely secure in myself. Now, I'm too terrified to drive on the highway to get to work. I stay home because I'm too afraid to travel fifteen measly miles to the office. This isn't me. This isn't who I used to be."

I asked Milo to complete the exercises you've just completed. When he finished, I asked him to take a look at the profile he'd drawn and highlight the thoughts, feelings, and actions he felt were most valuable in his past persona. Then I asked Milo to find ten or more adjectives that described the kind of person who had those thoughts, feelings, actions, and fears. He came up with words like *self-reliant, trusting, strong,* and *smart.* He also used the word *adventurous.* I asked Milo to consider how those qualities would fit into his life today, and how they would change his life if he embodied them. He studied the list and then said thoughtfully, "I can use all of those qualities today. They are gifts that were mine before and can still be mine. Now that I'm physically healed, I'm becoming more self-reliant again, and I'm trusting myself more to believe that I'm going to be okay. I'm getting stronger." He smiled broadly and continued, "It would be so fantastic if I could feel adventurous again. That was really one of the keys to who I was."

As you worked through the last few pages, you constructed an image of who you once were or might have been. While your circumstances may have changed, the past aspects of your identity that you most valued or would have valued can become part of your present. How is this possible? Those aspects are intangible, which means they are indestructible. Trauma cannot eradicate them; only your response to trauma can neutralize their presence. Healing offers opportunities to make the choice to honor those past valuable elements and so begin the process of reclaiming them.

This final step pulls all the details about the past together into a picture that means something to you today. As you work through the following list, record your thoughts and answers in your notebook.

- Looking back at the answers you provided to the first set of exercises, highlight the thoughts, feelings, actions, and fears that seem valuable to you. Whether that's enormous value or slight value, put together a fresh list.
- Taken as a whole, what do these characteristics say about you? Why is that meaningful?
- What do you admire about these characteristics?
- Reflect on the qualities and choose ten or more objective adjectives (consult a dictionary or thesaurus for help with variety) that describe a person with the characteristics you have identified.
- For each adjective, describe how incorporating it into your life on a consistent basis would change how you think, feel, and behave.

- For each adjective, identify one action you could take to embody that element in a physical way.
- In the upcoming week, find a way to incorporate each element into your behavior at least once.

Milo took this process to heart—and all the way back to work. He decided it would be "adventurous" to get back on the highway. Enlisting the help and support of family and friends, he began scheduling practice drives at low-traffic times on the highway, first with others driving and then eventually with him behind the wheel. Over a period of weeks, he built up similar actions corresponding to all of the other characteristics he identified, until he finally felt "more like a self that can be out and safe in the world." Today he has resumed his regular work schedule and is planning his first adventurous trip. It will be in the United States but across state lines, which for now, Milo feels, is adventure enough. "It's a big step in the right direction," he reports. "One day I'll break out my passport again, but only after I have some smaller trips behind me."

From the exercises above, you now have a clear picture of your past self as it feels most comfortable to you. The clarity of what has been lost may be more stark than before. It's at this point that processing grief and anger becomes important. In order to move on to developing your present and future selves, it will help to release the past with love and connection.

Respond to the Loss of Identity

> The person I liked the most, the compassionate, loving person I gave to everyone, is who I was and who I still am. This is the person that keeps removing the veil, peeling the layers away, and remains humbled by all the support and love I have received through the process of healing.
>
> —*Eileen (Silent Recovery)*

Shortly after my trauma, I returned to my "normal" life as an eighth-grader. The only problem was that nothing felt normal at all. I may have looked the same on the outside, but on the inside everything had changed. I worried about how I could keep myself safe and whether I would be able to protect myself in the future. Because these questions were so disturbing and lacked concrete answers, I shifted away from the present and back toward the past. My mission became going back to being my old self—the one who had never experienced a traumatic moment. I thought if I just could be her again, I'd be able to reduce the inner turmoil and slip back into a simple life.

In terms of academic focus, friends, music, and extracurricular activities, I tried as hard as I could to be who I had been before. Of course, no matter what I did, it was as if I were standing on one side of an enormous canyon and "She" were on the other. I learned that I could *imitate* the old me, but it didn't feel as if I was living in her mind or body. I became enormously frustrated and irritated. To combat these feelings, I tried pretending the trauma hadn't happened. Then, I pretended that even if it had happened, it hadn't affected me. Faced with the ever-growing divide between my past and present selves, I finally came to understand that not only had trauma happened, but it had left its mark—one that I couldn't remove or resist.

As time went on, this inner disconnection became debilitating. I missed the simplicity of the old me. I missed how comfortable she had felt, how connected to herself she had been, and her lack of fears. The more I tried to get back to her, the further disconnected I became, from both my old self and my new self, too. I shifted into a place filled with grief, anger, isolation, and disappointment. My mood swings, anxiety, and sadness increased. In my journal, I continually scrawled, "Who am I?????" as I sought answers that would lessen my sense of fragmentation. Soon it was the ache for this lost self that became a driving force in how I felt.

THE MEANING OF GRIEF

While expression of grief is individual, universal components include disappointment, rage, fear, sadness, guilt, and despair. However it shows up for you, at the bottom of grief (and the anger associated with it) is something you might not expect: *love*. As a matter of fact, the depth of your love is proportionate to your grief. The more you love and value who you were or could have been, the more grief you will feel—at first. Allowing yourself to recognize this emotion puts you in touch with what is important to you, which allows you to begin reclaiming it. Creating new connections and experiences restores what you have lost and offers an opportunity for you to move into the feeling of having and being that which you most value.

After the Boston bombings in 2013, a female dance instructor lost her left leg below the knee. As she explained in post-amputation interviews, dancing "is the one thing that I do, that when I do it I don't feel like I should be doing anything else." Dancers use a unique set of muscles and tendons to roll and pivot on the edges of their feet to achieve their enormous degree of artistry. She wasn't sure that a prosthetic device would allow her to be the dancer she once was. While a part of her identity as a dancer had been lost, her livelihood was also being challenged. This survivor was candid about her grief and anger. In interviews, she admitted to grief upon hearing that her leg was gone. "I just lost it," she reported. She also admitted to bouts of anger that incited her to throw water bottles and her walker across the room. Still, faced with the losses, she vowed to continue teaching dance no matter what.

What I love about this story is the survivor's commitment to acknowledging the pain of losing her past self, and also her commitment to developing a new one. You can do this too. While the idea of approaching grief can feel frightening due to the intensity of your emotional response, the truth is that given the right belief in yourself, you do have the strength to manage and move through anything you think or feel.

One effective way to access your fundamental strength is to answer this question:

What key positive and healthy characteristics allowed you to survive through your trauma, and to cope as you have until today?

Perhaps you can readily identify the strong qualities you possess. When you do, explore a little further by asking yourself:

- How have I accessed my strengths when I have needed them?
- What actions or experiences can I create that allow me to utilize those strengths today?

Alternatively, if in this moment you simply cannot see a single positive strength, try this:

- Ask a friend what she or he sees.
- Imagine you know someone just like you who has endured the same trauma and in the same way. Tell yourself the story of what this person did to survive. From this detached perspective, what strengths do you notice?

Part of the transition through grief is acknowledging and validating the pain that goes along with losing something you love. It's letting the ache come, embodying it, breathing it in, and then breathing it out again. By doing so, you begin reclaiming the love and releasing the loss. Once you release, you begin to live; when you live, you reclaim and restore.

THE MEANING OF ANGER

Anger is a reaction to a perceived threat to yourself, a loved one, your physical property, or even your self-image or identity. When you feel anger, you can think of it as an alarm letting you know something feels wrong. It makes absolute sense that anger might come up when thinking about your past. If anger is a defense mechanism, then it will present itself as the antidote to any feelings of fear associated with intense emotions, memories, or other material related to the past. Also, anything that reminds you of danger in the past can connect you to a need to protect yourself in the present. There's also this: It's very unfair that you had to survive your trauma. Feeling a sense of being wronged can bring up a feeling of threat. For all of these reasons, feelings of fury may become even stronger during your recovery efforts as you bring into consciousness more of your own self and any truths you've been avoiding or suppressing.

My client Larry had a temper so quick it flared with the intensity of a sonic boom: fast and lethal. Everyone in his family had learned to steer clear of him, and friends had drifted away because his wrath was undependable. When we met, Larry was sure it would be impossible to reduce his anger. "This is who I am, so don't think you're going to change me!" he declared.

Aberrant coping behaviors like anger (or addiction, cutting, bingeing/purging, etc.) are a sure sign that things feel out of control and you're trying to maintain some semblance of holding yourself together. Resolving the coping response can begin with identifying its necessity, then making alterations that bring about more healthy feelings of strength, confidence, trust, safety, and control. While the end purpose may be to change those behaviors, a starting point is recognizing why you need them, plus how they originate, which is where Larry and I began our work together.

If your reactive behavior comes from a perceived necessity to protect yourself, it can be inappropriate to ask yourself to just give it up. Change is best achieved organically through a gradual evolution rather than by lopping off a behavior like an unruly strand of hair. Instead of immediately asking Larry to control himself, we began a process of examining the daily interpretations that led to thoughts that activated his angry behavior. What we discovered was that from morning to night, Larry was full of examples of how he was being mistreated, maligned, disappointed by and maliciously acted upon by others. In fact, his level of anger was proportionate to the degree to which he felt threatened.

After establishing Larry's point of view, I asked him to observe and catalogue others' offensive actions throughout the next week and prioritize them from least to most egregious. The next time we met, he had quite a list! Together we examined Larry's interpretations of each situation. For each offensive example cited, I asked him to offer two new interpretations of the same events. Although he was initially resistant, Larry eventually came around to playing what he called "The Reinterpretation Game" (TRG). With increasingly adept consciousness and creativity, Larry began to discover that while situations initially seemed to present only information that showed how wrongly he was being treated, in fact there was evidence for entirely different interpretations of every instance. The more he practiced, the more Larry could see that, for every perceived slight, there was often an opposite and equally convincing explanation. By expanding his perspective in the safe and calm moments of our sessions, Larry developed his ability to apply the same skills in more tension-filled moments outside our work. Soon he reported being able to lessen his anger by pausing his reaction to play TRG. In most cases he could find another way to look at the situation, which allowed him to choose a more effective and controlled reaction.

Right now you may be thinking that when your anger comes on, it is so intense that it eliminates your control to the point it's impossible to get it back. I know that feeling; it's human, not something special to the post-trauma world. What makes it more challenging for you is that with post-trauma symptoms or PTSD, you're already coping and using your mental energy in so many ways that there is little left over to hook your anger and reel it back into the boat of reason. Your challenge in this area will be to:

- Use techniques from Chapter 2 even in these moments (particularly deep breathing, mindfulness, the Ninety-Second Rule, Take a Time Out, and even some elements of meditation).
- Make practical in-the-moment choices to delay your response.
- Open up internal space that allows you to make different choices by finding a healthy way to tolerate and release your emotion.

Your first aim in this area is to acknowledge that the *feeling* of anger may present itself without your control, sort of the way your mind notices a pesky mosquito. Your second intention is to recognize that whether or not you *express* anger is most definitely under your control; you can squash the mosquito or skillfully wave it away—the choice is up to you.

HOW TO PROCESS GRIEF AND ANGER

> Yoga: [T]he movement allowed the energy to move through me and release my emotions. I began to feel and grieve my losses . . . Much of my grieving was done on the mat. I could tear up, release, and reconnect with my body.
>
> —*Laura*

To feel functional, Derrick runs—literally. He jogs five miles first thing in the morning "to shake off the nightmares." All day he runs from patient to patient in his busy orthodontics practice. Then he runs ten miles at night "to get my body relaxed enough to sleep" before going out for dinner with friends. When I ask Derrick how often he sits still at home—quietly, alone—he looks alarmed. "Oh, I couldn't do that," he says. "If I did, I'd have to feel things. I don't want to feel anything."

Derrick's response is common, and completely understandable. In a world where dysregulated body functions amplify emotions, the sensation of being out of control easily arises. Despite the discomfort, expanding yourself and *feeling what is* constitutes the basis for substantial progress in recovery. The real truth about you and your capacity to manage emotions is that you are designed to ebb and flow with feeling. You saw in Chapter 2 that a thought produces chemical releases in the brain that peak and then wane in ninety seconds. The value of knowing this fact lies in your ability to trust that whatever you feel will always change. Emotions have zero capability to sustain themselves. They constantly transform, and while a feeling may last longer than ninety seconds *because you continue to have thoughts that release the chemical,* when you tire of that thought or shift your attention, your emotion will shift as well.

Imagine, Embody, Absorb

It would be natural for you to suppress, ignore, and avoid all the grief and anger associated with trauma. Now is the time to stop that. You have to feel in order to heal. Whether you've numbed out your grief for a long time or given in to acting out on your anger, implementing the following exercise will serve as an introduction to recognizing uncomfortable emotion and discovering how to stay in that space with strength, focus, and clarity.

Note: Before you begin, make a pact with yourself that if any feelings become too intense, you will cease the exercise, focus on your breathing, and picture in your mind a person, place, or thing that makes you feel a sense of calm, love, or happiness. For this purpose, you might even keep a picture of that object close at hand.

1. Sit in a quiet, safe space.
2. Close your eyes and breathe in deeply and slowly. (Use the "Change Your Physiology in Two Minutes" technique from Chapter 2.)
3. Go inside yourself and imagine you are sitting in a serene and beautiful room. Take some time to use all five of your senses to become acquainted with the room.
4. Take a deep breath in and let it go, slowly. Again.
5. Notice what in the room makes you feel safe and secure. Bring it closer to you, so close you can touch it. Feel the weight, texture and temperature of it.
6. Invite your grief about the past to come into this moment. Feel it getting near.
7. Imagine it takes the form and shape of a person.
8. Welcome this self into your mind, body, and heart.
9. Imagine that self sits down close to you.

10. What does that feel like?

11. Study that self's face, clothing, hairstyle, and any other details.

12. What do you sense, know, see, and hear?

13. What message does this self have for you?

14. Invite this self to share thoughts or ideas with you.

15. Ask, "What do you want me to know?"

16. Ask, "Why is this important?"

17. Ask, "What do you want me to do?"

18. Remain in connection and conversation with this self until the visit feels ready to end. Thank this self for its messages.

19. Embrace this person. Imagine that when you do, she or he shrinks down to an inch, and lands in your heart. Whisper to her or him, "I love you and I am always with you."

20. Slowly withdraw yourself from the serene room and bring yourself back to an awareness of the present moment and the physical space you are in. Focus on the natural flow of your breath. When you are ready, count from one to four. Open your eyes.

21. In your notebook, write down everything you remember, especially noting what you have been asked to do and any ideas you have for following through.

Repeat this exercise for anger by inviting your anger about the past to come into the present moment, sit down, and speak to you.

Your very big self now contains the much smaller feeling inside you. How does that feel? What is different about this feeling? How will this difference change what you feel and think going forward? For both grief and anger, practice this process until you truly sense the feeling settle inside your body in a more comfortable way. You can continue the dialogue within you from this one-inside-the-other position.

Note: If this process brings up extreme feelings, break down the individual steps into even smaller increments. When you sit down to do the exercise, do just one of the elements, and then with each subsequent sitting add one more element until you've worked through all the steps.

You might also imagine that this other self enters your space but remains very far from you, perhaps across the room or even across town. Invite her or him to slowly advance toward you, one measured step at a time. Pause between each step to assess how you feel, to breathe, and to regulate your response. Continue the process until the self is directly in front of you and you can look into her or his eyes. Offer welcome, acknowledgment, and validation.

Change the Picture

One of the reasons emotions feel as intense as they do is because your mind represents them in internal pictures that seem to be, among other things, very close to you, enormous, bright, in Technicolor, or clearly focused, offering a view as if you're looking out through your own eyes. Reducing the intensity can be as easy as changing the pictures in your mind.

1. Close your eyes and allow the feeling of grief to become present in your body.
2. As the emotion settles in your body, pay attention to the picture(s) that form in your mind.
3. Notice the size, coloring, sharpness, and nearness of the image(s).
4. Take a step back out of the picture so that you see yourself in the picture (instead of looking out through your own eyes).
5. Push the picture away from you as far as it will comfortably go. (Do this in increments: Push it across the room, then across the street, etc.)
6. If there's more than one picture, stack them so that they merge into one. If there is one photo, split it into two or more images.
7. Shrink the picture(s) by 50 percent.
8. Drain all of the color out of the image or images so that they become black and white. (If they were already black and white, drain out one or the other color so that the screen is either all black or all white.)
9. Shrink the picture(s) by 50 percent.

10. Fuzz up the image(s) by changing the focus, the way you would with a camera lens.

11. Now shrink the picture(s) by 50 percent.

12. Darken the picture(s) as if the lights are going down in a theater.

13. Push the image or images as far away as they will go.

14. Now make the picture(s) as small as possible.

15. Again, push the image or images as far away as they will go.

16. Imagine you can destroy this final tiny speck any way that feels right to you. How would you do it? Go ahead and do that now.

17. Take a deep breath in. Say to yourself five to ten times, "I am confidently making important changes." (It's all right if you resist believing this. Repeat it anyway.)

18. Slowly bring yourself back to an awareness of the present moment and the physical space you are in. Focus on the natural flow of your breath. When you are ready, count from one to four. Open your eyes.

Repeat this exercise for anger.

Note: You can use this exercise repeatedly for any type of emotion you wish to quell, anywhere, at any time.

For added power in changing how you feel while changing the pictures in your mind, insert the following nine steps after the third step in the "Change the Picture" exercise outlined above. Then, continue with the fourth step in the "Change The Picture" exercise. (You can also use the exercise below as a stand-alone intervention whenever you feel a disturbing feeling.)

1. If it feels comfortable, close your eyes.

2. Feel the uncomfortable feeling.

3. Identify where in your body you feel the feeling most strongly.

4. Imagine it has a size, shape, and color. Just by focusing your attention on the feeling let those details reveal themselves to you.

5. All emotions spin. Focus on the feeling and notice whether it spins forward, backward, clockwise, or counterclockwise.

6. By focusing your attention on the shape of the feeling that you

identified, slow down the spinning. Then, make it spin in the opposite direction.

7. Increase the spinning in this new direction until it reaches a speed that feels comfortable .

8. *Optional:* Count from one to four while doubling the speed of the spinning on each count.

9. Imagine you can set the spinning at this increased speed by conjuring up an image of something that feels really, really good.

Gather the Love

Earlier, on page 99, you built a picture of your prior self, or who you would have liked to be if you'd had the chance. Review your notes and answers. You harbor a great affection for aspects of this alternative self. What are they, specifically? Clarification begins the process of reembodying them.

Envision

1. Find a quiet and safe space.

2. If it feels comfortable, close your eyes.

3. Take a moment to envision the person you have described.

4. Imagine that she or he comes into the room and sits down opposite you.

5. Notice how she or he dresses, walks, talks, and moves.

6. Notice your emotional and physical reactions to being face to face.

7. When you see this past/alternative self, notice where the grief or sadness originates.

8. What part of your body is it in? Why does your body hold it here?

9. What part of your mind is it in? Why does your mind hold it here?

10. In your notebook, make a list of answers to this question: "What specific thoughts, ideas, and facts cause you to feel sadness when

looking at this person?" During the span of at least ten minutes, note as many answers as come to mind.

Evaluate

For each thought, idea, or fact you listed in step ten above, identify what you love about it. Be as specific and detailed as possible and answer these questions in your notebook:

- What makes that so special?
- Why is it valuable?
- Why was this (or could this have been) important in the past?
- How will it benefit you in the life you want to live today?

Choose one of the items and decide how you can live it for at least thirty seconds (or more if you feel comfortable) three times in the next week. When you achieve this, increase the frequency to once a day for a week, and then twice a day. Then add in the same process for another item on the list, and so on.

Honor What You Love

I have been able to feel more connected to my identity . . . by coming back home to my body. I work with a wonderful dance movement therapist and have started to heal this trauma through moving, breathing, and honoring my authentic self.

—*Stephanie Cornell*

In the previous exercises, you've gathered and reconnected to what is important to you about your past self or who you could have been. Now you're in the perfect position to deepen that connection. When you honor someone, it means you feel a deep sense of admiration for who they are and the qualities, abilities, and achievements they represent. After trauma, we have a tendency to honor the bad, especially the horror. In healing, you learn to honor the good. The essence of this process is honoring yourself. Who you used to be or could have been deserves to be recognized, respected, and celebrated. It is an important part of you that, like any departed entity, lives on in your mind and heart. While you cannot go back to who you were or could have been, you can honor the memory and idea of that self in any moment you choose.

For this exercise, devise a plan (that you will follow through on) for honoring your past self's existence. You can do this quietly on your own, or you can engage friends, family, and other connections to share the experience with you. Use your notebook to outline and flesh out your ideas. Ask yourself, "What can I do to honor my past self?"

To get you started, I'll offer some ideas:

- **Imagine that your past self is a celebrity** who is going to speak at an event for which you are the emcee. Write the introduction you would read, detailing all the terrific attributes and accomplishments of this person.
- **Plan an outing (or an entire day!) that your past self would truly enjoy.** Go for a meal, see a movie, shop in a different part of town, go to a toy store, drive to a location with a spectacular view. At each point in the outing, imagine your past self with you, grinning, smiling, and shivering with excitement.
- **Spend a day at home doing activities your former self would choose.** You may be much older than this past self. Forget about how silly any activity might seem; the aim is to honor your past self—the activities may be very silly indeed. If you are imagining a self that is very young, this might mean watching children's television or playing a game of tic-tac-toe or hopscotch. It might mean surfing the net to find music from *Free to Be . . . You and Me* and singing along, making origami, or spending the day gluing macaroni to a piece of cardboard. If your past self is adolescent, this might look like spending the day in your bedroom with the stereo

blasting your favorite bands from high school. You get the idea; go back in time and have some fun!

- **Throw a birthday party for your past self.** What kind of party would it be? What themes, activities, and foods would be appropriate? Invite your friends to come over and celebrate that self's special day in a way that will always be remembered.

- **Declare a national holiday.** If you were going to declare that a week from today is National _____ Day in honor of your past self, what would that be? In your notebook, fill in the blank and jot down some ideas. Then form a plan to execute this honor exercise.

Bring the Past Into the Present

> I started remembering what I enjoyed prior to the trauma and connected that to the self-soothing activities I have repeated since then, such as decorating, caring for pets, plants, exercise. Most of all I started learning to trust myself by caring for myself.
>
> —*Carol*

Oliver was ten when his father inexplicably disappeared, leaving his mom Josie as the sole caretaker of Oliver and his six-year-old sister. Josie, however, had a drug addiction that squandered any money she made as a cashier at the local grocery store. To supplement her income, Josie brought home strange men who drifted in and out of the house at odd hours of the day and night. Multiple times Oliver inadvertently witnessed his mother performing both traditional and aberrant sexual acts.

When Oliver was fifteen, Josie's boyfriend, Javier, moved into the house and assumed headship of the family. For the next two years he formed an uneasy but somewhat caring relationship with both Oliver and his sister. Despite Javier's presence and unbeknownst to him, Josie continued turning tricks. On a sunny day in August, one of her regular customers, Marty, showed up at the house. Strung out on heroin, he demanded to see Josie; Javier asked him to leave. When Marty stood his ground, Javier threatened force and chased Marty out into the driveway, where Marty pulled a gun and shot Javier at point-blank range. Javier dropped to the ground and died while Oliver watched from a tire swing in the front yard.

"It wasn't like my life had been so easy since Javier had been in the picture," Oliver explains. "But there was a sort of consistency in knowing there would be food on the table and we were safe." He pauses, his head hanging, hands clasped in his lap. Finally he looks up and says, "I felt responsible for Javier's death. I saw the whole thing and didn't do anything to prevent it."

To distract himself from the feelings of guilt and grief, Oliver turned to drugs.

"I was always feeling so keyed up, so wired. A friend suggested I do some pot to mellow out. Well, it mellowed me out, all right! I became so mellow when I was high that I felt completely disconnected from myself. I became overwhelmed by the sensation of peace—and then, panic. The feeling of peace was so unfamiliar it completely freaked me out. Under the influence of the marijuana, I couldn't take any real action to reduce the fear. I was trapped in this strange state in a secluded part of the woods where I'd gone to get high and be alone. The panic lasted for hours. Actually, it's never fully gone away."

Today, Oliver himself has a teenage son and is divorced from a promiscuous woman he married at a time when he "just wanted something that seemed familiar." As he moves through the process of releasing the past, he's discovering some very strong ties to the boy he was before his father left. Oliver's dad was a bricklayer, and Oliver remembers the enormousness of his father's hands and their callouses as he tickled Oliver when he came home at the end of the day. With his dad around, Oliver felt safe, secure, even loved. As he relates a story about his father waking him at four in the morning to go fishing—just before his father disappeared—Oliver breaks down weeping. "I miss that happy little kid!"

While "that happy little kid" seems disconnected enough for Oliver to miss him, the truth is that he's so near that the very idea of him brings Oliver to tears. From this, Oliver discovers something incredibly important: That happy little boy is alive and well inside of him. One moment the boy is lost to the past; the next he is found deeply embedded in the present. Knowing and feeling this begins Oliver's process of reconnecting to that lost self and finding ways to bring his feel-good properties into today, which allows Oliver to repossess qualities he values.

Like Oliver, you have access to your past self in who you are today. Your identity resembles an endless string of Russian dolls, each smaller (younger) self housed within the larger (older) self. There is the You since the trauma, inside of which is the You during your trauma, inside of which is the You in the days leading up to your trauma, inside of which is the You in the year before your trauma, and the year before that, and so on.

Some of your past selves contain moments that feel good and qualities that would benefit you today. While your break with a past self may seem sheer and the disconnection and distance vast, the fact is that you remain intimately connected to all of your former selves. They are a part of your cellular biology and neural pathways. If you have a memory of or feel desire for any of them, they are accessible to you. Your visceral sense of the memory or desire is proof of their presence and their attempt to make contact with your consciousness and invite you to respond.

Enmeshed in the work of surviving survival, it's easy to sense or feel losses but not take time to inspect what they mean or from where they originate or how to resolve them. The more you ignore the messages being sent forward from the past, the more those former past selves will try to get your attention through intensified feelings. The loss becomes deeper and more painful. The experiences of your past selves, however, combine to make you who you are today, which means that their positive qualities are within you even when they feel withheld from your present experience. Feeling a lack of connection, though painful, is only an illusion.

Your Past + Your Present = Your Future

There are many ways to use your past selves in your present healing work. In the exercise you're about to do, you'll make contact with one specific past self; this can be the lost one you've already identified, or a new one you'd like to repossess. All of this work will entail forming a new connection between your past and present selves. In the future, you can use this exercise to explore and connect with any prior self that may have relevance to your recovery progress.

To begin, take a look back to page 103 and see how you answered the question *What is valuable about your past self?* You made a list of ten adjectives that begins describing who you were or could have been. You also explored how you would feel and act differently if you had those qualities now. It's time for you to embrace those aspects of who you were or could have been in the past—and significantly incorporate them into your present.

MAKE CONTACT WITH YOUR LOST PAST SELF

I took a chance and enrolled in a children's writing program . . .
[C]ompleted nine months later, [it] helped me to realize that trauma may have changed me but my writing was and will remain my voice in this world.

—Jill Einsnaugle

Getting in touch with your past self (or who you could have been) activates your imagination in creative ways. Embracing and embodying that past self begins with acknowledging it, reaching out, and opening a dialogue. Play with the following exercise as much as possible. The objective is to connect to your lost past self so that you identify qualities, traits, or characteristics you would like to connect with and embody today. You can repeat the exercise multiple times with different intentions and even, later, different selves.

After you have experienced this exercise and connected to the past self you've been relating to (real or imagined) since the beginning of this chapter, move on to the next step.

Travel Back in Time

Think of your lost past self: the one you most miss, admire, long for, find inspiration in, or feel strongly about. This is the self that you are going to make contact with now.

1. Sit still, and quietly close your eyes if that feels comfortable.
2. Breathe deeply and slowly.
3. Go inside yourself and imagine you are sitting in a serene and beautiful room. Take some time to use all five of your senses to become acquainted with the room.
4. Take a deep breath in and let it go, slowly. Again.
5. Notice what in the room makes you feel safe and secure. Bring it closer to you, so close you can touch it. Feel the weight, texture and temperature of it.
6. On the ground, imagine that the timeline of your life stretches out in opposite directions, into the past and into the future. You are in the present. Place a marker to hold your spot—perhaps a flag, a flower, a shoe, or a sign.
7. If it feels comfortable, imagine you can float up above your timeline and begin moving back into the past at any increments or intervals that feel right to you. (Alternatively, if floating doesn't feel comfortable, walk on the ground of your timeline back into the past.) One month . . . one year . . . one decade . . . As you pass each block of time, imagine you can look (down) into your timeline and see yourself at that age.
8. There will be many selves in your past; continue traveling back until you reach a place in your timeline when you encounter the self you most miss or wish you'd had a chance to be. Slowly drift (down) into that moment. How do things look from this perspective?

9. If this is your first time doing this exercise, you might choose to simply observe. Then:

10. Notice why this self feels important. What can you teach this self? What can it teach you? Engage in a dialogue. Remain here as long as feels comfortable.

11. If it feels appropriate, invite this past self to come forward with you to the present. Hold hands and prepare to travel together.

12. Float back up above your timeline and then gently drift (or walk in your timeline) back to the marker you placed in the present moment. When you reach it, float back down into the present moment. If you have brought the past self with you, imagine what she or he will do here in your world. How will you help her or him feel safe and fit in? Picture these future actions as if they are a movie on the screen in your mind. Sense yourself moving through the actions you imagine necessary.

13. When you feel you have experienced this exercise as much as you would like, take a deep breath in through your nose and out through your mouth. Count from one to four. Open your eyes. Notice how you feel. In your notebook, transcribe what you have noticed, learned, felt or thought.

You have many past selves, several of whom may contain valuable information. You can repeat this exercise as many times as you wish, either to revisit the self you identified the first time or to find new ones. When you are comfortable with the exercise, invite any self that interests you or that wishes to step forward to engage in a dialogue. Discover what important resources, skills, thoughts, ideas, needs, and messages she or he possesses.

Note: As you do this exercise, you may make contact with a past self that feels grief, sadness, anger, loss, or disconnection. As much as your task here is to reconnect to the self or selves who can help you restore elements that are important to you, you can also help other past selves find resolution for the pain of their experience, plus the distance or break between you. If you discover a self that needs your help, pause and engage in a dialogue about what she or he wants you to know or needs from you. Think back to all of the survivors' stories you've read so far and see which one contains seeds for how you can soothe your past self. Would it be by holding that self as Rick did, or settling that self into your present-day environment as Augusta did? Alternatively, you can allow that self to tell you what she or he needs or use your imagination and creativity to devise a resolution.

Drill Down

The more you clarify who your lost self is and the more information you receive, the more expanded your vision becomes, which means you can more easily connect to, embrace, embody, and integrate the self you identified in the exercise above into who you are today. Since the exercises in the "Build a Picture of the Past" section of this chapter, you have gained much deeper insights into your lost self. The following steps will take some time and are designed to help you update your original vision while also becoming more deeply acquainted with this former self. In your notebook, fill in the blanks with as many answers as possible for each sentence:

- This self likes to eat _____.
- This self likes to listen to _____ music.
- This self likes to wear _____.
- This self likes to vacation _____.
- This self likes to work _____.
- This self likes to have _____ friends.
- This self likes to spend time doing _____.
- This self's favorite sound is _____.
- This self likes to spend time with _____.
- This self likes to live _____.
- This self likes has a dream to _____.
- This self wants (to) _____.

- This self regrets _____.
- This self loves _____.
- This self likes _____.
- This self dislikes _____.
- This self's hobbies _____.
- This self wishes _____.
- This self hopes _____.
- This self believes _____.
- This self does not _____.
- This self always _____.
- This self enjoys _____.
- This self hates _____.
- This self feels confident about _____.
- This self feels uncertain about _____.
- This self thinks _____ is funny.
- This self is often surprised by _____.
- This self would never _____.
- This self would always _____.
- This self is delighted _____.
- This self laughs when _____.
- This self cries when _____.
- This self feels threatened by _____.
- This self positively believes _____ about herself/himself.
- This self negatively believes _____ about herself/himself.
- This self is always right about _____.

What other elements define this past self? Let your mind roam in any direction. Add as many defining statements to this list as you can.

Deepen the Connection

Bridge the distance between you and this past self by putting conscious and deliberate language and clarity to your connection: Write a letter of introduction. The letter can be about anything and include any details you feel would be beneficial and appropriate to share if you were getting in touch with a long-lost friend for the first time.

An outline of the letter might look like this (but feel free to make your own outline):

- Introduce yourself.
- Explain why you want to connect.
- Describe what you value about this past self.
- Outline how you can benefit from connecting/living/working together.
- Issue an invitation (to connect further, spend time together, etc.).

While you're writing, consider answering these questions:

- What do you want to say to this past self?
- What do you want her or him to know?
- How can you help her or him?
- How can she or he help you?
- How can a deeper connection benefit you both?
- What questions would you like her or him to answer?
- How do you envision working together? When?

When you finish the letter, read it to yourself out loud, preferably in front of a mirror. Then, sit in a chair, imagine that your past self sits beside or across from you, and read the letter to your past self. What is her or his response?

BIRTH THIS PAST SELF INTO THE PRESENT

> I call back all the fragmented pieces kindly, gently with love, and
> nonjudgment . . . I breathe in a smile, the new me, and release out the old
> patterns and beliefs that no longer serve my Divine Mind, Divine Heart.
>
> —*Sue*

Your "persona" is that aspect of your character that is presented to others; it is the *you* that you show to the world. The foundation of reconstructing your identity lies in the strength of your being able to exhibit to the outside world the truth of who you are. With the clarity and connection you've built, it will feel increasingly natural to bring this past self into the present. Doing so depends on creating physical experiences that engage your past self's thoughts, ideas, beliefs, and perspective. I'll suggest a few ways to get you started, and then you will expand the process by creating the kinds of experiences you (and your past self) would most like to have:

Think of Your Past Self as a Character

You can deepen the power of your imagination by giving yourself real experiences that support the ideas in your mind about the qualities and characteristics you'd like to exhibit. Imagine you've been cast in the role of your most meaningful past self in a movie. You must practice being in character. For one week (or as long as you like), dress, eat, walk, talk, listen, do, and think the way this other self does.

To prepare yourself for this, do what all actors do when preparing for a new role: Develop a rich backstory. In your notebook, complete the following description (and add any other elements that feel important to you) to solidly create your physical vision of the character of your past self:

- Provide this character's name.
- Describe the history of this character.

- Describe what's most important to this character.
- Describe the belief that most drives this personality.
- Describe this character's greatest fear, and where it comes from.
- Describe how this character handles or addresses that fear.
- Describe what makes this character ecstatically happy.
- Describe what makes this character feel calm, content, confident, and empowered.
- Make a music mix that you can listen to as you prepare to play this role. Eat this character's favorite foods and wear her or his style of clothing.
- Describe how this character walks. Practice in the privacy of your home.
- Describe this character's purpose or mission.
- Describe this character's attitude.
- List some of this character's favorite words.
- List any other defining qualities of this character that would be important for you to embody in this role.

Now that you have prepared for your role, go act it out! Practice being in character as often and for as long as it feels right to you. Then begin using the attitudes and actions you develop in character when you are back in your normal daily self.

Think of Your Past Self as a Partner

One of the greatest aspects of having a friend, confidant, lover, or spouse is the fact that we have a sounding board—someone with whom to exchange ideas and from whom to receive insights, input, and advice. Your past self is *full* of such things!

For one week (or as long as you like), consult this other self before you make any choice or take any action. Whenever you find yourself analyzing a problem, making a decision, or interpreting the meaning of an experience, turn to this self and ask for an opinion. For a simple process, try this:

1. When you need advice, pause what you're doing and go inside yourself.
2. Imagine that this self enters the room you are in.
3. Engage this self in a conversation that fully explores the topic until you have reached a satisfying conclusion.

This exercise can be done while you're conscious and awake, and also while you sleep. Before bed, simply ask your past self a specific question and then be ready to receive the answer through a dream or thought in the night, or through a symbol or idea in the morning. Make sure to immediately write down the information you receive. It takes thirty-eight seconds for a thought to record in memory, so if you are tired and your mind doesn't focus, the answer will be lost if you fail to jot it down.

Think of Your Past Self as a Playmate

The work of recovery is tough, isolating, and energy draining. Sometimes the best thing you can do is take a break! By allowing your mind to empty of anything trauma related and fill instead with pleasurable distractions, you can actually amp up your healing commitment, dedication, and inner exploration and development. Science has proven that the benefits of play (both from exercises that provide relaxation and from those that provide stimulation) include the release of mood-elevating endorphins; a renewed sense of connection; improved mental health and memory; development of a sense of community and trust; increased problem-solving skills, adaptability, and learning; and stimulated growth of the cerebral cortex. In other words, setting aside playtime is like taking a whole slew of vitamins for your brain.

One way to further deepen your present relationship with your past self is by incorporating into your process a sense of play. This other self is a terrific resource and companion in this area. Set aside some time to spend a few hours (or more) playing with this self in some way. In coordinating your itinerary, consider:

- What kind of activities does this self enjoy?
- Where can you go to engage in these activities?
- What props can you purchase to facilitate this type of fun?

In this phase, your mission is to step into the world of your past self. What other actions can you take to experience the world, your life, your relationships, and your work through the qualities and characteristics of your past self?

INTEGRATE YOUR PAST SELF INTO DAILY LIFE

Like a frozen flower, you are gently unthawing. Release all expectations for how these experiences will go, and suspend all judgment. The point is purely to make contact and begin reclaiming lost elements from the past as often as possible in the present. Feeling the fullness of what you want to feel comes over a period of time. To enhance the efficacy and functioning of the neural pathways created by the above exercises, set a daily schedule for engaging in some or all aspects of them.

Exploring how to integrate your past into your present can sometimes be tricky. You may find that you can't access ideas, memories, feelings, thoughts, or actions the way you used to or expect to. That's perfectly all right. Present-day fears or other psychological circumstances may erect immediate obstacles. For example, Tonya, a woman very tied to the physical beauty of her body, enjoyed doing anything athletic. She particularly loved the feeling of running. After a plastic surgery debacle left her trapped in a body that was unexpectedly deformed, however, Tonya hated the feel of her body; the idea of running induced extreme panic and anxiety. In order to reclaim elements of her past self and activate the good feelings without activating the bad ones, at first Tonya chose to rely on imagination instead of actual action: She spent several minutes every day in a quiet space with her eyes closed imagining herself running her old route. Developing a tight focus, Tonya discovered that she could not only shift herself into a great exercise of imagination that helped train her brain, but also access the feeling she used to love of freely inhabiting her body, feeling its strength, and enjoying the vista of the natural world along the route. For a long time, this was as far as Tonya took the exercise, until she reached a place in her post-trauma identity construction in which she felt, though not in love with her new body, enough at peace with it to go for a bike ride and then a hike.

The Take-Aways

[O]ur inner child is our subconscious where all of our traumatic histories are stored—these cause blocks and work against us. Once you acknowledge and nurture your inner child, you can then work together in harmony to heal and essentially move mountains.

—*Treyce Montoya, MPsyD*

- Feeling disconnected from or disturbed by your lost self withholds positive, strong, and supportive elements from who you are in the present.
- In order to move on to developing your present and future selves, it will help to release the past with love and connection.
- At the bottom of grief (and the anger associated with it) is something you might not expect: *love.*
- It would be natural for you to suppress, ignore, and avoid all the grief and anger associated with trauma. Now is the time to stop that. You have to feel in order to heal.
- The experiences of your past selves combine to make you who you are today, which means that their positive qualities are within you even when they feel withheld from your present experience.

Who Have You Become After Trauma?

VALIDATE YOURSELF NOW

Move out of victimization and into empowerment [by] facing the fear right in the face. "Kiss it on the lips!" as Dr. Michael Beckwith says. Avoiding the issue, the perpetrator, etc., keeps you trapped.

—*Nancy B. Irwin, PsyD*

At the end of my trauma, I vividly remember walking away from the hospital knowing I had survived. I understood that the event was over and that the likelihood that it would happen again, although possible, was small if I took careful steps to be safe. The problem was, while I could say to myself, "That happened in the past"—while logically and analytically I *knew* that in the present moment I was safe—it didn't *feel* as if everything was in the past. It felt as if everything was still ongoing. That is, threat and danger existed everywhere—which, technically, they did. I walked through the halls of junior high school and our family home consciously trying not to focus on fear, the what-ifs, the how-wills, or any other kind of catastrophic thinking. I tried to forget what had happened, what could happen, and what I was afraid would happen again. I tried to define myself *against* my trauma by defying its existence and effect.

But I know you can guess what actually did happen: I became obsessed and a bit compulsive about doing all of that, which meant that the effects of trauma really did come to define me almost completely. I focused on both remembering and forgetting at the same time. I meticulously developed behaviors that helped me feel safe and in control. I became enormously rigid in my thoughts and actions. I became anorexic. I often refused doctors even when I needed one. I established routines that had to be adhered to; if they weren't, I'd have a meltdown. I didn't like change, feared surprises, and flat out despised anything that made me feel as if someone else had more control than I did. The older I grew, the more these behaviors became extreme and self-destructive. I was diagnosed with advanced osteoporosis, partly due to malnutrition. I had emergency surgery when a sinus infection reached the blood-brain barrier. Meanwhile, my thoughts, feelings, actions, and behaviors deepened my negative self-definition by connecting me more and more to who I was as a survivor.

How do you define yourself? The explorations you will encounter in this chapter will help you fully craft your current identity statement. In completing this you'll go below the surface of what you immediately know to explore who you are in a deeper way. Right now, it's time to frame your initial working self-definition. Even if this feels disturbing, uncomfortable, and just plain unhappy, finish this step; it is your baseline. Remember that even if you are frustrated and irritated with yourself today, there are still good and positive things about you; include them in your description. By the end of the chapter, it will be important to be able to look back, so even if you're tempted to skip this exercise— do it anyway!

I am _____

_____

_____

That was a challenging assignment. Kudos to you for facing up to it and getting it done. It's that kind of action-taking that brings results and forward motion. With this description, you have a concrete way to begin looking at your identity. What do you see? How does this identity feel? What surprises you about it? What do you love? What do you hate? You can use these questions to form a connection between you and how you see yourself. These types of assessments activate your brain's creativity and can help you further define, refine, and shape who you are and who you will become.

Clearly, as you saw in my self-description above, my habits and behaviors after trauma became more than a little out of control. They continued to change me (even more than the trauma itself) into a completely different person. What had happened to me—and is it happening to you?

The "New Normal"

I have learned to accept myself for who I am, including my faults. Once I forgave and let peace into my life, I was able to learn about myself and realize who I was. After time I realized life was better and I was better. I was able to feel happy again.

—Sparky

Each week in the newsletter I send out to subscribers, I focus on one aspect of recovery. Sometimes I offer a scientific fact or a tip; other times, I provide a recovery option or personal challenge for the upcoming week. The purpose is always to highlight how to be proactive in overcoming the past. One week I offered a survey and asked subscribers to share their largest obstacles and issues in living with post-trauma and PTSD symptoms. I received hundreds of responses outlining and detailing frustrations and adaptations in regard to what many described as the "new normal": a life driven by symptoms, adaptations, coping mechanisms, and altered belief patterns. The new normal affects every survivor and is the origin of the changes you've seen in yourself.

Without a doubt, trauma forces you to recognize things about the world and yourself that you may not have known, or didn't want to include in your life view. It brings front and center the truth about your safety, your ability to control events and people around you, and even your ability to respond to threats. The alterations you put in place to deal with this new knowledge usher in the new normal, where setting up boundaries and programs that ensure safety becomes a priority and any breach highlights your ultimate lack of control. Naturally, this knowledge increases your need for control, and so you might find yourself expanding your methods and developing more detailed plans, actions, and behaviors that you hope will give you the sensation you seek. In doing all of this, you create your personal new normal, which is often a lifestyle devoted to a negative and fearful perspective.

The following self-assessment offers just some of the many observations I hear from survivors about what their new normal looks like. Many of them relate to how I experienced my own new normal. I wonder how many will feel familiar to you. With this self-assessment, which provides a list of characteristics that are easily recognized and organized, you launch your personal, unique process of taking a good, long look at who you are. The purpose is to get a full vision of the breadth and depth of your new normal. This will help later in the chapter as you consider who you've become minute by minute, and also in your overall life.

A word of advice: Living the post-trauma lifestyle takes its toll on everyone, including the people around you. Often we don't see in ourselves what is blatantly obvious to others. It was a shock to me when my family told me I had become utterly controlling. I thought I was just being well organized and a good planner; they saw me frantically trying to control every detail of every family outing and having a meltdown if I didn't get my way. Outside perspective can be useful in illuminating not only what you can't or don't see, but what you don't *want* to see, either. To expand and deepen this assessment, share it with a trusted friend or family member.

SELF-ASSESSMENT #1

The chart on the next page provides a simple way to begin observing where things are fundamentally going off track and to begin clarifying what is in your power to address. How many of these attributes do you recognize in yourself? Place a check mark to the left of the phrases that define you. I've left some empty spaces for you to fill in your own ideas.

Successful trauma recovery causes changes in all of the areas on this assessment. In your process, are you addressing each of these five categories? Take some time to study the assessment and identify specifically how many uncomfortable elements you're dealing with. Add up the number of check marks you have in each category and place the number in the box that says "Total Number." Then, prioritize the categories by numbering them 1 to 5 from *most check marks* to least. Place the number for each category in the check box beside it in the final line of the chart. Categories labeled 1 and 2 will show you areas where you are most out of alignment with a healthy experience. If it feels appropriate, you can choose to give more time and attention to the high-mark categories in an effort to make progress in these areas.

Fill out the following sections to complete the self-assessment.

» Which two categories have the most high marks?

　　1 —

　　2 —

» How comfortable do you feel about addressing progress in these areas? Rate your level of comfort on a scale of 1 to 10, where 10 is most comfortable:

　　1 —

　　2 —

» For each category, what would have to happen for you to move up one notch on the scale (to feel more comfortable)?

　　1 —

　　2 —

Emotional State	Self-Perception	Feelings
Uncontrollable rage	"I'm crazy."	Out of control
Fear	"I'm worthless."	Unsupported
Inability to think clearly	"Everything is harder for me than for other people."	Frustrated that others don't understand
Deep-rooted pain	"I'm so unique and individual no one else can understand what I've gone through and am going through now."	Worthlessness
Anxiety	"I have no purpose."	Unsafe
Emotional numbing	"I am weak, fragile, and vulnerable."	Vulnerable and fragile
Dissociation	"I don't know/like who I am anymore."	Lack of confidence
Disconnection from self and others	"I can't be helped or saved."	Sad
Dealing with intrusive memories	"All of this awfulness is who I really am."	Overwhelmed
Easily angered	"I'm a loser."	All alone
Irritable	"I'm pathetic."	Stuck/frozen
Highly avoidant	"I'm unlovable."	Desperate
Hypervigilant	"I'm beyond saving."	Hopeless
Depression	"I'm broken and can't be fixed."	Self-doubt
Lack of self-awareness	"I have to accept that I'll be this damaged forever."	Low self-esteem
Easily flustered	"The old me is dead."	Misunderstood
Obsessing over small details you would never have thought about before	"I hate myself."	Ready to give up
Suicidal thoughts	"I'm useless and don't deserve to be alive."	Inauthentic
Panic	"I didn't deserve to survive."	Fearful of things that would not have frightened me before
Emotional mood swings	"I'm a burden to my family and friends."	Defeated
Total Number:	Total Number:	Total Number:

Behavior	Physical State
Afraid to go out of the house/agoraphobic	Muscle and joint pain
Faking normal	Fatigue
Push people away	Fibromyalgia
Flashbacks	Insomnia
Can't keep commitments	Brain fog
Uncomfortable dealing with uncertainty	Loss of job/income
Inability to trust myself or others	Lack of energy (mental and/or physical)
Inability to forgive myself or others	Mentally/intellectually impaired
Self-sabotage	Sleeplessness
Inability to take action	Digestive issues
Loss of ability to make decisions	Dysregulation of organ function
Addictive behaviors involving food, sex, money, drugs, alcohol	Hair loss
Loss of ability to do things I used to do	Teeth grinding
Frequently triggered	Overweight
Difficulty releasing and regulating emotions	Underweight
Inability to relax in public	Malnourished
Trouble dealing with/accepting change	High blood pressure
Unable to function if things don't go the way I expected	Headaches/migraines
Loss of interest in everything/ things that used to matter	Diarrhea
Need to make decisions for everyone, not just myself	Ulcers
Total Number:	Total Number:

» What known options (that you have not yet tried) do you
have for making that happen?

I —

2 —

» Which new option do you feel ready to try now?

I —

2 —

» Who can help you do this and how?

I —

2 —

Choose a date and time to take an action. Share your intention with
a trusted friend. Ask him or her to check in with you to make sure you've
followed through. When you have completed the action, use the following scale to reassess your progress:

- **If you rate yourself one notch higher**, move through the
  process again, asking yourself what it would take to move
  yourself up another notch. Follow through the steps repeatedly until you reach a 10.
- **If you rate yourself the same**, revise your answer for what it
  would take to move up one notch. Try a different action and
  wait to see the results.
- **If you rate yourself lower**, suspend your work in this area
  and focus instead on bringing yourself back to neutral. Ask
  yourself, "What do I need to feel more at peace in this area?"
  Use your skills and resources to make proactive decisions to
  bring results.

Coping with and managing symptoms from a vague awareness of
their details leaves the problem in control and continues to render you
powerless. Defining and refining who you are today helps shift the balance of power and requires constant effort and attention. Use the self-assessment chart to identify where you want to focus in terms of changing

who you are, how you feel, and the way you behave. The chart can also be used to keep track of what actions you're taking to make focus a priority, plus the progress you achieve. Work with all of this slowly and individually. Resist the temptation to approach many elements at once; this can induce brain freeze and stall your efforts. Instead, choose one element from each of your priority categories to focus your efforts on.

SELF-ASSESSMENT #2

> One thing that has made me feel connected is . . . finding someone who could validate my trauma. Validation was that "ahhh" moment for me . . . [It] was the release that helped me to press forward to enter into the fight as a victim but determined to come out a survivor.
>
> —*K. Justice*

Of course, the first new-normal self-assessment doesn't represent the whole of who you are; it represents only the negative aspects you experience. But trauma (and also your recovery process) has taught and developed in you important and good things too. It has activated qualities that you might not have had without this experience. While you wouldn't choose trauma as a growth incentive, you *have* experienced trauma, so you might as well become conscious of the good ways it has forced you to evolve and the positive qualities you've retained despite its intrusion. From this important information you can develop skills that support your future transformation and help you more easily create it.

Furthering your self-assessment requires balancing the picture. There are positive aspects of who you are today. What are they? Fill in the following chart to expand your self-definition.

Emotional State	Self-Perception	Feelings
Placid	"I'm sensible."	In control in some or many moments
Courageous	"I'm worthwhile."	Loved and supported
Able to think ahead	"I can easily handle most things."	Confident that others understand
Able to feel gratitude	"I'm unique and individual because of how I choose to express myself."	Valuable
Moments of serenity	"My purpose is _____."	Safe
Emotionally connected	"I am strong, tough, and powerful."	Secure and unbreakable
Able to maintain being present	"I know and like who I am."	Confident
Moments of connection to self and others	"I am constantly evolving and getting better."	Joyful
Able to manage memories without distress	"I am a person who is much greater than my past."	Unflappable
Able to maintain a sense of neutral	"I'm a winner."	Part of a collective human group
Nice	"I'm admirable."	Fluid
Able to face what needs to be faced	"I'm lovable."	Satisfied
Secure	"I can be healed."	Hopeful
Happy	"I can overcome the past."	Certain
Self-aware	"I am always capable of change."	High self-esteem
Calm	"I can choose who I want to be."	Understood
Able to shift attention away from uncomfortable thoughts	"I love myself."	Perseverant
Life-affirming sensations	"I have gifts to share with this world."	Authentic
Contentment	"I deserve to live and be alive."	Brave
Emotional even keel	"I'm a blessing to my family and friends."	Indomitable
Total Number:	Total Number:	Total Number:

Behavior	Physical State
Compassion	Conscious
Moments of real connection	Alert
Reaching out to others	Aware
Ability to be present	Muscular
Dependability	Toned
Ability to be spontaneous	Fit
Trust in specifically chosen people	Soft/smooth skin
Willingness to forgive myself and others for specific issues	Ideal weight
Self-compassion	Restful sleep
Ability to take action	Comfortable body processes, e.g. digestion
Ability to think things through and plan	Healthy organ function
Balanced attitude toward temptations	Happy hair
Engagement in things I like to do and that make me feel good	Lack of jaw tension
Ability to stay calm for periods of time	Clear head
Ability to identify, connect with, and express emotions	Relaxed body
Ability to be out in public and feel comfortable	Healthy nutrition
Ability to handle change	Healthy blood pressure
Flexibility when things do not go as expected	Healthy immune system
Sustaining interest in things that are important	Relaxed breath
Able to be responsible for personal decisions	Energetic
Total Number:	Total Number:

Looking at the assessment above, you can see specifically how many comfortable elements you actually possess, even if they are fleeting. Construction of your post-trauma identity benefits greatly from expanding your physical and emotional experience of this list. In fact, doing so can have a terrific effect on any post-trauma issues. As the balance tips in favor of the positive list, the negative list begins to shift, weaken, and often reduce. Many times I've spoken with survivors who believe you have to heal the bad in order to feel the good. But the reverse can also be true: Accessing the good can help heal the bad by changing your perspective, which transforms what you think, alters how you feel, and helps to rewire your brain. In this way, recognizing and expanding your experience of the good in you becomes an important aspect of both constructing your post-trauma identity and your overall healing.

In this new assessment, add up the number of check marks in each category and place the number in the box that says "Total Number." Then prioritize the categories by numbering them 1 to 5 from *least check marks* to most. Place the number for each category in the check box beside it in the final line of the chart. For categories 3 to 5, you're already doing well, and you'll probably naturally continue your evolution in these areas. For categories 1 and 2, it's time to focus some attention to round out your experience.

Fill out the following sections to complete the self-assessment.

> » What two categories have the most high priority?
>> 1 –
>>
>> 2 –
>
> » How focused do you feel on making progress in these areas?
> Rate your focus on a scale of 1 to 10, where 10 is most focused:
>> 1 –
>>
>> 2 –
>
> » For each category, what would have to happen for you to
> move up one notch on the scale?
>> 1 –
>>
>> 2 –

» What known options (that you have not yet tried) do you have for making that happen?

    1 —

    2 —

» Which new option do you feel ready to try now?

    1 —

    2 —

» Who can help you do this, and how?

    1 —

    2 —

Choose a date and time to take an action. Share your intention with a trusted friend. Ask him or her to check in with you to make sure you've followed through. In each category, choose one element to work on at a time.

Define Yourself Now

[I am] learning that my experience doesn't define who I am but simply is something that occurred that had impact on me. Who I am is determined by the choices that I make following the experience, and those are based on my core values and beliefs and how I process the traumatic experience.

—Jeff Presnal

By filling in both assessments, you've begun the real work of conceptualizing who you are. There are, to be sure, many more elements that can define you. Feel free to create your own extended assessment in your notebook. Considering all of the elements from both charts now, how do these added elements change your initial self-description on page 134? What had you forgotten about or overlooked? Revise your statement now:

I am

_____

_____

_____

Let's take this a little further and become even more specific and multi-dimensional. Based on who feel yourself to be today, make a list of the following:

- **_Context._** What types of environments combine to affect your identity? Work, home, religious, elective organizations/associations, spiritual, social, private? Circle your choices and add any others that apply to you. How does each choice support or suppress aspects of your self-definition?

_____

_____

_____

_____

- **_Narrative._** List five to ten defining moments in your life. What positive and negative qualities have they brought out in you? Create an equal numbered list for positives and negatives relating to each moment.

_____

_____

_____

_____

- **_Values._** What principles and standards do you feel are important to have in your life? Examples include compassion, freedom, gratitude, love, family, enthusiasm, self-development, risk-taking, balance, trustworthiness, security, and faith. There are many lists of value words online. If you find your mind blank in answering this question, do some research and bring back your findings to make a list here:

- Another way to assess your values is to answer the question, "What do you want to be known for?" Your answer can include actions, experiences, contributions, discoveries, skills, public interactions, private effects, relationships, and so forth. You can choose today what you will be known for at the end of your life. What do you want to be known for? Note your answers:

- *Other factors.* Outside context, narrative, and values, what other descriptors do you feel are important in defining you? Add them here:

While an accurate self-definition may begin with the new-normal elements, it also includes the larger aspects of who you are. Examine both self-assessments, plus the context, narrative, values, and other descriptive factors you've chosen to highlight. Take some time to reflect on what most defines who you are. Be honest and observational. Suspend all judgment.

This self-definition will be done in your notebook. When you are ready, follow these steps:

1. It can be difficult to detach enough to see yourself clearly from the "I" perspective. For this part of the exercise, imagine you are a friend of yours. Describe yourself in the third person (e.g., "This man is _____" or "This woman has _____"). Imagine you are reporting what you see to an audience that has no prior conception of who you are.

2. It's much easier to adapt your description to an "I" perspective when you have completely fleshed it out in the third person. When you finish your third-person description, revise it by replacing all third-person pronouns and references with "I," "myself," or "me".

Note: How you describe yourself will deepen, expand, become more focused, and evolve as you continue to facilitate the development of your post-trauma identity. Your mission with this exercise is only to begin flexing your muscle of self-description. Which means, feel free to be awkward, wrong, unfamiliar, uncertain, and unsure. Until you become more adept in this area, identity can feel like a very intangible essence; the work you engage in here seeks to make it more tangible. Still, the transmutation of idea into reality takes time. However you fulfill this exercise is perfect—as are you in every moment, even the ones that feel all wrong.

In constructing your post-trauma identity, there are two parallel tracks to work with. The first is the *microview,* a focus on the small details of daily living. Becoming acutely aware of this aspect of who you are allows you to see your survivor self with clarity in any individual moment. A large part of this centers on becoming conscious of experience, cause, and effect. The second track represents the *macroview,* an overview of your whole self in the larger context of your life beyond trauma. In this perspective, you discover and refine who you are and how you want to show up in the world at large. When you address both levels and bring them into alignment with your desires and each other, you create a wholly integrated and functional persona based on your choices, decisions, and actions. Your job will be to stay attuned to both the microview and the macroview to make sure that what happens on each level positively contributes to the overall vision of who you want to be.

PRACTICE CONSCIOUS SELF-AWARENESS

> Redefining is difficult. My connection with animals helps. It is an unconditional love few people can support, but [animals] do.
>
> —*JennJones*

When you take the time to practice paced breathing, you change your psychological state by changing your neurophysiology. When you take the time to practice *conscious self-awareness*, you can change your psychological state by altering your perceptions, interpretations, and self-definition. Self-awareness means being alert about what it means to be you in any moment. Being conscious means being awake and aware of your surroundings—not for the threat that they represent, but just as the fact of the environment and context in which you exist. Combining these elements offers a strategy for more centered groundedness, connection, and control, plus reduced tendencies for dissociation and disconnection. It also offers the opportunity to develop what I call "anti-trauma habits": practices that support your (1) "I can handle it!" belief system, (2) ability to exist in the world with calm alertness, and (3) knowledge that you will appropriately notice and respond to real threat and danger. In combination, these elements form a specific type of person and strategy for living: one that offers consistency in and familiarity with yourself from day to day.

After Selena was mugged at gunpoint during her first year in a major city (she'd grown up in a very rural environment), she found that she couldn't bear to be alone—not home, not out; nowhere did she feel comfortable to be by herself. She constantly needed the presence of a friend and readily admitted that she always had to be hugging someone, even for the smallest reason. If a friend had a good day or a bad one, Selena hugged her. If someone was late to meet her at a prearranged destination, she hugged him for apologizing. In any situation, Selena looked for and found a reason to have this kind of reassuring physical contact. The problem arose when friends weren't available. If Selena's need to be near to and touched by someone she trusted couldn't be met, she panicked, experienced enormous emotional meltdowns, and embarrassed herself by tracking down people through a flurry of phone calls and texts and sometimes even by following them to physical locations.

When we first began working together, Selena acknowledged these behaviors and felt they were out of her control; she accepted them as her new-normal mode of operating.

"I need to feel safe," she sniffed. "These things make me feel safe. If it annoys some people or seems bizarre to others, that's too bad."

"Do these behaviors feel good to you?" I asked.

"No, it's like I'm compelled by some invisible force. But not doing these behaviors makes me feel even worse."

"Beliefs drive all of your behaviors. What idea or thought makes you feel the need to be so constantly connected to other people?"

Selena shrugged her shoulders, but when I remained silent, she shifted her eyes to a picture across the room and began to think. Eventually she said, "I feel safer around other people because they'll protect me if anything bad starts to happen."

"And what will you be doing?"

"Nothing. That's why that guy was able to mug me; I didn't respond. I can't trust myself to protect me."

In this instant, Selena's willingness to be self-aware and conscious brought her to a moment of crucial clarity. Discovering that her survival mechanism was being fueled in large part by her belief that she could not be counted on was a monumental turning point in Selena's post-trauma identity construction. With that information, it was clear that she needed to focus on replacing the belief "I can't protect myself" with the more positive belief "I am capable of protecting myself in every moment," and taking actions that would bring that belief into reality.

Immediately, Selena developed and implemented ways to train her focus on the new belief, including placing Post-it pages all over her apartment. She also entered a self-defense class and a kickboxing class. She liked how it felt in her body to feel strong and able to make defensive and powerful moves. She put herself on a reduced schedule of phone calls and texts to friends whose feedback let her know they appreciated the lesser degree of intense contact. In addition, Selena made a conscious effort to hug people only when a hug was required. While she still experienced tension walking home alone at night, Selena was able to assess her options and then chart a well-lit path from building to building without calling or texting a friend.

Over the period of time that Selena focused on making these changes, she found herself shifting into a different internal space. She felt more dependable and centered. Instead of walking with her eyes darting from side to side, seeking danger, she stared straight ahead and walked with a sense of powerful purpose. Becoming more conscious of what had been driving her allowed Selena to make changes that more effectively developed her feelings of safety and control, plus helped her relinquish the inappropriate post-trauma habits she had established. In achieving this, she developed a self-definition dedicated to the idea, among others, of being a woman who protects herself.

BECOME YOUR OWN COACH

Listen to your gut/instincts every time. They will always
lead you to the next place you need to be.

—Vanessa

How you approach ideas, problems, and challenges defines you. As you clarify that definition, you have an opportunity to refine your thought processes, which can lead to changes on a deep level that release you from old patterns and propel you into new actions.

Successfully reconstructing your identity begins on the most interior level by honoring, respecting, and supporting who you are. This comes from self-knowledge, self-love, inner connection, and dedication to meeting yourself where you are—that is, accepting who you are in this moment with the understanding that you can and will have opportunities to change in future moments. It also depends on implementing plans designed to continue your personal growth and development. One way to develop your strength and stay on track is to consistently ask yourself *empowering questions:* queries whose answers require a full sentence rather than a simple yes or no and that lead to ideas for action-taking. Empowering questions begin with *Who, What, When, Where, How,* or occasionally *Why* (be careful not to stagnate in rumination). For example:

- **What** people, experiences, or things would support my identity transformation journey?
- **Who** could listen to my self-definition ideas and offer helpful suggestions for achieving my vision?
- **Where** could I go outside my home that would offer a good setting to think things through?
- **How** can I feel more organized in this process?
- **When** will I take the action this requires?
- **Why** do I feel stuck or held back in this work?

When trauma and posttraumatic stress leave you feeling inert and stagnant, empowering questions jump-start your engine by encouraging you to be selective in how you think, make decisions, and take actions. By utilizing empowering questions, you can give yourself guidance based on a thought process that expands rather than contracts your thinking. For the next twenty-four hours, focus on putting in place a habit of asking yourself empowering questions for every decision, uncomfortable feeling, or challenge you face. Then extend that practice over the course of the next thirty days.

ASSESS WHO YOU ARE

What helps me is my belief in God, his presence which I have felt.

—Laura

Selena's healing progress continued. The stronger she felt, the more willing she became to examine who she was. As she did this, she was surprised to find things she liked about herself. One day as we were discussing good decisions she had made over her lifetime, and how they had paved the way for the good decisions she was making in recovery, she tilted her head to the side and said, "You know, the decision I made during the mugging, to be quiet . . . I've always felt that anyone worth respecting makes an effort to save herself. But, he had a knife, which really frightened me. He held it near my neck. I was terrified he would deliberately stab me, or cut me by mistake if I moved or surprised him. I decided letting him mug me was safer than fighting him. I think my silence . . . is why I survived. It was a good decision."

This revelation changed both Selena's memory of the event and also her perception of herself. She saw that even in a bad moment, she had made a good decision. She began examining and revising all of her negative self-views. Then she started deliberately looking for the good in who she was. It was easy to find, because being a survivor comes with many admirable qualities. The more Selena looked, the more she found, until her self-concept was no longer built around the cowardice, mistakes, and shortcomings she saw in her trauma and post-trauma behavior but instead focused on her ability to make intuitively good decisions, feel connected to family and friends, and protect herself.

Want to know who you really are? In the present moment, start noticing the details of how you make daily choices and take daily actions. Identifying patterns helps illuminate your motivations, internal drivers (those deep programs that direct you toward or away from experiences), values, and decision-making practices. With this information, you'll know more than simply what your emotional or physical state looks like; you'll know the *why* behind it and *how* you achieved it—which means you'll also find clues for how to change that state when and if you choose to do so. To expand your self-perception in this way, focus on the following six categories:

- *What do you think?* Self-talk is extremely revealing about who you are at any moment. It's the ticker tape of your mind, loaded with symbols about your perspective and interpretation second by second. Do you have a negative stream of consciousness? A suspicious one? A self-critical one? Are you always apologizing? Or, are you positive and optimistic? Immediately you may think you know how to describe your inner dialogue, but the truth is that until you actively listen, you don't have a full view of its function. The language you use, the tone of your inner voice, and where you place your focus and for how long all contribute to your thought processes. To discover the perspective of your inner voice, try this: For a week, listen to the way you talk to yourself. You might even take notes on repeated words or phrases, tones, and focus. Then ask, "What would make this voice more supportive, helpful, and compassionate?"

- *What do you feel?* Feelings, especially intense ones, let you identify ideas that are important to remember and pay attention to. Admittedly, your mind after trauma may seem overrun with such ideas. Let's step back from that negative thought and observe the purpose of a feeling. Your brain perceives something and makes a picture, your mind interprets the picture and forms a thought, and that thought creates a feeling. The purpose is to make sure you receive information. For every intense feeling, ask yourself, "What is a part of me trying to help me notice, learn, or understand?"

- *What do you believe?* Beliefs are the foundation of all of your behaviors, thoughts, feelings, perceptions, interpretations, and actions. They are ingrained in your subconscious mind, which informs 100 percent of who you are. The foun-

dation of your beliefs is programmed into your brain from
the ages of zero to three, and all the way up to age seven,
after which you can alter old and develop new beliefs either
by choice, repetition, or intense experiences. What beliefs are
operating in how you see the world on a daily basis? Whenever you feel uncomfortable, ask yourself, "What do I believe
is true in this moment?" Verify its truth, then switch your
attention to a more self-supporting belief.

- **What do you fear?** Of course, trauma puts in place many
  new fears, which may compound fears that already existed.
  In the heightened post-trauma world where threat and danger
  seem to exist in every moment, you're probably already very
  aware of the big fears you harbor. What about the smaller
  ones? As you move through the day, ask yourself, "What am I
  afraid of in this moment?" Explore the 5Ws (*who, what, where,
  where, why*—plus *how*) to identify what the deep fear is really
  about. Then switch to problem-solving mode by making a
  plan to reduce the fear. Investigate what it would take to
  lessen the fear and then take actions to do so.

- **How do you behave?** You are genetically hardwired to read
  the body language and actions of others. From the information your senses receive, you determine whether to more fully
  engage or disengage from another person, how to predict his
  or her behavior, and how to determine your own course of
  action. Turning the tables on yourself—observing your own
  behavior from start to finish in any situation—tunes you into
  triggers and responses, plus alternative actions that can shift
  you into a place of strength, safety, and control. Ask yourself,
  "What pushes my buttons?" "What interpretation caused me
  to respond this way?" "What else might be going on in this
  situation?" and "How else can I handle this?"

- **What do you wish for?** Even in the midst of your post-
  trauma pain, you have dreams. What are they? When you feel
  drawn to something, hope for something, yearn and long for

something, that's a very life-affirming part of you rising up to make contact. It is a part untouched by trauma—a pure part that despite what has happened still wants to feel good. Acknowledging, engaging, and giving that part what it wants in healthy ways reaffirms your connection to life, and your willingness to create it. Ask yourself, "If I could have, be, or experience anything, what would it be?" List as many things as possible. Then, start making choices and taking actions to create one desired outcome at a time.

Conscious self-awareness promotes a daily habit that builds your ability to be in control in moments that both do and don't matter, primarily because it builds your ability to be present in a state of curiosity and reflection. It also helps you learn from a deep sense of who exactly you are. Looking for clues about yourself shifts you into more observation and less evaluation of the circumstances. It also refocuses your attention from threat to factual information and from external to internal experiences. The more you practice this in noncritical moments, the more effortlessly you will apply the process and its benefits in moments that are more crucial.

Each day over the next week, choose three random low-stress moments and three random high(er)-stress moments to halt what you're doing. Become consciously aware of what's happening in the moment and answer the following questions:

- What do I think about this situation?
- What do I feel about this situation?
- What do I believe about myself in this situation?
- What is my greatest source of discomfort in this situation?
- What actions can I take to lessen that discomfort?
- What do I wish for in this moment?
- What actions can I take to move me closer to that?

To easily remember this process, write out the questions on a note card you can carry with you at all times.

To build a sense of the full insight this exercise offers, keep a journal each day with your answers to the questions. When the week concludes, pause and take a step back. Assess what you've written. What kind of person do you see?

_____

_____

_____

_____

What have you discovered?

_____

_____

_____

_____

Connect to Your Core Self

> My wonderful network of friends and family who love me and support me so thoroughly . . . remind me on a daily basis of all the things that make me "me," of all my strengths, and of my capacity to give and receive love, help, confidence, inspiration, and all of the good stuff.
>
> —*Susana A.*

Mark and his father, Archie, both loved to tell a good joke.

"The hallmark of my dad was his ability to tell a joke anywhere, anytime, in any mood," Mark remembers. "It didn't matter if you were totally ticked off. When he told a joke, you couldn't help but laugh. His happiness was infectious and unending."

Owners of an air-conditioning business Archie had inherited from his own father, the men spent every day together growing the company, building the business—and making each other laugh. While Mark was proud to carry on the family tradition, he was also proud to be an amateur musician; he frequently played guitar for a local rock band on week-ends. His love of music and performing had been with him since he was fourteen, when he attended his first rock concert and fell in love with the feeling of the music, the crowd, the venue, and the sense of instant community. With savings from a summer job mowing lawns, Mark bought a six-string and taught himself to play. Over the next two decades, Mark was very aware that when he was on stage with his instrument, "I knew exactly who I was. Those were the moments that took the rest of my good life and made it awesome."

One day when Mark was thirty-seven, he and his father went up in a small private plane. His father's favorite hobby was flying, and he was an accomplished amateur pilot. On this particular day they flew out over the Atlantic Ocean off the coast of New Jersey. The sky was bright blue, clouds floated high, and the air was pristine with the smell of autumn. The flight was smooth until there was a loud bang and the plane catapulted into a free fall. Unable to regain control of the plane, Archie attempted to crash-land in an open field. Only Mark survived.

A year later, Mark found himself in a pit of despair. His guilt for surviving, his sadness over losing his father, and the long rehabilitation of his broken ribs, pelvis, and legs all contributed to a personal transformation from the jovial son-of-Archie Mark had been to a man he and his family barely recognized. He refused to work or even enter the office he had once shared with his dad. He became silent, unsocial, disoriented, and disconnected. He packed away his guitar and spent his days playing video games in the basement.

It was Mark's wife, desperate to ease her husband's suffering, who set up his initial appointment with me. At one of our sessions, when I asked, "Throughout your life, what activity has made you feel most alive?" there was a slight delay, and then a half-smile crept onto Mark's face.

As an element of himself that had always brought Mark a sense of wholeness and soothing, the guitar represented a bridge back to a part of himself that felt good, life-affirming, and connected to a deep sense of purpose. It also seemed like a part he had lost contact with, maybe forever. Cautiously, Mark picked up the guitar and began playing daily.

First he only played songs that were Archie's favorites. Naturally, this seemed to deepen his depression. For balance, I encouraged Mark to use the guitar as a means to reconnect to his most essential self. This meant more than just playing Archie's favorites but his own as well, plus exploring the guitar as a means to express his post-trauma thoughts and feelings. Slowly the guitar became the focal point of Mark's post-trauma identity work. After a period of contemplation, Mark began writing lyrics and composing music. He wrote a song in honor of Archie, and about the crash, and about life after the crash. The more he leaned into the space of his guitar, the more he found himself, his music, and his voice. Ultimately, he wrote enough material to record an album, which he self-produced. Today Mark is back on stage with the band, has launched a small indie record label, and works as a booking agent.

Mark's post-trauma identity evolution is a great example of how the process can go beyond self-reconnection to designing a whole life around what makes you feel most like your core authentic self, the one unafraid to do and be and stand up for what creates a feeling of being alive regardless of opinions or expectations or past experiences. With the freedom to choose outside the family business tradition, Mark tapped into his own real interests. Beyond the plane crash and the loss of Archie, in the most authentic part of who Mark is lies his love of his guitar. It is a love full of anabolic (positive, synthesizing) energy that creates a focus on Mark's natural gifts, strengths, and source of joy. These three elements are powerful places from which to create your self-definition.

Shifting from powerless to powerful includes shifting from feeling bad about who you are to feeling good. One way to do this is by turning your attention to doing what you're good at so that you (re)develop your sense of *self-efficacy*. One of the most insidious aspects of life after trauma is the way past events make you question your ability to handle things in the present. Whereas you may have felt strong, calm, and dependable before, or may wish you'd had a chance to develop those qualities, now you feel uncertain, insecure, and undependable. A main purpose in constructing your post-trauma identity is to draw out your sense of being able to plan and produce an intended result. Consistently engaging in experiences that allow you to feel effective helps form neural pathways not only for that feeling but for the skills themselves.

For now, set aside where you've come from, who or what has impacted you, and what you have believed until today. This is a new moment. This is the beginning of a new "new normal" in which what you want, choose, and take actions toward is what you create, because beneath it all still exists a core you. It's time for that self to be revived and take the lead.

WHAT ARE YOU GOOD AT?

Even if your trauma happened at birth, there have been moments in your lifetime that you have discovered a natural skill. By examining your dominant skills, you have an opportunity now to define yourself in a way that extends who you already naturally were or had the potential to be:

1. Take yourself to a quiet space and close your eyes.
2. Take a few deep, slow breaths. Pay attention to how your body feels when the air moves in and out.
3. Imagine the timeline of your life stretching into the future and the past in opposite directions.
4. Imagine that you can place a marker at the present moment, then, if it feels comfortable, float up above the timeline.
5. Float (or walk) back through the years of your life all the way to the first year you can remember.
6. Slowly move forward year to year, searching out the moments you felt strong and powerful in activities that were healthy and safe.
7. Imagine that you have a basket; for each moment you discover, name the skill and place it in your basket.
8. Continue moving toward the present moment and hover over the marker. Examine the items you placed in your basket. Take some time to name each one and feel the feeling it produces in you.
9. When you have thoroughly examined the contents of the basket,

bring it with you as you float back down (or step) into the present moment. Slowly bring yourself to an awareness of the physical moment you're in. Notice the sounds, the temperature and the feeling of the air, and the smells in the room. Take a deep, releasing breath. When you're ready, open your eyes.

Picture your basket in your mind. Write down the skills you named and placed in it:

_____

_____

_____

_____

For each skill, note the activity you were doing that brought it out:

_____

_____

_____

_____

Take some time to reflect and compose your thoughts. What about those activities and skills made you feel so effective?

_____

_____

_____

_____

How often do you do those activities (or similar ones) today? Why or why not?

_____

_____

_____

_____

What would have to happen for you to work (more of) these activities (or similar ones) into your schedule?

_____

_____

_____

_____

How can you deepen and expand your daily practice and experience of those activities?

_____

_____

_____

Make a schedule for incorporating more of these activities with the specific intention of experiencing and focusing on how they make you feel.

WHAT MAKES YOU FEEL JOYFUL?

[What makes me feel joyful is] doing the things that bring me enjoyment and pleasure. In my case, I like to create things. I started crocheting.

—Daisy

At the moment of my greatest post-trauma despair, I felt numb and beyond saving in any way that would allow joy to be a possibility. Then a small voice in my mind said, "Try." As in, "Try to feel joy; let's just see if it can be done." Although I was doubtful, I made a commitment to try to feel joy at least once per day. It didn't have to be big, earth-shattering joy; it just had to be a small, quiet instance of it.

In trying to figure out what I could do that would bring joy, I already knew the little things. I could play with my dog, or take a walk on the beach. Suddenly, they weren't enough. Something in me kept pushing for a different type of experience, one I wasn't used to and that wasn't so accessible; one that pushed me outside of my head (and my house!) rather than allowed me to stay in it. After looking for the right thing to do, I stumbled upon the fact that when I dance, I feel free and joyful in a way I never do when I do anything else. Immediately I signed up for ballroom dance classes every day of the week. A freestyle dancer (think nightclubs in New York City), I had never partner-danced in my life. When I walked into the first class—disheveled and exhausted from another sleepless night—I felt trepidatious, out of place, and more than a little apprehensive about whether or not I'd be able to keep up with this group of strangers. It turned out to be one of the best decisions I ever made in recovery.

Not only did dancing every day set me up to connect with a part of myself that felt joyful and free, it helped me keep a schedule, be present, and connect my mind and body, and it offered an escape from the hourly thoughts about my awful past, painful present, and dark future. More than that, the daily buildup of joy started training my brain to *look forward to pleasure*, something I hadn't done since before my trauma. It also taught me that my joyful self did exist; she just needed to be invited to show up. The more I engaged with her, the more I learned that there was more to me than the effects of trauma. Plus, the more I experienced the feeling of joy, the more connected I felt to who I could be and the strength of that person. The result was that I developed more courage, which made me braver in my recovery quest. By the time I reached freedom, I had redefined myself from someone emotionally dead to a woman who can feel soaring bouts of joy. It was a redefinition that came from the deepest part of my core self and continues to inform my identity today: Not only do I still dance weekly for pleasure, but I also sporadically teach and perform.

I've come to believe so much in the benefits of the joy quest process that I began using it with clients. Lois discovered her joyful self back in the saddle of a Harley-Davidson motorcycle. Denny discovered his joy pounding over the waves of the Atlantic on a Jet Ski. Jolene, Patricia, and Corrie all reclaimed their joy through intense gardening. Steve retrieved it by returning to his faith and prayer.

Creating your joy connection can be as simple as giving yourself permission to feel good and as complex as trial and error. Because joy is an innate instinct, you can trace elements of it back through your life. For example, what made you feel joy as a child often still engenders those feelings when you're an adult. Thus, finding joy might mean examining what you loved as a kid. Conversely, if you're like Lois, whose childhood was so riddled with abuse she couldn't think back to it and look for any joy, your mind may naturally resist looking for joy the distant past. In Lois' case, we started from the present moment and sought the last moment of joy she had experienced as an adult, which was motorcycling at 90 miles per hour on the back roads of her small Colorado town. Lois no longer owned her Harley, so she borrowed a friend's for biweekly rides. Later in her recovery, Lois sent me a picture of herself as a five-year-old on the back of her father's motorcycle. When she found the photo, she realized that as a little girl she had loved those rides because they gave her a reprieve from the abuse she sustained at the hands of her mother. Even in Lois's case, what the little girl loved provided the same delight for the sixty-year-old woman she became.

Everyone has moments of joy (even if it is as simple as the taste of ice cream, or the freedom of finally leaving home for good), so release the impulse to say your life has never known a moment of joy—it has and your job is to identify when that was and what conditions and actions created it. You may identify several options for accessing that feeling, or you may just stumble upon one.

Explore Your Timeline

A timeline is a great way to begin your joy exploration:

1. Take yourself to a quiet space and close your eyes.
2. Take a few deep breaths. Pay attention to how your body feels as the air moves in and out.
3. Imagine the timeline of your life stretching into the future and the past in opposite directions.
4. Imagine that you can place a marker at the present moment, and then (if it feels comfortable) float up above the timeline.
5. Float (or walk) back through the years of your life all the way to the first year you can remember.

6. Slowly move forward year to year, searching out the moments you felt a sense of joy in activities that were healthy and safe.

7. Imagine you have a basket; for each moment you discover, name the source of joy and place it in your basket.

8. Continue moving toward the present moment and hover over the marker. Examine the items you placed in your basket. Take some time to name each one and feel the feeling it produces in you.

9. When you have thoroughly examined the contents of the basket, bring it with you as you float back down (or step) into the present moment.

10. Slowly bring yourself back to an awareness of the physical moment you're in. Notice the sounds, the temperature and the feeling of the air, and the smells in the room. Take a deep, releasing breath. When you're ready, open your eyes.

Picture your basket in your mind. Write down the joyful moments you placed in it:

_____

_____

_____

_____

Take some time to reflect and compose your thoughts. What about those moments made you feel so joyful?

_____

_____

_____

_____

What can you do today that creates joyful circumstances in your life? Compile a list of the joy options you discovered and how they are available to you now. Include a (tentative) schedule of when you can engage in them.

_____

_____

Be creative in how you access these activities. While you may not always be able to, say, go horseback riding in your favorite meadow, what else can you do to experience the joy of that action? Visualizing the experience in your mind, viewing riding videos online, or riding a bull at your local country bar might provide a creative alternative for days you can't get to the most desired activity. Give yourself a weekly challenge to incorporate one source of joy into your life. When this feels comfortable, increase it to daily.

Note: In addition to your timeline discoveries, there may be activities you've always thought would make you feel enormous pleasure. Now is the time to try them! Make a list of what they would be, research how you can experience them, and add them to your list of options.

WHAT HAVE YOU ALWAYS WANTED TO TRY?

Sofie lived in a small town in South Carolina. A cancer survivor who had undergone chemotherapy, radiation, and several surgeries by the time she was cancer free, Sofie had lost her job, many of her friends, and any sense of direction in life. At age sixty-two, she felt herself succumbing to a deep depression as she tried to figure out how to start over.

"I'm not even close to the person I was before my diagnosis," she explained. "My priorities are different; my values are different. Because of all this, the world doesn't look familiar anymore. I can't find my place."

Sofie had come a long way since beginning to redefine her post-trauma identity and was ready to take bigger actions to reclaim her full sense of self: She was ready to *celebrate* who she was. For Sofie, celebrating herself meant setting aside time each day to do one of her favorite things: spend time in the simplicity of nature—and feed a paddling of ducks at the pond near her house.

"I walk to the pond at sunrise every day," Sofie said excitedly. "The ducks are waiting for me. They know I'm bringing food. As I break off the pieces of bread, they come very close and wait for me to drop the pieces where they can reach them. Some ducks are even getting brave enough to take the bread from my hand. Every morning it's like a party just for me."

The good feelings Sofie experienced became something she looked forward to every day. They were a motivating force to get her out of bed in the morning. They were so pleasurable that Sofie starting going to the pond again in the afternoon. The more she offered those good feelings a way to present themselves, the more willingly and frequently they did so. Sofie's lingering depression lifted enough for her to begin thinking about the world outside her head. We discussed how much she enjoyed feeling as if she was doing something meaningful when she fed the ducks. As she became emotionally stronger, we began discussing how she could engage with that meaningful feeling more often.

Sofie remembered that as a child she had always loved caring for animals and had even wanted to become a veterinarian. When low family funds and an early marriage made that ideal impossible, she shelved her first love and developed a more practical career as an administrative assistant. Faced with the idea of starting her life over from a new place, however, Sofie decided to focus on expanding her experience of joy by pursuing meaningful time with more animals.

Sofie's hometown contained a no-kill animal shelter that frequently put out a call for volunteers and foster homes. To ease herself into a more structured schedule, Sofie committed to five hours of volunteering per week. After a month of seeing that the hours felt comfortable, she increased to ten hours. Six weeks later she began fostering dogs that came into the shelter. The experience was a terrific avenue for Sofie to engage with the self she admired and enjoyed in ways that allowed her to grow. She made a difference in the animals' experience on a daily basis, but that wasn't all. Sofie's natural and professional abilities for organization allowed her to contribute ideas and systems for overhauling the way the shelter and its staff operated and make them more efficient. Colleagues began coming to Sofie with questions and requests for assistance. Soon, her volunteer hours had increased to twenty per week. She told me with a big smile, "I'm back! Or, I did it: I figured out how to shift out of my old trauma self and feeling bad into a new self that's all about feeling good in the present. I'm part of a team. I matter!" Indeed, Sofie came to matter so much that when a position at the shelter opened, they hired her.

What have you always wanted to try but been too afraid to attempt? As Sofie discovered, internal growth and personal development require stretching and challenging yourself. Yes, going outside your comfort zone—and being able to handle and master that space—can feel uncomfortable and even dangerous. Still, trying something new is a great way to develop and reignite courage and learn about how possible it is for you to succeed in ways that feel good.

Try this:

1. Take some time to make a list of ten activities you would like to try.
2. Categorize the items on the list as "immediately" (I), "soon" (S), or "later" (L) to represent how quickly you can engage in these activities.
3. For each item on the "I" list, write out the steps it would take for you to engage in it.
4. Take a look at your list and your schedule, and begin placing activities from each list on your calendar.
5. Share with a trusted friend your intention to act on this schedule. When you do, share the results.

HOW DO YOU RELEASE YOUR "FUN FREAK"?

Recovering your life after trauma is serious business. Living, however, is not. Being serious all the time may seem like the "right" thing to do, but consider this: Your brain hungers for diversity. In fact, it functions more optimally when it has a range of experiences. Remaining utterly serious as you construct your post-trauma identity both dampens your brain's functioning and suppresses the real energy of your core self, which is designed for joy. It is imperative that you take time off, indulge your wish to have a good time, and liberate your "fun freak" so that this part of you can support and encourage the outcomes you're seeking to create.

Following the flow of energy—good feelings—is an organic and holistic way to begin rediscovering who you are today, what's important to you, why it's important, how you can build your life around it, and how to express your true self in the world. Plus, it shows you who you are *already* by helping you restore your sense of yourself as someone who can have a good time. So much of trauma recovery is about who you want to and will become. It's easy to write off who you are today because up until now that self has been solely focused on unhappy and uncomfortable feelings. Celebrating that self means offering it time on the stage of your life. Creating experiences, entering relationships, and seeking situations and opportunities that allow you to spend more time in and with a self you love, admire, and feel good inhabiting are great ways to celebrate yourself.

Looking back at the explorations you've done in this and earlier chapters, you are beginning to see glimpses (if not entire streaks) of a fully present self that waits in the shadows for you to invite it to come out. Tentatively at first, and then with increasing gusto and comfort, begin enlarging your feel-good feelings so that they extend from one brief situation to others throughout the day. You need to have fun. You need to have a good time. Doing these things stirs your creativity and restores your energy. To define a structure for this process, answer the following prompts in your notebook:

When I feel good . . .

- What's happening in my body?
- What's happening in my mind?
- How am I interacting with myself, others, and the world that makes me feel this way?
- What other situations would allow me to engage with this feeling?
- How can I work more of these experiences into my daily or weekly schedule?
- What kind of people share this pleasure with me? How can I find more of them?
- How can I do this kind of activity and make a difference for someone else?
- How can I feel this feeling while making a difference for or sharing it with someone else?
- How can I engage in this activity more frequently and for longer periods of time?
- What skills am I exhibiting in this feel-good activity? Where else would such skills be appreciated?

Use your answers as prompts for devising a schedule of new actions.

WHO ARE YOU REALLY?

If you'd been in my head during the years I struggled after my trauma, you would have heard definitions that included, "I am pathetic. I am useless. I am hopeless. I am crazy. I don't know who I am." It won't surprise you to hear that the more I thought those things, the more I became and wholly embodied them. The problem was, those statements weren't an accurate description of the whole of who I was.

The ideas you form about yourself today form the foundation for who you will turn into tomorrow. Let today mark the day that you begin redefining yourself in ways that are meaningful and optimistic. It's time to create a new self-definition. Based on what you intuitively think and feel in this moment (resist looking back at your previous self-definitions), and based on everything you've learned in this chapter, pause for a moment and write out your updated self-description:

I am

Read your definition out loud and examine each of the words you chose. Are they fair and accurately representative of who you are? Do they suspend judgment and present true facts? Are the positive aspects of you represented? Make any necessary revisions. Then refer back to the first definition you wrote on page 134 earlier in this chapter. How do the two compare?

The Take-Aways

> The healthiest advice I can offer for reclaiming your precious self is this: Your old story is not the ONLY story. Beneath your personal stories of pain and suffering, you can access wholeness, joy, and compassion. You can learn to put your energy where your joy lives.
> —*Shann Vander Leek*

- Even if you are frustrated and irritated with yourself today, there are still good and positive things about you.
- When you take the time to practice *conscious self-awareness*, you can change your psychological state by altering your perceptions, interpretations, and self-definition.

- When trauma and posttraumatic stress leave you feeling inert and stagnant, empowering questions jump-start your engine by encouraging you to be selective in how you think, make decisions, and take actions.
- Conscious self-awareness promotes a daily habit that builds your ability to be in control in moments that both do and don't matter, primarily because it builds your ability to be present in a state of curiosity and reflection.
- Following the flow of energy—good feelings—is an organic and holistic way to begin rediscovering who you are today, what's important to you, why it's important, how you can build your life around it, and how to express your true self in the world.

Who Do You Want to Be?

A BLUEPRINT FOR YOUR FUTURE SELF

*A trauma survivor's struggle is to make sense of the unimaginable.
As the survivor connects the dots of trauma, she reclaims
what was once fragmented and lost . . . The journey results in
a reconstruction of a new and different sense of self.*

—Deborah Serani, PsyD

Grady had a big problem: As a hurricane survivor, he had worked hard for several years to reduce and eliminate many of his PTSD symptoms. Although he was very clear on who he had become in response to trauma, thirty-year-old Grady found himself at a crossroads in recovery and felt stalled. If he had a choice, who did he really want to be?

"I was so confused I didn't know what to do. I couldn't continue the life I'd developed because it was based on all kinds of avoidance tactics. I finally felt safe and in control, but I didn't know what that meant in terms of how I wanted to live or who I wanted to be in six months, a year, or even five years."

Grady set out on a quest to determine his future identity. He tried dating women similar to his friends' girlfriends and dressing the way his colleagues did; he even bought the same car his father owned in an attempt to step into a ready-to-wear self-definition. Unfortunately, nothing felt right.

"I was just playing with other people's details, which was fine at first, but then I never developed a single idea that was built on my own vision of how things should be because—I didn't have a vision!"

One of the biggest problems after trauma is that you become so focused on the past that the future seems impossible to imagine. Yet constructing your post-trauma identity and reclaiming your life means imagining and then creating the future you desire. It's critical to start shifting your gaze away from pain, danger, and healing and direct it toward something positive and constructive. Now is the time to create a blueprint for a future self that is exactly who you would choose to be. With that vision in place, you will know what you're moving toward, plus you'll be able to identify what actions, experiences, and alterations are necessary for your post-trauma identity construction to reach its full potential.

For a moment right now, close your eyes, and imagine who you will be when your recovery journey ends and your post-trauma identity (while ever evolving) becomes stable. Imagine how you will behave, walk, talk, dress, work, travel, love, rest, play, and anything else that comes to mind. How clearly and vividly do you see that person? How well can you hear the sound of your future voice? How will it feel to be the future you?

When I ask clients to do this exercise, I receive a variety of responses, from quick intakes of breath to scowls to looks of sheer panic. Some diligently try to complete the exercise. They close their eyes, settle their bodies, and do their best to will an image and sensations to appear. Often this activity prompts irritation, frustration, fear, and even desperation. If these (or any other) avoidance responses feel familiar when you engage in this exercise, relax—that's completely normal. Stand up for a moment and stretch. Take a deep breath, hold it, and let it go. Scrunch your shoulders up and then back down from your ears. You're doing just fine. The purpose of this activity is only to get a baseline of where your imagination is so that you know where you need to build it from. Imagining things as different from how they presently are can be incredibly difficult at first. Who and how you are seem so familiar and comfortable (especially in their safety values) that eschewing the details of them may seem crazy, or at the very least impossible. But the whole reason you picked up this book is because you want things to change. There is a part of you that is not only willing for things to be different, but also has the vision for what that difference will be. Connecting to that part and its vision is essential.

At this point, you have taken a good look at and honored your Before self. You have also become very acquainted with and celebrated your After self. It's time to begin thinking about the next and final step: meeting your Now self.

Many survivors reach this point and recoil from their absence of knowledge about their future selves. When Jared is asked to describe his future self, for example, he replies, "That's impossible; I can't do it." A combat veteran, Jared is highly trained to anticipate. However, he finds it difficult to apply that skill to his own future. He's not alone. For a long time the majority of your energy has been directed toward and siphoned off by anticipating every future danger and threat. You have probably spent what amounts to hours picturing the next attack, drama, or incident, plus your response to danger or how to avoid it. You have probably seen all of that as big as an IMAX movie screen in your mind, in great detail and in 3-D Technicolor, that even includes sounds, smells, and tastes that you can feel in your body. Without making yourself extremely uncomfortable, for five seconds dip into your mind and let it show you dangerous and unpleasant things that might happen in your future. Try it now. I'll wait. I bet your mind does this with very little effort.

Was I right? Are you able to vividly imagine bad things happening? I thought so. That was actually a trick question, because it lends itself to your negativity bias. We all can imagine the worst with great proficiency. But here's what you just learned with that exercise: Your ability to imagine the future is alive and well. With great ease, you were able to conjure up a picture full of details. Now, let's apply that skill to your future *good* instead of potential bad experience.

Develop Your Daydreaming

When was the last time you sat around and daydreamed about something good happening? You can train your brain to increase its ability in this area by focusing on this fun task.

1. Sit in a quiet space and close your eyes.
2. Think of something you would like to experience in the future. That can mean a delicious ice cream sundae five hours from now or a fabulous vacation next year or entering a committed and loving relationship.
3. Focus on each of your five senses one at a time: imagine what that future moment will look like . . . what you believe it will feel like to be you in that moment . . . what that moment will smell like . . . what that moment will taste like . . . what sounds you will hear.
4. After you've spent time focusing on each individual sense, allow yourself to be still and notice the whole scene with all of the details synthesized.
5. Notice what other details reveal themselves to you. Notice how the daydream takes on a life of its own, either by remaining still, so you can enjoy one specific aspect or moment, or by becoming a movie that plays all by itself.
6. If during this daydream you've been watching yourself from afar, spend a few moments stepping into yourself in the daydream. Feel your arms, legs, hands, feet, torso and head slip into those of the person you see in the daydream. Now, experience it all again from the perspective of looking out through your own eyes and being in this body.

The only way you will change is if you make it happen. While others can support and help you, only you can create the changes you wish to experience. Achieving outcomes in post-trauma recovery—and especially in constructing your ready-to-wear identity—requires making choices in alignment with your desires. When you first approach this part of the post-trauma identity construction process, it can seem as if you lack direction. That's easily remedied with specific focus. For the rest of this chapter, you will design your Now self blueprint and learn to begin living it.

Focus on Change You Choose

I would go browsing through huge shopping centres . . . Through doing this I discovered my post-trauma taste in fashion, food, and homewares.
—Sharon Thorndike

Change you don't choose is an inevitable element of life after trauma. Creating change you *do* choose is an equally substantial aspect of recovery. Reclaiming your sense of self and constructing a post-trauma identity combines clarity of vision with the power of choice, and moves forward according to how well formed the plan for putting those choices in place is (i.e., how feasible it is). Today you can choose to create change. Accomplishing this relies on connecting with what you want and why you want it, and on developing the idea of how having it will change your life.

KNOW WHAT YOU WANT

When you're seated at a restaurant, the first thing you're given is a menu so that you can decide what you want to eat. The first thing you will be asked is, "What do you want to drink?" If you don't answer the question, what will happen? You'll get plain tap water with ice. Will you be happy with that? Will that quench your thirst or enhance your experience of the meal? If the answer is yes, then feel free to hydrate; at this point in the meal you're already getting what you want and you need take no further action. Probably, though, you don't want plain tap water with ice. You want bottled water, or soda, or iced tea, or beer, or a glass of wine, or even tap water without ice. When you sit down, you are prepared to share with the waitstaff exactly what you want to drink. In fact, you may have thought ahead and decided before you even entered the restaurant. Next, you peruse the menu, identify what you want to eat, and share that equally easily. You may ask the waitperson for recommendations or consult companions at the table, but in the end you weigh your options, imagine what each dish would taste like, and decide what seems best to you. The point is, you already have a strategy (mental pictures, thought and action processes) for thinking ahead, deciding what you want, and being satisfied with what you receive.

In some cases the idea of making choices can be triggering. If you experience a cascade of overwhelming and uncomfortable feelings from just the thought of making a choice, pause for a moment and step back. In your past there may have been unfair or inappropriate pressures surrounding choices, or unfortunate outcomes because of choices you made. Or, you may find that because of how trauma affects your brain you don't easily process information and so making choices has become exceedingly difficult. If any of this describes your response to the idea of making choices then chunk down the concept to an idea that is more comfortable and familiar: Identify something that you easily choose on a daily basis. For example, perhaps you choose the exact moment you get out of bed, or your clothes, or what station you listen to on the radio. Maybe you choose your shampoo or the type of toothpaste you use or even when to go to the bathroom. The truth is, all day you're making choices so easily you forget to appreciate that you do have a strategy for imagining what you want (an outfit, clean hair, fresh breath) and then making choices to create the desired outcome.

While your discomfort with making choices is valid I'm asking you to consciously decide to (temporarily) set aside the history that created it. Here's why: At the core of who you are is a person constantly making choices (including the choice to open this book) throughout every day. It's that fact—and only that salient fact—that matters in this chapter. Your job going forward will be to train your focus on the success of the small, inconsequential choices you make in every moment. When you're preparing to make bigger choices it helps to be connected to your simple 'strategy' for choice making. That is, how you successfully make choices, and the fact that you do make them often in many positive ways. How do you make the choices you do make all day? Start paying attention to how you choose one shirt over the others in your closet. Notice what pictures you see in your mind, what your hear in your head, and how your body feels when you choose that first morning beverage you drink. Focusing your awareness in this area will tap you into a rhythm of choice-making that you can use in your work throughout this chapter.

At the heart of making any (large or small) choice is a motivating desire. You want to please yourself, someone else or the situation. You have a clear mission that helps you make the decision and take the action to complete the choice. The same is true for your post-trauma identity construction. In order to be successful, you need to be enormously clear on what you want and willing to take actions that create it. In this case, that means concretely imagining the end result so that you embody your desire, discovering how to translate that into reality, and telling your brain what it needs to do to help you. The specifics of your desire are essential so that you create results that match what you really want versus what would just be nice, or okay. Consider this sentence:

I want to feel better.

Sort of, blah, isn't it? What does it mean to feel better, specifically? Does that relate to an emotional, intellectual, or spiritual experience? How will things be different if you feel that way? What needs to change in order for you to feel that way? The questions go on and on. There's no blueprint here for how to achieve "better," or even for what "better" truly is.

Now, consider this sentence:

I want to feel at peace with the past, deeply connected to who I am and my internal self in the present, and full of anticipation for the strong, courageous, joyful, free, and productive person I am becoming in every moment so that I can achieve a promotion at work, take a Caribbean vacation with friends, and finally meet my soul mate.

What a big difference! With this sentence you know how you want to feel about the past and can ask yourself empowering questions about what would make that happen. You also know what you want in the present and can put in place a plan for feeling those things. Plus, you're very aware of problem-solving to create that rather fantastic-sounding future. With this kind of specificity, your clarity, choices, and actions improve more than a thousand percent, which means so does the likelihood of your achieving it all.

KNOW WHY YOU WANT IT

Making any kind of change brings unforeseen and unexpected challenges. There will be days when you feel you don't deserve to succeed, don't have what it takes, and want to give up. The first key to keeping yourself motivated lies in your *emotional buy-in,* which relates to the strength of your emotional connection to your desired outcomes.

Your whole life, you've achieved things because they were important you. From learning to tie your shoes (because you valued independence and maturity) to learning to ride a bicycle or even drive a car (because you valued being able to transport yourself), you've succeeded at things because you felt and sometimes even consciously knew why they mattered to you.

What happens when you set out to do something that *doesn't* matter to you? I'll give you an example:

I was once interviewed by a reporter, Dana, about the value of having a coach. As part of the interview, we did a sample coaching session. Dana expressed the desire to lose ten pounds. As I coached her around this subject and we explored her emotional buy-in, Dana experienced a huge revelation. She had thought weight loss was an objective she kept failing at because she just didn't have any willpower. However, when we discussed the things she valued in her life (cooking with her chef husband, dining out with friends), it became clear that her level of engagement in activities that kept the ten pounds on was something she was unprepared to give up. She wanted to overeat while cooking with her husband; that was part of the fun. She wanted to overeat and drink with friends; that was how they made cherished memories. Likewise, the activities that would take off the ten pounds would interfere with other activities she valued. With a tight schedule, something would have to go to make room for exercise on the calendar, but Dana wasn't willing to eliminate anything already on the docket. She rated every present activity as more important than an exercise regimen. "I get it now," Dana smiled. "I haven't lost the weight because I don't really want to!"

When Dana decides to increase the importance of weight loss in her life, she will be able to lose any number of pounds she desires. At that point, her emotional buy-in will open her creativity and flexibility so that it isn't an either/or situation of giving up things she values to reach success, but of finding ways to balance the values. Dana will find ways of connecting with her husband and friends other than overeating and drinking. She'll be willing to get up one hour earlier to carve out time from her schedule for the gym. She'll do these things because the desired outcome is emotionally in alignment with what she values.

How is this idea showing up in your post-trauma lifestyle? What are you choosing to do, or not do? Both the positive and negative things in which you engage in order to feel safe or heal are not always easy. Yet, even by approaching rather than avoiding the tasks you've created a degree of success. Look back at the more challenging things you've done. Why were you able to achieve them? The answer is because the outcomes were enormously important to you. How important is the outcome of your post-trauma identity?

Sustaining a super-conscious connection between what you want and why you want it offers fuel for your process in other important ways. First, neuroplasticity increases when you engage in activities that are valuable to you. The more you value your identity processes, the more you encourage your brain to turn on in supportive ways. Second, when there's a compelling reason to face the challenges and move through them, it becomes much easier to remain motivated and committed. Third, when you're aware of why you want something, you connect how you feel to how you think. This is a powerful combination, a little like the mind-body feedback loop. In this feel-think synapse, you wire together feelings that motivate action with thoughts that direct the action. See the difference in these situations:

Kyra's process constantly starts and stalls. She recognizes the work that has to be done but just can't seem to get herself to consistently engage with it. When I ask her why she's working with me, she answers, "Well, you know, because . . ." When I gently nudge her to be more specific, she replies, "'Cause who wants to live like this?" When I ask again why our work is important to her, she simply shrugs her shoulders. I know there are reasons Kyra feels it's important for her to feel better, so our first action will be finding them. Until Kyra is willing to tap into what she values, she will probably continue to see herself stall because she's not willing to engage in a sense of why the work is worthwhile.

Anita, too, used to see herself start and stop many times in her quest to recover and redefine herself. Then she became very focused on why success was so important to her: "My daughter needs a mother she can interact with, someone who's not lost in her own head and can't connect with her. When I heal, I'll be able to be the mother she deserves, and that day is going to feel so good!"

When Anita began thinking about this statement on days she seemed defeated, she felt instantly grounded and energized. Her path became less rocky and more consistent. She began carrying a small photograph of herself and her daughter. In moments of despair or weakness, she focused on the picture for strength and courage.

Forecast Outcomes

> The number one thing that has helped me stay connected to my (new) identity is art. When I "cracked," I opened the door to becoming an artist and changed my full name. I am now a part of an international group of creatives.
>
> —*Molly (Kahikatea) Marshall*

My brother has a thirty-five-foot yacht on which we've spent many family vacations. When we lived in New York City, we rode the boat to Montauk, Providence, Martha's Vineyard, and Nantucket. Now that we live in South Florida, we've taken the boat to the Bahamas, Miami, and the Keys. These are all long trips that take us far offshore. Before we even leave the dock, my brother hunkers down in the cabin to consult his computer programs, the radar, and weather channels to see what lies ahead and ensure our safety. If his research shows thunderstorms directly in the path we're about to travel, he may delay the trip. Or, he might consult his charts and discover an alternative route to navigate around any trouble. Whether we're embarking on a short fishing trip or an extended vacation, my brother constantly forecasts the weather and makes choices based on the information he receives.

In navigating your post-trauma identity construction, it's important for you to do the same sort of procedure: Chart your course and then look ahead and make sure the coast is clear. You can easily do this by thinking into your future, assessing what you see there and making any adjustments in advance or along the way depending on what you experience.

You met Dorothy in Chapter 2, my client who wouldn't get out of bed and watched the same movie over and over all day. When we began working together, we outlined the problems, imagined the outcomes she wanted, and then checked to make sure that the solutions were in alignment with her real desires. We discovered something important that, had we not uncovered it, could have planted an enormous obstacle in Dorothy's progress and possibly halted it altogether: Post-trauma symptoms were keeping Dorothy safe from her toxic family. She explained, "If I'm too sick to do anything, then my parents won't call and demand that

I come help them with something. My sister won't dump her responsibilities on me, and my brother won't just show up here and expect to crash for however long it takes him to scrape up enough money to get out."

Suddenly a partial motivation for Dorothy's limiting and uncomfortable post-trauma lifestyle revealed itself as armor. If we reformed who she was without any other intervention, we'd be opening her up to danger. Before we did any deep identity-altering work, we constructed a process that would keep Dorothy safe when she was feeling better. For her, this meant conceiving and erecting boundaries, practicing them, and engaging her husband as part of her boundary-defining team so that she felt supported. The more confident Dorothy became that she could defend herself against her family and maintain her safety, the more comfortable she became with healing and the post-trauma identity construction process.

When considering your own recovery, it would be beneficial to ask yourself some questions about how the outcomes will affect your life. With each answer you will be able to pause, take a step back, reflect, assess, and choose how to proceed. Sometimes the answers will confirm that you're on the right path, clear skies ahead. Other times the answers will let you know that you're heading into stormy weather that there's no way to skirt; best not to leave the dock yet. At still other times, you'll know you're headed into stormy weather and it would be better to find an alternative route. Dorothy achieved all of her original desires, but first we took a side route to put in place boundaries necessary to ensure the safety of her final destination.

At this point you're ready to develop a detailed list of desired outcomes that you can begin using to create the technical aspects of your post-trauma identity construction plan. Later in this chapter you'll develop a deliberate strategy for executing that plan. Here you'll make a preliminary blueprint by pulling together and applying the concepts of choice, understanding, and forecasting. If you run out of space in this book as you complete the following exercises, continue in your notebook.

Choose

In this step, you begin deciding who you want your future self to be, specifically.

Step One:

How do you want others to perceive you? Imagine you are a friend of yours looking at you from afar. Describe your future self from this external perspective, beginning with the phrase, "If I were to describe [insert your name], I would say he/she is _____."

Step Two:

If you could choose who you will become (which you can), who would that be? Craft an "I am" statement around that now. Based on all that you've learned, your present self "I am" statement (from the end of Chapter 4), and your hopes and dreams, write a description of the future identity you wish to inhabit *as if you were already doing so.* Be bold, lean in, and go for it! (You can always revise this statement later as you continue to develop what you think, want, feel, and believe.)

I am _____

Understand

To keep up your motivation and commitment during the discovery ahead, it's critical to have emotional buy-in and be clear about why you're doing all of this. When you emotionally resonate with your vision in a positive way, you receive feedback that you're on the right track.

Look at the descriptions you wrote in the "Choose" exercises. Notice the overall vision that appears. Why is it important to you to become this person? Write as many reasons as you can think of.

Forecast

Think of your own, your friends', and your family members' reactions to the new you. What will they like about it? What will they admire? How will the changes benefit them, or take away something from them? How much will the changes be appreciated or rejected? Why? How will you respond to that?

Looking ahead will help you anticipate any obstacles that will need to be addressed, plus give you a taste of the pleasures that await you. Throughout the rest of this chapter (and your life), you can use the following questions to forecast results and identify whether or not they are in line with the outcomes you desire. Be excessively specific in your answers; consider all options, facts, details, and ideas.

Refer again to your descriptions in the "Choose" exercise. When you achieve the actions necessary to create this vision of yourself, how will your life change?

Use the questions below to check for resonance of the proposed blueprint with your future self. Write the answers in your notebook.

- What will happen if I achieve this identity?
- What won't happen if I achieve it?
- What will happen if I don't achieve it?
- What won't happen if I don't achieve it?
- What do I get to have or keep by having my present identity?
- How does that benefit me?
- How does that benefit those around me?
- How will the changes I wish to make benefit me?
- How will the changes I wish to make benefit others?
- How do I know it's worth becoming my future self?
- In which situations does it feel okay to keep my present identity?
- In which situations does it not feel okay to keep my present identity?
- Where does it feel appropriate to have my present identity?
- Where does it feel appropriate to have my post-trauma identity?
- With whom does it feel more appropriate to keep my present identity?
- With whom does it feel more appropriate to achieve my post-trauma identity?
- How will achieving my post-trauma identity affect my life?
- How will achieving my post-trauma identity affect my family?
- How will achieving my post-trauma identity affect my friends?
- How will achieving my post-trauma identity affect my job and colleagues?
- What will be different as a result of achieving my post-trauma identity?

What feedback are you receiving as a result of these questions? Is it safe for you to proceed with the plan, or do you need to make a detour to put in place other elements essential for your success before moving ahead?

Draft the Blueprint

> I've spent years redesigning who I am because ultimately it's my choice. I realized at an early age that I can use difficult experiences . . . as catalysts to help shape me into the person I want to be. Those difficult moments either make me or break me; the choice is always mine how I direct the effects of those moments. At the end of the day, I decide who I am.
>
> —*Heidi* (Dr. Sousse)

Paul survived a car wreck in which the left side of his body was crushed. After months in the hospital and even more in rehab, his body finally resumed its healthy shape and function. However, Paul discovered, to his chagrin, that his mind wasn't quite so resilient. He harbored deep fears and insecurities about his ability to be safe while traveling even the smallest distance in the car. The enormously intense emotions of anxiety and anticipation began hours before he had to get into the car and continued for hours afterward, even when he had experienced a successful trip. In addition to the effects of the trauma itself, it seemed that the accident had triggered all of his insecurities; those related to the accident were compounded by increased feelings of need and loneliness that had been with him since childhood.

When Paul finally reached the point in his recovery that it was time to create the blueprint for his future self, he didn't know how to translate the ideas in his vision into experiences for his mind and body.

"That future self seems so far away," he said, "as if he's not really ever going to be me; he's just a figment of my imagination."

Paul felt overwhelmed, shut down, and stuck. His recovery threatened to stall until he began taking small steps to implement simple actions designed to transition his ideas into reality in ways that were comfortable, safe, and incremental. Together we designed a process that brought his future self closer to his daily experience and then right into his present. We began by utilizing Paul's imagination.

A friend of mine is a pro golfer. When he talks about how he learned to be as good as he is, he's quick to mention his use of visualization. His pathway to learning to hit the sweet spot of the ball included hours off the course simply sitting in a quiet space and visualizing success: the setup for the shot, the arc of the swing, the connection of club and ball; the turn of his hips; the flight of the ball toward the cup. Every professional athlete learns to use the power of imagination to create patterns in the brain that correspond to what the mind and body will experience in the external world. Your future self is a culmination of how you set up the shot, swing the club, and connect to the ball.

Paul and I first employed this skill in the area of helping him to comfortably drive down the street. In his blueprint of his future self, Paul had included the ability to drive as safely and securely as he always had. We chose a beginning and ending location, did five minutes of preparatory breathwork to create a sense of calm and present-moment, inner connection and proceeded with a driving visualization exercise. Paul closed his eyes, focused internally to see the landscape, and narrated for me as he "drove" from home to the grocery store.

"I'm backing down the driveway," he said. "I'm pausing for a woman to walk by with her dog. I'm slowly backing out into the street and turning the wheel to the left to straighten out. I'm putting my foot lightly on the accelerator. There's no one behind me. I'm going to slowly roll to the stop sign . . ." and so on until Paul had "reached" the grocery store a few miles away. Then he turned around and drove back, narrating the journey for me the whole way. When he finished the exercise, Paul opened his eyes and offered a huge smile. "That felt pretty good! I can do that!"

After practicing a few more times with me, Paul gained enough confidence to continue the exercise a few times a day at home. The more he practiced, the better he felt. The benefits were immediate: he reported reduced stress at the thought of driving; an increased belief in his ability to drive safely, calmly, and with clarity of mind; and a shift to positive anticipation for the driving experience.

As Paul continued the imagination exercises, I also asked him to solidify his vision of his future self by making it into a reality in non-challenging ways. This process included surrounding himself with objects, visual aids, and experiences designed to create a context for his internal desires in the external world. He cut out a picture of his dream car from a magazine and pinned it to his bulletin board. He replaced his favorite driving mug (which had been destroyed in the accident) and put the new mug on his desk. He began practicing the visualization while sitting in his car inside the closed garage, then graduated to opening the garage door. He developed strong driving-related affirmations based on what he *already* believed about his ability to achieve his driving mission, and also created focused "I am" identity statements to continue training his brain to learn how to be, see, think, and act like the confident driver he wanted to be.

The benefits of Paul's actions accumulated until he began feeling comfortable enough to actually drive the car down the driveway, and then around the block. When his confidence grew in this area, he extended his practice drives to trips to the grocery store, just as he had imagined. Gradually, Paul's comfort behind the wheel increased, until he could drive anywhere without breaking into a cold sweat. Today Paul owns the car whose picture he pinned to his bulletin board and drives it with both confidence and a sense of pride. The car represents his Now self, plus his achievement in becoming that man.

All of the work you've been doing in this book has been geared toward clearing a space within yourself to make the changes you desire. Merely becoming aware of the proposed changes isn't enough to make them appear. To create, meet, and merge with your future self, you will need to liberate the ideas from your mind and birth your future self into the reality of your daily life.

Imagine

When you imagine your future self, it may, as Paul's did, seem distant and very separate. Suspend judgment and follow the following steps.

Step One:

Think of your future self. Allow a picture of that self to form in your mind and body so that you see and/or sense it. How does it feel? Does it seem close or far away? Pause to deeply experience this vision.

Imagine that by focusing on the image, it moves closer to you. Pretend you are a magnet and draw the image even closer to you still.

How close can you bring that future self? See if you can:

- Bring it close enough to shake hands as you stand face to face.
- Allow it to stand beside you, shoulder to shoulder.
- Allow it to stand a few inches in front of you with its back to you.
- Step forward and easily melt yourself into the body before you: feel your feet slipping into those feet; your arms, back, and chest slipping into that self's body; your head easily fitting into that head so that you can see through the eyes of your future self.

How different do things look and feel from this location and perspective?

Step Two:

Choose an activity that this future self would do. That can be something as simple as walk down the street with a fearless attitude or as complex as negotiate a lucrative deal. Set aside ten minutes per day to quietly—with your eyes closed—imagine the entire scene in vivid detail. Notice what you're wearing, saying, feeling, thinking, sensing, smelling, seeing, and doing. Notice details of others involved in the scene.

Repeatedly reexperience the first exercise and play the full scene(s) of the second exercise from start to finish in your mind at least once or even up to three times per day for at least thirty consecutive days.

Solidify

I'm going to suggest that you do something now that you may feel is a little challenging. As you move through the exercise, remember to craft the details according to your level of comfort. Once you get going, you can increase that level anytime you wish. At all times, be creative! Think outside the box, have fun, be silly, and follow the good feelings.

To solidify something is to make it strong or united. In your case, it means uniting ideas in your mind with reality in your world. Doing this will allow you to see, touch, and feel those details. Implementing any or all of these exercises (or other ideas you have) will help you convert your experience from interior fantasy to exterior experience.

- **Create a vision board or bulletin board or even cover your refrigerator** with aspects and elements of your future self. Training your brain for what you want to experience helps focus it on getting those things for you.
- **Buy, create, or borrow physical objects** that represent tastes, activities, likes, and desires of your future self and place at least one in each room of your home. Once a week, shuffle the items to new locations so that you continue to keep your awareness of their presence at a conscious level.
- **Create experiences** that your future self would want and enjoy. You may do these in smaller or less time-consuming ways than you will in the future, but engage in at least one activity weekly or even daily.
- **Choose five words** (adjectives or nouns) that describe your future self. Write a series of "I am" statements that orient you to that self (e.g., "I am confident," "I am comfortable," "I am a successful business owner"). Review these statements

at the very least when you wake and right before you go to sleep—and as many times throughout the day as you wish. It's unnecessary for you to believe these statements; it's only necessary for them to be in your mind's radar. If it feels more comfortable to you, amend the statement to, "I am open to
_____."

DEVELOP ACTIONABLE DESIRES

I started by creating an identity . . . when I started a business designing and building tree houses . . . This allowed me safety and time to seek my true identity, which started by forgiving God. This led to meditation, and from that came a sense that I belonged in the world and in all the roles of my life, and slowly I am becoming comfortable in my own skin.

—John

In the language of achieving, many people use the word *goals;* I don't. In fact, you haven't seen the word *goal* at all in this book until this moment. Historically, goals are what you *work* toward. They're what you're hoping to reach disconnected from the reasons you're taking the actions and the emotions driving you to do so. Plus, you have to put out a lot of effort to get there. I prefer the word *desires,* which keeps you constantly connected to what you wish for and introduces an outcome that flows from what you want rather than dangles just out of reach. *Desire* is a word that calls up dreams and keeps you focused there throughout the process of applying the plan. Equal to the power of the phrase "I choose" in connecting you to a sense of your self-efficacy, "I desire" connects you to the power of what you wish for. It's from here that you can create your ultimate vision of yourself, your life, and your world.

I first met Sam when he joined one of my PTSD support groups. At the time, he was in his late forties, and his multiple traumas had involved child abuse and domestic violence. In our pre-group interview he burst out angrily that he didn't know why he had reached out to me, since he felt he couldn't be saved. Still, he said, "a part of me hopes. I'm slightly optimistic that you will able to help me."

When I asked Sam his biggest concern, he explained that he was having difficulty staying present. "When I'm in a situation that seems even remotely threatening or uncomfortable, my mind just drifts away. It's very embarrassing because then the people around me have to poke me, shout, or say something offensive to get my focus back. I want to be the kind of man who feels comfortable wherever he is, and one that can manage any situation by being wholly present and able to respond appropriately."

On Sam's first day in the group, we began chipping away on this single desire: learning to become more present and in control of staying that way. A year later, through achieving a series of smaller outcomes, he had mastered this skill and identified his next desire as getting a job. Having sold his stake in a business for a large sum, Sam had not worked in six years while struggling with post-trauma and PTSD symptoms. With his ability to be present confirmed, he deemed it time to begin redeveloping his mind's ability to process. He set about training his brain (using, among other things, free exercises on Lumosity.com), working with a job placement counselor, and continuing to develop his ability to be present, confident, and effective. He looked for opportunities to exercise his voice and desires. Rather than take it for granted that people and things were the way they seemed, he questioned everyone and everything. In this way, he reduced his fears and increased his confidence. He began working with Toastmasters, going to job fairs, and practicing mock professional interviews. Step by step, Sam continued to develop himself. Eighteen months after we began working together, he had not only landed a new job in a career he loved, but he had also had the clarity and confidence to negotiate his salary to a level higher than expected.

The strength of Sam's process is that he's always clear on the next desire. When he achieves one objective, he naturally looks for the most organic successor. This willingness to be so desire oriented keeps Sam on track and also maintains his focus on both the immediate wish and its ultimate outcome.

The early part of trauma recovery is always about triage: learning how to identify priorities and comfort zones, find a sense of safety and control, and exercise your strength and focus to face fear instead of running from it. Since then, you may have fallen into a pattern of just doing the next thing that occurred to you, which is a great way to progress and perfectly suits trauma recovery—until you get where you are now.

Constructing your post-trauma identity requires you to identify specific desires so that you deliberately construct aspects and elements of the person you want to become. Today, you're more safe and in control than at any point in your recovery. You have more of a sense of your self-efficacy, clarity, and wishes. This part of recovery isn't driven by basic survival needs. Instead, it's driven by your vision and decisions. In fact, what you decide today is who you will be tomorrow and the day after that, which makes your decisions today of prime importance.

Although the specificity of looking ahead may seem challenging, it can be achieved by asking yourself one simple question:

When I'm trauma (and PTSD) free, what do I want to be true about me?

Fully answering this question in detail covers all of your hoped for qualities, plus your context, narrative, and values. It describes the wished-for details of the *you* who will emerge from this journey. It also outlines your desires so that you can see them clearly and in specific categories that you can use to develop your blueprint from this moment on.

Explore your answers to the following outcomes questions as extensively as possible. Answer the questions by free writing in your notebook for five minutes or more at a time. (Free writing happens when you keep your pen constantly moving without worrying about spelling, grammar or syntax. Focus your mind only on answering the question. When you get stuck in the flow of ideas repetitively write the last phrase or sentence until a new thought enters your mind.) Reread what you've written and then summarize the ideas in one or two sentences that most effectively get across the main point.

Thoughts

- When your recovery is complete, what do you want to be true about your thoughts about yourself? What thoughts will those be, specifically?
- When your recovery is complete, what do you want to be true about your thoughts about others? (Consider your thoughts both about people you know and about strangers.) What thoughts will those be, specifically?
- When your recovery is complete, what do you want to be true about your thoughts about the world at large? What thoughts will those be, specifically?

Feelings

- When your recovery is complete, what do you want to be true about your feelings about yourself? What feelings will those be, specifically?
- When your recovery is complete, what do you want to be true about your feelings about others? (Consider your feelings both toward people you know and toward strangers.) What feelings will those be, specifically?
- When your recovery is complete, what do you want to be true about your feelings about the world at large? What feelings will those be, specifically?

Behavior

- When your recovery is complete, what do you want to be true about your behavior toward yourself? What behaviors will those be, specifically?
- When your recovery is complete, what do you want to be true about your behavior toward others? (Consider your behavior

both toward people you know and toward strangers.) What behaviors will those be, specifically?

- When your recovery is complete, what do you want to be true about your behavior toward the world at large? What behaviors will those be, specifically?

Beliefs

- When your recovery is complete, what do you want to be true about your beliefs about yourself? What beliefs will those be, specifically?
- When your recovery is complete, what do you want to be true about your beliefs about others? (Consider your beliefs both about people you know and about strangers.) What beliefs will those be, specifically?
- When your recovery is complete, what do you want to be true about your beliefs about the world at large? What beliefs will those be, specifically?

Actions

- When your recovery is complete, what do you want to be true about your actions in support of yourself? (Consider things like self-care, self-talk, and protection.) What actions will those be, specifically?
- When your recovery is complete, what do you want to be true about your actions toward others? (Consider your actions both toward people you know and toward strangers.) What actions will those be, specifically?
- When your recovery is complete, what do you want to be true about your actions toward the world at large? What actions will those be, specifically?

In the beginning, your desired outcomes may feel very far away, overwhelming, unreachable, and beyond your current capacity. If that's the case, try this simple exercise:

1. Find a quiet, safe place and close your eyes.
2. Think about the end result that you desire.
3. Imagine how it will feel to have it.
4. Focus on that feeling and allow it to grow in your consciousness.
5. An image corresponds with this outcome. Allow it to materialize in your mind. The image may be of an entire scene, or just a fragment or detail. It may be a literal representation or a symbolic one, focused or blurry, light or dim or even just a sensation. Any way that the image appears is perfectly fine.
6. Now slowly bring that image closer to you. Gently pull or will it to move from where it is to half the distance closer. When you have done that, pause. How does that feel? If it feels okay, good, or even better, continue with the process again and again until you have closed the distance entirely.
7. If bringing the picture closer does not feel good, pause and ask yourself, "What is uncomfortable about this?" Revisit the outcomes questions on page 187.

Note: For some people, moving the picture farther away will feel better because they do not actually want that outcome so much as they think they want it. If this is you, revisit the "Forecast" exercise and create a vision of your future self that aligns what you want with what feels good to you. Then try the exercise above again.

While for the majority of people bringing positive things closer feels better, for a small percentage of the population even when the desire is true and comfortable things feel better when the picture moves away rather than when it moves closer. This is just a matter of personal calibration; how your brain represents things. If this is you (i.e., if your desires and plans are well formed but you feel the picture's emotion more intensely as you move it away from you), trust your instincts and play with the picture in the way that feels best.

OUTLINE YOUR INITIAL STRATEGY

Creating an authentic connection through yourself to others is the key
for finding your way back to yourself . . . Taking the chance to let your
true self be known, rather than simply revealing what you think others
want to see, means embracing the courage to connect with others.

—*Dena Rosenbloom, PhD*

Outlining a plan for achieving what you want can help you not only organize but de-stress by creating order out of the chaos of ideas. For each of the recovery desires that you set (and for every desire you have for the rest of your life), success depends on how you approach it. In Sam's process, this was particularly important. In order to achieve the most recovery possible, he knew it would be necessary to become fully present. Due to the cumulative effect of multiple traumas, however, Sam had developed a coping mechanism that held him safely and securely in a dissociated state. Those moments when others had to snap him out of it were painful and left Sam feeling fragile and exposed. Earlier I mentioned that Sam created smaller successes in order to achieve the bigger outcome. Following are a series of steps that you can apply to do the same with your individual desires.

START WITH THE END IN MIND

[I am] slowly learning that I do have choices, experimenting with exercising
choices, and having compassion for myself and others when things go "wrong."

—*Flora Yurold*

The most powerful way to bring anything into your life is to have a clear idea of what you want the end result to be. In creating your recovery and post-trauma identity, for each specific area you choose to focus on we begin with the end so that you always have in mind what you're moving toward. This strategy engages your reticular activating system (the part of your brain that controls your overall level of consciousness) to look for ways to accomplish the end result, keeps you focused and on track, supports your determination and perseverance through challenges, and orients you to a starting point from which you can develop a plan.

For Sam, this step meant becoming familiar with what success would look like if he were to be very present all the time. Over a period of days, he built on all the exercises you've experienced in previous pages to formulate a well-defined and descriptive image and feeling of success. For him, this meant imagining himself being able to converse with friends or strangers in private or in public in a way that allowed him to feel confident, connected to his strength, and able to focus. When Sam had a clear image of this, we knew he was starting with the end in mind.

Building on your self-description on page 185, spend some time focusing on the end result you desire. Close your eyes and allow yourself to to connect with the vision. When the picture appears, play with it:

- Make it larger.
- Make it clearer.
- Make it brighter.
- Make it even more technicolored.
- Bring it closer to you.
- Have it surround you from 360 degrees.
- Add a soundtrack.
- Let the still picture morph into a moving picture; let the scene play to conclusion.

Continue massaging the picture until you have not only a picture but also a keen feeling that accompanies it. The more connected you are to the end result, the more your mind will help you facilitate it.

Often you may sense or feel the idea of what you want the end to be, but you may not be able to see the full picture at all. In these moments, you can begin creating your blueprint by reverse engineering the whole picture:

1. Vertically crease an 8.5- x 11-inch sheet of paper. Above the left column, write "Dislike." Above the right column, write "Like."
2. In the "Dislike" column, write down every single thing about yourself that you wish were different. This can include behaviors, beliefs, attitudes, physical attributes, emotions, post-trauma symptoms, and so forth.
3. For every item in the "Dislike" column, write the opposite, more desired attribute in the "Like" column.
4. When you have completed both lists, fold the paper along the crease so that you can see only the "Like" column. Take a moment for a long, slow read. This is your vision of the future you according to what is most important to you today.

CHUNK IT DOWN

It wasn't until I started therapy . . . that I truly started to figure out who I was. A big part of it has been through volunteering and helping others through difficult times, and my incredible therapist.

—*Angie Boudreau, Toronto, Canada*

Being aware that you want to make a change is the first step to achieving it. Seeing the whole picture, however, can be overwhelming, especially if the end result looks dramatically different from who you are or what you experience today. Reducing and overcoming that feeling results from identifying what actions need to be undertaken. The easiest way to discover the necessary steps is to unravel the end result. We do this by looking at the final outcome and asking, "What has to happen to get me here?"

For Sam, the end result meant that he was calm, was able to easily focus in a conversation, could manage and contain his arousal response, and was able to hear and respond to others' comments. Together we explored those outcomes and talked through what events had to occur so that they could be achieved. Sam's thought process went something like this (I've added the underlining to emphasize the action steps):

In order to be calm, I would have to feel safe, which means I'd have to be with people I trust, at least somewhat and on a basic level; I have to make sure that the people I'm conversing with feel comfortable to me. I have to begin making better choices about who I allow to talk to me. I also have to establish better personal boundaries, because lack of that often makes me feel vulnerable and this gets me in trouble, which means I need to really define what my personal boundaries are.

I also need to feel connected to myself, which means being clear on what makes me feel present, which I know is a feeling that I exist in my body instead of out of it. The times I feel most in my body are when I'm with my animals, my dog or my horse. So, to develop that feeling and learn to get into and stay in it, I probably need to spend more time consciously being aware of how I feel, think, act, believe, and behave around my animals. Then, I can take those skills and employ them around humans.

From these simple discoveries, Sam began outlining changes and actions that would move him forward. From the outline, we set about prioritizing which things had to happen first, second, third, and so forth. Eventually Sam settled on the first step as exploring his definition of trust. From there he grew his process to include all the identified steps necessary to create all the outcomes.

When you begin with the end result, you can clearly and pretty immediately identify major developmental events. You can further break down those events until you have taken the one big outcome and broken it into elements that feel manageable and achievable.

Step One

Turn to a fresh page in your notebook. Transcribe your description of your future self from the "Choose" exercise on page 185 (and include any tweaks you've made since the original). Then write the question, "What has to happen to get me here?" Write out as many events, changes, choices, actions and experiences as you can think of that need to occur.

When you have exhausted your ideas, take a step back, pause, reflect, and assess what seems most important to do first, second, third, and so forth. Number the steps in order of their priority.

Step Two

Label a separate piece of paper for each numbered event and write out every step that will have to happen to get you from where you are today to that end result. You can write out the steps from today forward, or you can start at the end (a future date) and work your way back to today. Some people like to do this as a flow chart, others like mind mapping, and others just like to write as many steps as occur to them and then organize and prioritize them later. Trust your intuition. Whichever method feels most comfortable is the best way to allow your mind to work.

SET MANAGEABLE DESIRES

From the previous exercises, you have compiled an enormous cache of action steps. This is an exciting place to be, and yet it, too, can feel overwhelming. At this point, it's time to give your post-trauma identity construction plan real structure by setting manageable objectives that make you feel excited, apprehensive, challenged, proactive, and in touch with the ability to succeed. Just having the list of necessary events isn't enough; you need to know how you will achieve them.

The AIM SMART! process helps you create a plan tuned around the "Acceptable minimum, Ideal, and Middle," using elements that are "Specific, Measurable, Attainable, Realistic, and Time oriented." It helps you prepare a solid strategy with a full range of considerations and built-in action steps that use your own check-in process as a guide for future action. Following the AIM SMART! process allows you to form a well-designed desire for any aspect of your post-trauma identity blueprint.

The process contains nine steps, each of which is detailed below. You'll notice that each step builds on the one before and poses a question for you to answer that further develops your action plan. I've chosen as an outcome "commitment to exercise" to give you an example of how the process works.

AIM Desire-Setting Steps	Example: Commitment to Exercise
A – What is the **"acceptable minimum"** achievement? To begin, decide what's the least you feel comfortable accomplishing.	Working out two days/week would be the smallest acceptable effort.
I – What is the **ideal**? On the flip side, it's also good to note what your wildest dream would be.	Working out six days/week.
M – What is in the **middle**? With the boundaries of the range intact, this step offers you a middle ground—a little more or a little less than the extreme.	Working out four days/week.

Now that you have solidified a range, you're ready to work out the nuts and bolts of your action plan.

SMART! Desire-Setting Steps	Example: Commitment to Exercise
S – Specific: The better defined your desires, the greater the chance that you will accomplish them. Specificity can be applied in a few ways:	
First, by being clear on the *what*, *when*, and *why* aspects of your desire and answering questions like "What are you going to do?" "When will you do it?" and "Why is this particular desire important to you?"	"I am going to work out consistently multiple times per week because I want to feel better about my body and proactively reduce stress."
Second, by summing up the desire in a detailed statement.	Specificity is the difference between "I'm going to exercise" and "Starting on the first day of next month, I am going to go to the gym at 8 a.m. on Mondays, Wednesdays, and Fridays to spend fifteen minutes on cardiac exercise and then thirty minutes weight lifting so that I lose my excess weight and strengthen, tone, and shape my body."
Third, by answering the question "What exactly is the very first step?"	"My very first step is to take out my calendar and scheduling in the time."
M – Measurable: You'll feel more connected to your desires—and more sure of your progress—when you have tangible proof that you've accomplished each step. This means that before you begin, you ask yourself, "How will I know I've been successful?" or "How will I know when I've achieved this step?"	"Tangible proof I've accomplished the first step will be calendar alarms set on my digital calendar that alert me via my cell phone and email, plus a written calendar on the refrigerator door."

A – Achievable: When focusing on your desires, you should expect to be stretched, but not incapacitated. Meaning, achieving the outcome should require work but not paralyze you. In this step, you check in to make sure you're setting a plan that is commensurate with where you are emotionally, physically, and intellectually. Ask yourself, "Is the initial step something I can do? If not, what is getting in the way?"	This would apply to deciding if the idea of creating a calendar is achievable. The answer might be, "Yes, I can draw the calendar and mark the days and times for exercise, plus program my online calendar to send out alerts." Or it might be, "No, I don't have time today because of an unexpected meeting that's been scheduled." Being clear on the good reason (not a flimsy excuse!) that something can't be done can reduce the stress of not achieving it while allowing you to make an alternate, achievable plan.
R – Reasonable: There are things you're prepared and ready to do, and things you aren't. To successfully achieve a desired result, it must be something you feel both willing and able to work toward. Ensuring that a plan is reasonable supports your motivation to put in the time and energy it takes to achieve it. For this step, ask yourself, "How feasible is it that I can do this at this time?"	"This step is very feasible, since I have some free time to set up the schedule this evening."
T – Time oriented: For you to be successful, your desires need to be grounded in a time frame. If you don't commit to a date and a time, your required actions and the outcome itself will always float just out of reach. Setting a time frame creates a sense of urgency that can unite with your motivation and produce momentum, which gives you a natural boost toward successful achievement. Here you might ask yourself, "By when, exactly, will I complete this step of the outcome?"	The answer might be, "Before I go to sleep tonight; 11 p.m."
! – Create a written statement that outlines/ summarizes the plan. Desire-setting brings together many fragments of the achievement process. The more you can see them—literally—the more easily successful you will be.	The written statement might look like this: "Before I go to sleep tonight, I will draw up and hang on the refrigerator an exercise schedule that commits me to at least two and at the most six workouts a week."

Once you complete the first of the actions toward your identified desire, consult your prioritized action list and use the AIM SMART! process to set yourself up to achieve the next step, and then the next, and then the one after that until you have completely achieved the original overall idea.

Achieving your desires will not always go smoothly. When you hit an obstacle or don't complete a step in the time or way that you had wished, be kind to yourself. You are human. The way you first envision completing an action may be lacking information that, as you receive it, changes the process. Remain flexible, continue checking in with yourself, and revamp your strategy. Use the AIM SMART! process to identify how to remove the obstacle. Or, reexamine the action step and see where you can tweak the process for more success. To design actions, ask yourself the following questions:

- What do I need to be able to do this?
- How do I know that I have those things?
- What am I lacking?
- How can I get what I need?
- Where can I get it?
- Who can help me get it?
- When can I get it?
- What will be the next step when I get it?

When working with AIM SMART! desires, you approach one objective at a time. Sam's foray into this process expanded his work in choosing the right people to be around. Isolating this one action as the first and most important to establish, he worked through the steps above by applying them to identifying the type of person he wished to spend time with. He chose the minimum and maximum levels of achievement, set a date and a first step, and checked in with himself to make sure this one action seemed like something he could tackle. When he affirmed that it was, he put in play the process to follow through.

With a clear vision of the many actions you can take to achieve your full post-trauma identity, you have an even bigger choice: Which one will you tackle first? There's no rule for how to move forward. Prioritizing desires can be accomplished by determining what seems to need to be done first, second, third, and so forth. Or, you can arrange actions according to what you feel you're ready to approach.

My personal favorite strategy: As often as possible, first do what you're good at. Take the actions that feel most comfortable and succeed at them by *facilitating simple successes.* Experiencing "little wins" goes into your brain's "I can do it!" column, which is like a shot of glucose that fills your brain with achievement energy. The more of this kind of energy you have, the more effective, confident, and able you'll feel when you approach more challenging tasks. With a track record of success, you'll flow into the higher-level challenges with more strength and will be more likely to handle the difficulties and still succeed.

Action Step

From your list of prioritized events in the previous exercise, choose one action that needs to be taken and put it through the AIM SMART! outline. Answer each step in the process with as much detail as possible. Then take the necessary steps to accomplish that outcome, and the one after that, and the one after that, and so on. Check in with yourself; ask what type of prioritizing feels appropriate for your process. It's completely reasonable to achieve any exercise over the course of several days.

BUILD SUPPORT

... knowing that I was not alone in a world where I thought I was some kind of freak having to fake it and cover up the truth for others, discovering that there were others out there like me and they called themselves survivors ...

—*Anonymous*

Even when you are organized and focused on a strategy, there may be days or experiences that make you doubt yourself or the possibility of the end results. Or there may be moments when it just would be so much easier to succeed if you had some help. It's for this reason that building a support system can make an enormous difference, not only in whether or not you succeed but also in how easily you do so. Support can come in the form of one person or many, from family and/or from friends, professional or personal. The real focus is on helping you to feel accompanied and believed in on your quest for transformation.

How much do the people around you believe in the changes you've decided to create? You already know how important your own belief in yourself is. That belief is equally important in those with whom you live, work, or socialize. These are the people with whom you create your world. American entrepreneur, author, and motivational speaker Jim Rohn said, "You are the average of the five people you spend the most time with." Whether you or they know it or not, your relationships influence how you feel, think, believe, act, behave, and experience life, and even how much you succeed. As much as you can (and there are limits to this, I know, since we don't choose our family or our coworkers), it's important to (1) develop a team of people who will support you in your post-trauma identity construction and help it to succeed, and (2) develop a plan to put in place boundaries so that you spend as little time as possible or no time at all with people who refuse to positively respect your vision.

Sam approached this subject by making a list of the people he knew who made him laugh, smile, or feel good, and were trusted friends. From this list (which was relatively short), he selected one person, Kevin, to take into his confidence, share his desires with, and ask for support in the form of texts, emails, telephone conversations, and get-togethers. The plan was not to overwhelm Kevin with constant emotional dumping or overwhelming neediness. Rather, it was to have one person Sam could count on to be positive and interested in and dedicated to helping him achieve whichever desire he approached.

Sam also made a list of people with whom he would *not* share his identity construction process. These people were often cold, disconnected, downright unkind, depressed, and demoralizing in their own perspectives. Sam noticed when he spoke to or spent time with them, he came away feeling a slew of negative emotions and a heightened sense of fear and danger. Some of these people were in his family, others were in the community, and some were at work.

Building a support team (or selecting a teammate) offered Sam an opportunity to assess what kinds of influences he wanted around him, plus who would most be able to help him stay focused and achieve his desires. Walking up the identity construction mountain is a lonely trek. Strategically placing supporters along the route lessens your isolation and can often provide a very meaningful and productive outside perspective. From the inside, you may be stuck at the point of a challenge that, when you share it with someone on your support team, has a simple solution readily identified from an external point of view.

When considering who you wish to invite onto Team Identity, ask yourself the following ten questions. Record your answers in your notebook:

- Whose presence makes me feel good even when I'm having a bad day?
- Who makes me feel safe when I feel threatened?
- Who makes me feel stronger and more confident?
- Who (always) believes in me?
- Who most wants to see me succeed?
- Whom do I trust to give me good advice?
- Who makes me feel calm and assured, even when I feel doubt?
- Who has personal skills that I admire?
- Who displays empathy, compassion, love, friendship, and understanding?

Action Step

Once you've thoroughly explored who you want to have in your support system, spend some time deciding, outlining, and thinking through what you want from each person, how you will express it to her or him, and when. From the list you develop, reach out to each person with a general request for support, or identify each person's strengths and impact on your world and ask her or him for specific support actions.

To identify people you want to keep *away from* your recovery process, answer these questions:

- Whose presence makes me feel bad every time I'm around her/him?
- Who makes me feel less strong and less confident?
- Who (always) believes I will fail?
- Who least wants to see me succeed?
- Who usually gives me bad advice?
- Who makes me feel anxious, panicky, threatened, uncomfortable, or in danger?
- Who has habits that are toxic to me?
- Who displays sarcasm, a lack of compassion, hatred, unkindness, or a lack of understanding?

With the people these answers highlight, find ways to put in place boundaries or cut off all contact so that you create a healing space without their negative influences.

DEVELOP ACCOUNTABILITY

It's safe to expect that you might outline your strategy and organize your plan and then find that . . . your energy fizzles out. Or, maybe your energy feels completely consumed and now you're drained. An alternative scenario: You develop all of these plans and then get cold feet. Whatever the case, it's entirely normal to get to a point where you know what you have to do but can't get yourself to follow through. It's in this moment that being held accountable by an outside source can be a life saver.

Accountability means feeling responsible to someone else for a promised action. An accountability buddy ratchets up the stakes because when you don't follow through, you're not just letting down yourself but someone else as well. Letting someone down or revealing yourself as less-than-on-task doesn't feel good. Since biologically you're designed to avoid bad feelings and seek rewards, the presence of an accountability buddy can tap into your neurophysiological structure, activating its processes in ways that enhance your ability to succeed. Being held accountable is a great motivator to give you that extra push to get out of "Do I have to?" or "I don't feel like it!" mode and into "Here I go!" mode. It's also an effective, free, and simple way to keep yourself focused, on track, and moving forward.

When Sam asked me to be his accountability buddy, I was thrilled to take such a productive role in his identity process. As Sam's coach, I was already helping him organize, identify, structure, and execute thoughts, plans, and actions in recovery. I often hold clients accountable for what we discuss when and if they specifically want me to do that. Sam wanted me to hold him accountable weekly for execution of the outcomes he and I discussed and expected him to approach. Knowing that I would be waiting for details of his progress kept Sam in a mindset that was geared toward action every day of every week. The benefits of this were evident in how quickly he set desires and met outcomes, until finally he had achieved so much of his overall vision that he decided to take the big plunge of relocating across the country to create his dream lifestyle.

Action Step

For each desire you choose to approach, ask yourself:

- Who is most depending on or expecting me to achieve this outcome?
- Who most wants to see me succeed at this outcome?
- Who will most benefit when I follow through on this?

Consider all of the answers that appear to you, and then choose someone who will hold you accountable. This can be someone on your support team or someone else entirely. The key is to feel that:

- When this person asks you if you have followed through, you will feel uncomfortable to reply, "No."
- When this person asks you if you have followed through, you will feel excited to reply, "Yes!"
- When you think of this person, you will feel motivated to achieve your self-set task, because what she or he thinks of you matters.

If you like consistency, you can choose one person who always holds you accountable. The beauty of accountability contacts, however, is that you can choose different people to be your accountability buddy for different tasks. For each step of every desire, ask yourself, "Who does this matter most to?" or "Who will benefit from my achieving this objective?" That's the person who you want holding you accountable, because it will be the person whose emotional investment is the largest, which means you'll feel more motivated to follow through.

GIVE YOURSELF PERMISSION

In his quest to set himself free, Sam bumped into a stumbling block that was very familiar to me. When he was successful at achieving even the smallest outcome (which meant he felt good and proud of himself and hopeful), those feelings were often followed by increased feelings of fear and apprehension and the thought that feeling better was dangerous.

"It's not okay to be okay," he reported. "If I'm not feeling bad, I feel vulnerable, like I'm not paying enough attention and something awful will happen to me. I feel safer when I feel miserable."

Sam was at the moment where he had to give himself permission to feel good, strong, capable, and okay in a world that lacked the heightened edge of anxiety. His initial reluctance makes perfect sense. After trauma, your neurobiological and psychological systems rewire to keep you safe. Feeling constantly on edge, aware, and hypervigilant may have developed in you a sense of control, too. The more you constrict and restrict your feelings and focus, the more you can hope to predict and avoid any threat. Of course, living like that is partly why you've been so miserable. When you look for threat, you always find it, and even create situations that fulfill the prophecy of your perspective.

Letting go of this kind of cycle can make you feel exposed to danger. If you're not looking for threat, who will be looking out for you? If you're not backing away from life to ensure your safety, how will you be sure to have it? Survivors often find fear so familiar that the absence of it seems terrifying. This is a trick of your mind and neurology. It will be up to you to change this patterned response. You will define a sense of safety partly through all of the shifts you've been developing up until this point. Partly, too, you will do this by expanding ways to feel safe because you know yourself as a person who is strong, effective, connected, and alive. Essentially, this is a shift from feeling safe because you feel afraid to feeling safe because you feel a sense of self-trust. As with everything, this is a process that does and should take time to develop and organically evolve. It may begin with your being mindful of the discomfort and using the actions outlined in Chapters 2 and 6 and Appendix A to release the emotion. In addition, you can give yourself *permission*.

Sam approached giving himself permission very cautiously. We talked about what it meant to live in a sense of self-imposed freedom. We discussed his fears, plus what the benefits and positive outcomes could be. We identified the desire, why it was important, and forecasted results. At first Sam didn't feel he could give himself permission to move forward.

"Isn't part of making sure you're safe remembering the past, and focusing on making sure it doesn't repeat itself?" he wanted to know.

Sam was right: there is a time for that behavior, usually immediately following a trauma. While looking back was at one point an important action, that time has passed. Think of it as a season; it's meant to reach a conclusion.

After careful consideration over a period of weeks, Sam decided he was ready to give himself permission to feel good and shift his perspective from the past and present to the future, full steam ahead. While making this decision didn't fully eradicate the fear, it did remind him to expect resistance, acknowledge its presence, respect the fear behind it (and even take specific actions to reduce it) and consciously choose to allow himself to experience the good that would come from the actions he was taking.

Without guarantees for what can, will, or may happen in the future, now is your opportunity to say, "I can handle it!" and shift to a new level of freedom.

RELEASE YOURSELF

Asking if you're ready to give yourself permission to be free may seem like a silly question. Of course you want to feel better! But giving yourself permission is about more than just saying you're ready to feel less bad; it's about saying you're ready to redesign your thinking from trauma focused to life focused. If you're not ready for this step, file away the idea and revisit it when you feel more secure. If you're ready to embrace some freedom, try this:

Giving yourself permission means more than saying in your mind, "Yes, I agree with this idea." When you give someone permission to do something, you formally authorize your consent for an action. And you do this through specific communication, which is what you need to do with yourself.

SAY IT OUT LOUD

Power comes into your process when ideas move out of your mind and into the real world. Saying anything out loud powerfully brings it into being. Think of a time that you've shown a person or a pet affection. If you just sat there thinking to yourself from across the room, "I really love that dog," how deep would the connection be between you and your feeling or you and the dog? Instead, if you speak kindly to the dog, rub its belly or stroke its back, and let it know what you think and how you feel, you will experience increased resonance and deeper feelings. In return, the dog will actively respond with both acknowledgment and return of affection. You benefit from this kind of interaction even when it's between one of your selves (e.g., your warrior self) and another (e.g., your fearful self).

If you're ready to give yourself permission, stand in front of a mirror. Take a good, direct look at yourself. Lock eyes with your reflection. Then read the following script:

(insert your name), you have worked very hard and for a very long time to keep yourself safe and to make the world more in control so that you avoid all threat. It's been a tough job and you've done it fantastically well. I admire you for how diligently you have stuck to the post-trauma processes and procedures you put in place. Now the time for all of that has ended. You have passed the test. You are able to survive; you and I know that as truly as we know your name is _____. You have what it takes to be aware and keep yourself safe. You also have what it takes to live a good, fun, joyful, productive, and really meaningful life. It's time for you to focus less on the past and more on the future. Today, _____, on this _____ day of the month _____ of the year _____, I give you permission to shed your survival behaviors and take on a new mission: loving how you live. I give you permission to move forward. I give you permission to feel better, and better, and even better still. I give you permission to feel free, and safe in your freedom. I give you permission to do all of this because you have earned it. And also, because it is okay to feel okay. I give you permission because I want you to be happy. I give you permission because it is time. I give you permission because I trust you. I give you permission because you deserve it. I give you permission because you are worthy. Most of all, I give you permission because I love you. Be free.

The first time you do this you may feel awkward or silly. Afterward you may not even believe that you have permission. Embrace whatever your response is. It will change and evolve over time if you continue to do the exercise daily.

Note: Put more power into this process by: (1) visualizing the self you saw in the mirror and reading the script out loud before you get out of bed in the morning and right before you turn out the light in bed at night, (2) asking a trusted friend or relationship to read it to you so that you hear a voice other than yours concurring with the idea, (3) creating your own script that makes you feel as deeply connected to this idea as possible.

WRITE IT OUT

The kinesthetic transfer from brain to body that occurs when you write carves into your experience a powerful kind of learning.

1. Write out the above script (or your own). Do this twice: once with your dominant hand, and once with your nondominant hand. Then place the completely legible version somewhere you can see it during the day.
2. With your dominant hand, in your notebook, write out your answers to the following questions:

   - If you were to give yourself permission to move forward into the future you, what would have to happen?
   - If you were to give yourself permission to let go of your overall perception of what keeps you safe—and develop a new perspective—what would that new perspective be?
   - How do you know it's time to give yourself permission?
   - What frightens you about giving yourself permission to be free?
   - What has to be done so that your fears are addressed and lessened and you feel more comfortable?

Use all of the tools you've learned throughout this book (including all of the preceding sections of this chapter) to address anything that's holding you back in this area and resolve it.

The Take-Aways

Connect with your passion and fire and see where it takes you post-trauma. It will bring you to new and beautiful places, but can also reconnect you to the person you were, and always are, at the deepest core of yourself, at the seat of your soul, and at the origin point of your joy. Use what you love to give you wings and take flight on a beautiful new journey of self.

—*Teresa B. Pasquale, LCSW, E-RYT 200*

- Constructing your post-trauma identity and reclaiming your life means imagining and then creating the future you desire.
- The only way you will change is if you make it happen; others can support and help, but only you can create the changes you wish to experience.
- To create, meet, and merge with your future self, you will need to liberate the ideas from your mind and birth your future self into the reality of your daily life.
- Constructing your post-trauma identity requires you to set specific desires so that you deliberately construct aspects and elements of the person you want to become.
- Experiencing "little wins" goes into your brain's "I can do it!" column, which is like a shot of glucose that fills your brain with achievement energy.

Ten Common Obstacles to Creating Your Post-Trauma Identity

> Find others who have been through similar levels of trauma, share with each other what you have been through and . . . its effects on you, and then ask each other what [you] have done and what [you] would suggest you do to deal with whatever is facing you.
>
> —*Mark Goulston, MD*

Xerxes is the kind of guy who gets things done. A money manager at a large investement banking firm Xerxes had joined the firm straight out of college and had been groomed and developed there, rising up the ranks for more than ten years. He had performed well, had a terrific salary and imagined his career and life moving forward with uninterrupted success. Imagine his utter devastation when the market collapsed and in one day he want from top dog to no job.

"I felt blindsided," he explained. "Everything I knew about who I was seemed to be stripped away in an instant. Gone was my title. Gone was the security and stability. Gone was the clear path. I had a wife and a family to support, an enormous mortgage to pay. I didn't know how I was going to do those things. The whole industry was imploding so it wasn't like finding a new job was going to be easy. For a while I stuck to the old schedule, getting up at 5am, commuting into New York City and then just sitting on a bench on Wall Street all day. I didn't want to tell anyone that my circumstances had changed. I was in a state of shock and disbelief."

Eventually, Xerxes did tell his family and friends what had happened and slowly started a job search. It took a year before Xerxes found a new position. By then a sense of anxiety, lack of certainty and financial insecurity had altered his behavior.

"I can't make myself calm down," he said. "I feel like any moment the bottom's going to fall out of my life again. I yell at my wife for spending money on even the tiniest thing. At the office I've become so uptight and obnoxious it's ruined my ability to have positive working relationships with my colleagues. Inside myself I feel like I'm always in emergency mode. This distorts my thinking and clouds my judgment, which affects the quality of my work which only makes me feel even more terrified that at any moment I'm going to get fired and find myself out of a job all over again."

Having achieved professional success early in life, Xerxes knows what it takes to bring commitment, dedication and action to a job. When he began his post-trauma identity construction, Xerxes set out to achieve it the way he would approach managing money: with focus, determination, organization, solid fundamental research and the belief that deliberately choosing and developing personal qualities is critical to success. With that much clarity, Xerxes was shocked six months later to find himself in a state of deep conflict.

"I take one tiny step forward and then five giant steps back," he complained. "I know what I need to do, but I can't always get myself to do it. Or if I do, I can't hold on to the changes."

Guaranteed, there will be days during your own post-trauma identity evolution when you feel like Xerxes. On those days, a couple of things will be important to remember:

First, *your feelings are separate from who you are.* They are ephemeral experiences caused by your thoughts. Regardless of whether or not your feelings feel forward or backward, you yourself remain stationary in the present.

Second, *while it may feel as if you're going backward, that's an impos-sibility:* going backward would mean going back in time, which you've already discovered you can't do. Technically, in every moment you are more knowledgeable, and more experienced than the moment before, which means you are definitely moving forward, even when feelings from the past show up in your present.

Third, *feelings can remind you of the past even when they exist solely in the present.* You may remember an earlier time when you felt this or that way in your struggle, but even in the moment you feel that memory you're still in the present. You can't go back to some past moment, place, or time. Instead, you are where you are, *here,* and just really not feeling good about it.

Fourth, *feeling like you're falling backward simply means things aren't going forward the way you expect;* it indicates a change in process. What has happened that is bringing different and unwanted results? This is easy to address by examining your expectations, beliefs, treatment approach, and actions—and tweaking any or all of them to produce more comfortable and positive results.

Fifth, *sensing a sudden shift backward is really your sensing a shift in your ability to manage the changes and challenges you experience.* This is a breakdown in your response process. Ask yourself where you're feeling a weakness. Is it in your body, emotions, mental faculties, relationships? Find the weak link in the chain of your strength and focus on fixing it.

In the midst of reversal feelings, it will be important to remember that even when you feel most agitated and disappointed, you are con-stantly facing the same two repetitive options: making a *choice* and taking an *action*. Working either side of the choice/action equation can shift you out of reverse and into full speed ahead.

To be sure, sometimes the idea of making a choice or taking an action will feel downright impossible. What to do then? Your work in this final chapter is meant to help your mind become more limber, flexi-ble, and resilient. Take a deep breath. Relax your body into an even more comfortable position and proceed into this chapter ready to develop another element of control. The following pages examine ten common problems you might encounter in developing your new self, plus their solutions. There are, of course, many ways to resolve each of the issues— the options would make up a whole new book! So here I'll offer only one idea for each problem. Then, I challenge you to create others. Using the exercises, you can gently propel yourself from feeling power*less* to feeling power*ful,* both in your identity discovery and in your overall trauma recovery too. You can approach this material from the perspective of diagnosing what's holding you back, or you can enter it for further exploration of how to effectively engage choices and actions.

#1 The Problem:
You are trying to maintain too much control.

> I have redefined and felt more connected to my identity through a daily
> commitment to walking in nature. I also paint intuitively and let go
> of all expectations and just let imagery emerge and surprise me.
>
> —*Lisa*

During your trauma, you learned something very important: Your safety depends on you. Since then, you've probably put that lesson to good use by scattering expectations throughout your day. Looking ahead and making assumptions about situations, circumstances, and outcomes allows you to plan for anything, right? Wrong. This kind of mental work can make you feel in control, but actually, it's a lot of activity with no authority. While you can control your expectations for the future, you cannot control the future itself. To gain real control, you have to *give up* control. This means giving up your expectations of how things will progress and what your experiences will be—and putting in place something much more powerful and effective.

THE SOLUTION:
MORE INTENTION, LESS EXPECTATION

An expectation is a strong belief that something will happen. The minute you place a control-seeking expectation on any situation (or yourself in it), you lock yourself into a rigid, inflexible, uncreative environment that can easily lead to shock, disappointment, blockage, and a sense of failure. An intention, however, is a softer way of looking ahead. An intention is merely your plan, purpose, aim, or objective. As life has already taught you, plans change. Your purpose, too, morphs depending on your desires and the details of any situation. When you focus on expectations, you focus on what is *out of your control.* When you focus on intentions, you focus on exactly what you *do* control: your approach to the moment you're in.

Set Individual Intentions

With every identity step, your objective is just to get the job done. It makes zero difference how you get it done or how many ways you attempt any task before you are successful. Ask yourself only to commit to pressing forward, to be willing to go into uncomfortable spaces, and to develop alternative, responsive (versus reactive) behaviors when you encounter any disturbing experience.

At the outset of every step, clearly define your focus by what you are attempting to achieve. Use the following process for any action or desire you have for the rest of your life:

- *What do I want?* Identify a desire. Write a detailed description of what you want to achieve.
- *Why is achieving this desire important to me?* List all the reasons why you want this oh so badly.
- *How will achieving this desire change my life?* Be very clear about what will change, both inside of yourself and also in your interaction with and place in the rest of the world.

Based on your answers to the three questions above, create your intention for this one desire by filling in the blanks:

I want

because

so that

With a refined, intention-driven focus, decision-making and action-taking become more effective and streamlined. At any moment of any day, you can pause and write out an intention to guide your choices and actions. When your head feels chaotic or you feel yourself slipping backward, an intention can act as an anchor to hold you in place while you recalculate your next move. For example, prior to taking any action, you can ask yourself, "How does this help me achieve my intention?" If you can answer that with legitimate evidence, then you will know how to proceed, or you will know to make a different choice. You can set an intention for one small identity action and also for recovery as a whole.

To deepen your interaction with any intention, follow these steps:

- When you think of the intention you described above and the desired objective, what one word represents all of this to you?

  _____

- **Incorporate this word into your world in as many ways as possible**. For example, use it as your focus when you practice meditation and breathwork. Find a physical object or picture of the word (of the word itself, or that represents the word to you) that you can place in a very visible area. Make it the wallpaper on your smartphone or the screensaver on your computer.

- **Translate that word into something you carry with you at all times.** When you feel pressures increase or notice yourself shifting out of intention and into expectation thinking, pause and reconnect with your intention by spending a few seconds or even a few minutes touching what you carry and contemplating its meaning and what action you can take to embody it.

- **Adopt as your daily mantra, "More intention, less expectation."** Success relies more on the small moments than on the big ones. Remember: Forget *how* you think something should go or the results it "should" bring and turn your energy toward *what* your approach to experiencing it will be.

- **In any spontaneous moment, ask yourself, "What's my intention?"** Prior to exploring an action, write out your intention in the most specific language possible. For example, you may write, "I am establishing boundaries because I want to clearly define my personal space so that I stop being exploited by other people." Very simple intention, plus a definitive action you can take.

Bringing this perspective of intention versus expectation into your recovery and post-trauma identity construction softens the harshness of your belief about how things "should" go and opens up your creativity in getting the results you seek. It also keeps you focused on the *what* (of your vision and approach), which is really where success begins.

#2 The Problem:
You feel overwhelmed by what you are trying to achieve.

> My hardest obstacle was accepting what had happened. One
> must do that in order to find bliss—and be in the present.
>
> —*Brent Forcier*

When you stand at the beginning of any intention, it's easy to look at the final outcome on the horizon and immediately be filled with a sense of "I can't do this!" It's at this exact moment that figuring out how to slowly put one foot in front of the other becomes critically important. You have a choice to make: You can try to achieve your objective all at once, or you can deconstruct the process so that it feels feasible, manageable, and organized.

THE SOLUTION: RECOGNIZE AND CHECK IN

Feelings of being overwhelmed diminish when you feel more proactive in the achievement process and all of its various steps. Learning to identify problems before they spiral out of control further refines your focus and leads to effective actions.

Implement Meaningful Check-Ins

Check-ins are useful in every aspect of identity restoration and particularly useful in the area of "overwhelm." Being aware simply means putting in place a daily or even hourly check-in where you stop the world for a few seconds and take an inventory of your present experience.

1. Ask, **"How do I feel right now?"** Be specific in your answer.
2. If you feel good, ask yourself, **"What's one thing I can do to make myself feel this feeling even more?"**
3. If you feel any kind of negative feeling, ask yourself, **"What's one thing that would lessen this feeling?"**

4. Whether you feel positively or negatively, continue to repeat the process until you feel better than you thought possible, or until the negative feeling has been dispelled as much as possible.

Implementing check-ins allows you to regain another element of control over your experience because it puts you in touch with the present moment. Doing this lessens any surprises. You will notice when a stressful feeling emerges and immediately act to dilute it. This empowered action on your part helps you develop more ability to regulate your emotions while also deepening your focus on how you move forward and in what way.

#3 The Problem: You are anxious and afraid.

> My Native American Spiritual practice has given me the most comfort throughout my journey of gathering myself back together . . . Working with the principles . . . has brought me back to a space within myself where I feel whole, grounded, and able to function in the world again.
>
> —*Tara Ladner, LMT, CWPC*

Fear is a normal part of any change-oriented process. In fact, resistance to change is a side effect of fear. As you consider (and sometimes, worry) about how your post-trauma identity alterations will affect you and your place in the world—and more importantly, about the possibilities they will open up—it's normal for fear to increase and your dedication to your process to decrease.

THE SOLUTION: LASSO THE FEAR

Regardless of your fear's source, there are ways to quell the constriction and open yourself up to forward progress. Think of fear as a stop sign. When you approach an intersection and see a stop sign, you remain calm and obey what you were taught when you learned to drive: Stop, check all ways to see oncoming traffic (aka threats), and then proceed with caution. You're already so very used to this process that you probably don't even think about it. You can talk to a companion while driving and deftly handle this activity, which means you can easily apply it to your post-trauma identity development.

Challenge Fact vs. Fiction Thinking

The trauma lifestyle is designed to keep you safe. In order to do that, it sees many things as a potential threat to your physical or emotional well-being—even things that aren't truly a real threat. For example, let's suppose that right before your trauma you heard a woodpecker hammering away at a nearby tree. Now every time you hear a woodpecker you immediately respond with fear, anxiety, and a search for safety.

Is it true that every time you hear a woodpecker, a trauma is about to occur? Of course not. To hear a woodpecker and sense danger is fiction thinking. Fact thinking relies on simple questions designed to bring you proof of reality:

- What is putting me in danger right now?
- How much of an actual threat is this?
- How do I know this is true?
- What proof do I have that this is true?
- Would an outside observer agree that this is true?
- What are the objective facts of my safety in this moment?
- What other, safe interpretations exist for the details of this moment?

The next time you feel fear or anxiety, challenge that experience by playing a game of "Fact or Fiction?"

1. Fold a piece of paper lengthwise and **write down all of the thoughts you have about your fear** (what the threat is, what the danger is, what might happen you, etc.).
2. **Objectively consider and assess each item** you've written down.

Apply the questions above. Write next to each fear "fact" or "fiction." To be a fact, something has to be definitively *true*. This means anyone else can look at the list and *without coaching from you* absolutely agree that those are the conclusive facts and the only interpretations and possible outcomes given the situation at hand.

3. Look over your list. **How many items are actually facts? How many turn out to be fiction** (meaning it may feel this way or you may see it this way, but the idea of real danger is false)?

4. **Make a new choice and take an action.** When you verify that something is fiction, it will change what you know about the moment you're in (although it may not immediately change how you *feel* about the moment you're in.) The new, factual situation offers you fresh choices that lead to new actions.

When you are active, you are empowered. Developing a habit of challenging fiction versus fact thinking means resetting your brain's filter to more accurately assess the world around you, including ways that you can choose and act so that you feel safe and able to protect yourself.

#4 The Problem: You feel stuck or stalled.

> I am very grateful . . . for the patience, . . . kindness and . . . humanity in people. The people . . . I care most about have forgiven me for things that I have done in response to my traumatic experiences . . . and have therefore made it easier for me to forgive myself.
>
> —*Sophia*

Restoring your sense of self doesn't happen in a straight line over a prescribed period of time. It's a little like traveling through a mountain range: There will be ups and downs, there will be good weather and bad weather, and it will require much sustained effort on your part.

Even when you're diligent, you may hit a patch when you feel you've reached a plateau and just can't seem to move forward. Some popular reasons for feeling stalled or stuck include:

- **Fear and anxiety** about whether or not you will be successful.
- **Resistance** to what you must do in order to gain what you want.
- **Avoidance** of uncomfortable feelings or thoughts.
- **Lack of support** in both professional or personal arenas.
- **Mistakes, slipups, or unexpected outcomes** that leave you feeling inadequate.
- **Exhaustion** when you've been working hard and need to rest.

Feeling inert is only a temporary situation. It is also an invitation to examine what is holding you back and make a plan to remove it.

THE SOLUTION: TRANSFORM RESISTANCE

Two common areas generate blocks in your progress. They both have to do with what motivates you to make choices and take actions.

Internal drivers are personal motivating forces that push you toward or away from choices, actions, and experiences. They are based on your unique view of the world and yourself in it. For example, your desire to feel good is an internal driver that moves you toward something. Likewise, your fear of feeling pain is an internal driver that moves you away from something. Internal drivers can be positive or negative—at any time. Your desire to feel good can lead you to schedule a massage for yourself (positive) or indulge in drugs (negative). Getting back into the flow of your post-trauma identity construction means acknowledging what has interrupted your progress, addressing that issue, and removing it through a recalibration process that assesses the driver, sees its negative effect, and cancels its influence.

Identify and Transform Internal Drivers

The first key to removing obstacles lies in properly and fully identifying them. For internal drivers, consider this checklist to begin developing clarity around where your blocks originate inside your own self. Circle all areas that intuitively feel as if they are holding you back. You know yourself better than anyone; feel free to add your own ideas to this list.

✓ Fear   ✓ Lack of confidence

✓ Shame   ✓ Low self-esteem

✓ Grief   ✓ Inadequacy

✓ Anxiety   ✓ Anger

✓ Insecurity   ✓ Denial

✓ Guilt   ✓ Future success

✓ Distorted perceptions   ✓ Past failure

For each driver you circled, ask yourself:

- How do I know this is what I'm feeling?
- What thought is creating that feeling?
- What new thought would be more appropriate?
- What needs to change so that the feeling is reduced?
- What would make that change happen?
- How can I do this?
- Who can help?

External drivers are influences from the outside world that affect your choices, actions, and experiences. These can include people, places, objects, and situations. For example, a spiritual experience of the arts or religion may inspire you to reach for a better way of life than you currently encounter. Or, a friend who worries that when you achieve your new self you will no longer be interested in continuing your present friendship may suggest ideas and actions that go against your healing choices. As with internal drivers, external drivers can be both positive or negative. How you acknowledge, embrace, and interact with them gives them power and influence.

Identify and Transform External Drivers

External drivers can come from any source outside your own head. Circle all that apply, and feel free to add any others that come to mind:

✓ Family   ✓ Environment
✓ Friends   ✓ Geography
✓ Relationships   ✓ World events
✓ Colleagues   ✓ Virtual experiences and contacts
✓ Employers   ✓ Culture
✓ Work   ✓ Religion
✓ Daily events   ✓ Community
✓ Financial concerns   ✓ Local events

For each driver you circled, ask yourself the following questions and record the answers in your notebook:

- How does this affect me?
- What does it make me feel?
- Why does it make me feel this way?
- How exactly does it hold me back?
- What would need to happen for me to be released?
- What would be the first step to making that release happen?
- Who or what could help me achieve this action?

#5 The Problem: You are full of self-criticism and doubt.

> I have decided to become the strong, confident, in-control person
> I always wanted to be even before trauma . . . my own attitude
> change in my own mind [is] how I now portray myself.
>
> —*Bernie Bowman*

It's very hard to fully love yourself when you're struggling with the effects of trauma and PTSD. First, you don't really like the dysfunctional, altered person you've become. Second, you're not thrilled with the powerless and hopeless way that you feel. Third, you see the world (and that includes yourself) through a dangerous and negative perspective. The result of all of this? Extreme self-criticism and a crushing amount of self-doubt, both of which can make transforming yourself even more challenging.

THE SOLUTION: DEVELOP SELF-COMPASSION

While it's entirely reasonable that you experience self-criticism and doubt, shifting into a more positive and self-supporting space is a necessity. When you change how you think about, treat, and speak to yourself, you increase your flexibility, plus dramatically add to your creativity in addressing any challenge. It all stems from being nicer, kinder, and more compassionate in your attitude toward the most important person today: You.

Thought Monitoring

You have approximately seventy thousand thoughts per day. How many of them are you aware of? How many are kind, supportive, and solution oriented? As you struggle with coping and life in general, it's entirely possible that your inner voice might lapse into a terrifically critical and destructive commentary. What's so sneaky about how you talk to yourself is that it's such a natural part of the dialogue in your head that you may not even notice it. Transforming means you must be very specific, which includes knowing the details about what goes on in your head. You need to be aware of how your thoughts sabotage you generally in daily life and specifically in your quest to redefine who you are. Try these methods to engage your active focus:

- *Eavesdrop on yourself.* Imagine that in your head there's a public address system that broadcasts every thought you have over a set of loud speakers. Find the knob that turns up the volume and start avidly listening to what's being broadcast. For the next twenty-four hours, specifically listen for every negative thought you have about yourself. Carry a small notebook or piece of paper with you. Every time you think something negative about yourself, write it down. The objective here is to develop your facility for hearing and noticing the flow of negative thoughts, from the most inane to the most combustive.

- *Notice what topics the thoughts focus on.* When the twenty-four hours is over, make some time to look over the full list of negative thoughts you wrote down. (Hold on to this list; we're going to use it later.) What patterns do you see?

- **Increase your awareness.** For the next four to seven days, put in place a practice of constantly monitoring your thoughts and inner dialogue. Try to become so intimately aware of your thoughts that you automatically notice the negativity as it pops up. As you develop this habit, simply notice the thoughts, say, "Cancel that!" and release them as if they were helium balloons.

Replace the Thought

When you eliminate anything, it will leave behind an open space. Ever hear the saying "Nature abhors a vacuum?" This means that every empty space naturally will be filled with something. What Nature does is fill empty spaces with the most familiar object. If you've canceled a thought and left that spot open, it will be filled with the old, familiar thought you just tried to eliminate.

When you feel comfortable that you are catching the negative thoughts and interrupting them with a good, strong, loud "Cancel that!" it's time to add a new action: *Fill that space with a new, positive thought.* Take the original negative thought and turn it into a positive statement about yourself. For example, "I'm such a loser; I can't remember anything" can become "I'm a diligent person who remembers as much as possible."

Take out the list you made earlier of the negative self-talk you observed. For each of the statements you wrote down, write a new positive statement to use as a replacement. Throughout this process use language that feels comfortable to you. You may change "I'm such a loser" to "I'm amazing" or "I'm doing the best I can." Shifting to positive language simply means a more comforting perspective. Play with the range of how emphatic the new vocabulary is and choose what feels good to you.

Acknowledging and actively shifting your negative self-talk reduces the angst you carry about yourself. In the replace and reframe process, you actively transform doubt into a more positive and supportive perspective. Following this process for thirty consecutive days will imprint it as a new habit in your brain. Continue the process and mark your progress as you notice your negative self-talk reducing. You can do this just by being aware, or by continuing to keep a list of your negative thoughts, week after week crossing out the ones you have replaced, and literally watching the list dwindle.

Note: When you have your negative self-talk under control, move forward by applying this process to your negative thoughts about others and then, the world. Simply follow the same steps as outlined above. By the time you have completed all three categories of thoughts (yourself, others, the world), you will have dramatically improved the environment in your mind. The benefits of this will extend from reduced anxiety to a heightened sense of well-being to increased flexibility to added creativity.

#6 The Problem: You are moving too fast.

> My counselor invited me to not just survive but to thrive. I had no idea what he meant. He took the next several years teaching me. I learned new ways of living and identifying myself a bit at a time. I am proud of surviving and I love thriving.
>
> —*We Are One by Ruth*

With the aftereffects of trauma or the symptoms of PTSD, you have learned to live at high speeds to race against danger, fend off expected threats, and make yourself feel in control. Since your desire is to transform yourself to advance your recovery, it can seem as if moving faster in that direction would be a good thing. You may believe that if you work faster, try harder, see more, do more, and attempt more, you'll heal more. Plus, there's the added issue that you wish you had been healed yesterday, which makes you feel as if you're losing time and more and more of yourself every day that the job's not done. In a world that's lost much of its meaning, redefining who you are becomes very meaningful, which can make you run after it even faster.

If you've tried racing ahead in recovery, you know what happens: The increased speed of the work—which naturally brings up uncomfortable material and moments, plus new growth situations to which you must become accustomed—hits you hard and sends you careening into a crash. If you've done this even once, you know how moving too fast can end up slowing you down instead.

THE SOLUTION: ADJUST YOUR PACE

If you're at a point where you feel you're experiencing the negative impact of moving too fast, now is a great time to put on the breaks. Slowing down needs to be addressed mentally, emotionally, and physically. When I work with clients, we always begin with the physical element, since that is the most accessible and also the most visceral.

Before you practice the exercise described below, keep this in mind: Slowing down may feel unfamiliar, which can be frightening. It can also allow things to come up that the presence of your usual speed has suppressed. Sometimes these elements may bring up feelings of fear, anxiety, panic, shortness of breath, sweating, heart palpitations, or other amplified reactions. To prevent and appropriately manage any negative reactions from any one of the following exercises, first:

- **Choose a physical location** in which you feel safe to explore these activities.
- **Ask a trusted person** to share this experience with you; invite her or him to accompany you in the moment of the work.

When you first begin playing with this process, you may feel inept, out of control, or silly, or you may even feel a sense of failure. Give yourself permission to be an amateur. You are about to learn a new skill; you are expected to give it your best shot—that's all. If it feels appropriate, go back to Problem #1 and build your intention for this process.

Slow Down Physically

Your mission here is to begin playing with how you experience your body and what it does. Find ways to slow down, including in how you:

✓ eat	✓ work
✓ shower	✓ read
✓ dress	✓ write
✓ walk	✓ meditate
✓ talk	✓ breathe
✓ have sex	✓ clean
✓ brush your teeth	✓ comb your hair

How slowly can you eat a sandwich? How long can you take getting dressed? When you do any activity more slowly, it gives you a chance to experience it at a deeper and potentially more meaningful level. It also shifts you into a place of choice, action and control.

- **Begin with a very short time frame.** Five minutes is a good amount of time for your first advance in this physical area. For example, see how slowly you can walk for five minutes, and then go back to walking at whatever is your normal speed. (If five minutes feels too long, shorten the length of time until you discover what feels comfortable.)
- **Extend your next slow-down experience.** If five minutes feels comfortable, then extend it to ten or fifteen minutes. Each time you feel comfortable at a certain amount of time for five consecutive attempts, add on another five or ten minutes. When you get up to sixty minutes, consider yourself titrated and freely play with the amount of increased time in whatever way feels appropriate to you. (To "titrate" means to increase in increments. For our purposes, successfully titrating means comfortably achieving an increased time frame five consecutive times.)

Slowing down physically trains your body to experience any moment in a new way. Since your body sends feedback to your mind, a physical sensation of slowness or stillness can inspire your mind to do the same.

Alternatively, slowing down can induce uncomfortable feelings. Respect the messages your mind and body send you. *Stop the exercise immediately* in the event of any abreaction (overwhelmingly negative response). Then:

- Check in with yourself; use your stress reduction tools (see the cheat sheet in Appendix A) to bring yourself back to homeostasis.

- Check in with your five senses; attend to your breathing and allow the momentary reflex response to naturally subside.
- Remind yourself you are safe.
- Call a friend or other support resource.
- Engage in an activity that makes you feel calm, centered, grounded, and really, really good.

Taking an action after a flood of emotion can act as a mental cleanse and help both your mind and body experience a sense of distance from the disturbance and reset. Ask, "What can I physically do right now that would make me feel better?" This might be playing with a pet, hugging a loved one, going for a walk, or jogging in place.

#7 The Problem: You lack balance.

The trauma and PTSD lifestyle has ingrained in you an outlook and arousal approach that thrives on stress, survival mechanisms, and an always-alert mode of operating. From this perspective, the absence of stress or an experience of fun and relaxation can seem downright dangerous. You may hear yourself saying, as Sam did in an earlier chapter, "It's not okay to feel okay!" Continuing to live this amped-up lifestyle, however, drains your mental focus, fatigues your emotions, and exhausts your physical energy.

THE SOLUTION: PRACTICE EQUILIBRIUM

Adding balance to your general lifestyle can create balance in your recovery process. Scheduling downtime and finding activities that reconnect you to a sense of joy, delight, connection, and pleasant distraction rejuvenate your physical energy and allow your mind to synthesize thoughts and information.

The tools discussed throughout this book are terrific processes to begin developing balance. Setting aside time to meditate or do breathwork every day is a simple practice that can bring substantial results that move you into a more balanced state. The exercises below are designed to help you further explore and creatively design a balance track that meets your individual needs.

Balance Your Life

In this area, the objective is to open your mind to experiences that make you feel engaged, joyfully alive, and connected to who you are in exciting, comfortable, and life-affirming ways. You work hard; you should be rewarded for that with time in which you are allowed to play. If you already incorporate downtime, let's kick it up a notch and make sure it's focused on things that feed you. Spending a few hours every night watching crime shows on television is, technically, downtime. However, it's not the most anabolic, energy-producing time. The purpose in balance is to give you a breather and also make that breather feed you in some positive, energy-infusing way.

If balance makes you feel uncomfortable, apply the tools you learned in the previous section about slowing down. As with all recovery processes, adding balance can be done slowly. Set an intention, gauge your responses with check-ins and tweak what you're doing by chunking down your practice until it feels manageable. This may also be a good time to enlist the support of a trusted friend or family member. Having someone with you while you add balance can provide a sense of safety and, in effect, balance your response to what comes up from this practice.

Read over the following suggestions and pick one that resonates with you. Using the AIM SMART! process (see Chapter 5), work the chosen activity into your schedule over the next week. Remember to be specific about how often and for how long each balanced action will last:

- Set aside twenty-four hours during which you do only what

you *want* to do. Make a list of healthy choices and spend the
time ticking them off one by one.

- Commit to an activity that makes you feel completely free,
  unaware of the passage of time, and full of good feelings
  when you engage in it.
- Purposely connect with one person or animal who matters to
  you.
- Read a good book.
- Take yourself (and others) to a movie.
- Consult a recipe book and cook a meal you've never tried
  before.
- Join a group that meets to do an activity that interests you.
- Spend a significant time outdoors.
- Deliberately connect with nature in a way that feels meaning-
  ful.
- Find a safe time and space in which it feels comfortable to
  take a nap.
- Sit in the sun and let your mind remember a time you felt a
  sense of peace, big or small.
- Do something you've always wanted to do but never took the
  time to do.
- Learn a new skill.
- Plan a day trip to a pleasant destination.
- Eliminate *should, have to, ought to,* and *must* from your vocab-
  ulary and replace them with *could, want, desire,* and *wish.*
  What kinds of experiences do these words relate to? Make a
  list and then engage in them one by one.

These ideas are prompts to get you started thinking about ways to balance. The objective is to put your mind into a situation in which you feel
good and that has zero to do with anything about the past, your present
work, or the future you're trying to create, and then to lose track of time.
In any form of balance, imagine you are taking yourself on a mini-vaca-
tion. What fun and pleasing thing do you want to do?

#8 The Problem: You lack commitment.

If you've been unsuccessful in following through or implementing changes, cut yourself some slack. While trauma impacts your brain's structure and function, the effects of those changes can also impact your ability to pull yourself together and do difficult things despite obstacles. There's no doubt about it, stress reduces willpower, a quality you need a lot of in order to complete your personal transformation. There are, however, ways to develop that skill and support the science of your brain while simultaneously strengthening your resolve to make choices and take actions.

THE SOLUTION: ACCESS YOUR WILLPOWER

A biological response that helps you find the motivation to do difficult things because they matter to you, willpower shifts your body into a specific empowered state. It is a strength you can train and a mode of brain operation you can shift into at will.

Ten-Minute Delay

Strengthening self-control, like any skill, is a process of building the muscles that help you achieve it. The promise and experience of instant gratification (reward) can hijack your brain, leading it to give in to temptation. You'll make better decisions and enjoy greater results if you take the frenzy out of your brain and replace it with calm control. When seeking relief from cravings and temptations that are unhealthy, delaying gratification can actually change the outcome, give you more control, positively impact how you feel, increase your self-worth, and translate into a willpower habit that helps you take wanted actions as much as it stops you from taking unwanted ones. Whether you find yourself wanting to do something that will bring a positive response or something that will bring a negative response, boost your ability to choose by training yourself to delay gratification. Six steps can help you practice reclaiming control:

1. **Agree** you can have what you want (the minute you do this, your stress hormones begin to reduce).
2. **Decide** to wait ten minutes before allowing yourself to have it.
3. **Distract** yourself by turning your attention to an entirely different activity or focus.
4. **Check in** with yourself after ten minutes have passed and assess a) your intention in the moment, b) how aligned your intention is with your ultimate desires for your well-being.
5. **Choose** whether or not to have what you thought you wanted.
6. **Act** on your choice with a sense of purpose and control.

Practicing this exercise firmly roots you in the present moment with a focus on desire, choice, and action—the three pillars of both identity construction and trauma recovery. Whenever you seek to increase your willpower in any area, there may be a part of you that "doesn't feel like it" when it comes to taking the necessary steps. Expect that—and dismiss it. "Feeling like it" (actually *wanting* to do what's necessary) often comes after taking the action. In fact, taking a good action will induce a new feeling that suddenly makes you want to do the right thing. For example, deciding to employ a ten-minute delay (a positive and in-control behavior) can lead you to either give in to the temptation in a smaller way later or make another, better choice entirely.

#9 The Problem: You lack self-trust.

Something that's helped me reconnect with myself has been to notice how my body reacts to situations and trust it to tell me when I've had enough. Trusting myself is an ongoing process, but I've found that I can actually heal faster and more fully when I stop pressuring myself to "feel better" and allow myself to just feel.

—*Viannah E. Duncan*

Naturally, trauma challenges your ability to trust your skills, responses, thoughts, actions, and perspective. Given the behaviors you may not understand, the emotions you feel at the mercy of, and the fears that seem to rule you, it can be difficult to embrace who you have become. Rather than acknowledging and validating why you behave, think, or feel the way you do, you probably find reasons to doubt the validity of your every move. In fact, you may, as I did, really hate yourself and treat yourself as unkindly as others do, wondering why you can't "just get over it" and attempting to force yourself to shed, evolve, or destroy the part of you that seems to have missed the message that the trauma has passed.

Not embracing all of who you are, including the things you don't like, deepens your internal disconnection, clouds your vision of desired change, and sets in place a precedent for splintering yourself. Even when you don't like something about who you are, it still maintains its right to be a relevant aspect of your whole self until you choose to change it. The more you resist embracing your flaws as easily as you do your strengths, the more you resist important parts of yourself and the more you slow down the healing process. It takes very little effort, energy, or focus to think, "I'm such an idiot. I am always afraid for no reason." It takes significantly more effort, energy, and focus to embrace who and how you are and say to yourself, "That's okay. I understand."

THE SOLUTION: GET TO KNOW YOURSELF AGAIN

Trauma changed you in significant ways and may have introduced you to the idea that you can't be counted on. Still, you possess many dependable qualities that are available at any time. Constructing your new self means knowing what those are, actively incorporating them into your daily experience, and developing a successful track record that allows you to depend on your ability to deliver. Give yourself a foundation for that process by following these steps:

Step One:

Crease four sheets of paper lengthwise into three columns. Label each individual page with one of the following categories: "Think," "Feel," "Believe," "Behave." Label the columns on each page "Positive Attribute," "I like this because . . .", and "The benefit is . . ."

In column one, list all the positive attributes you possess in the area of that page's category. For example, on the "Think" page in the "Positive Attributes" column, you might write *creative, solution oriented, kind to myself, conscious, clear, able to assess, focused,* and so forth.

In the "I like this because . . ." column, list why you like each attribute you've identified. For example, on the "Think" page you might write *I can trust myself to be aware, I support and love myself, I find answers to problems, I think through difficult things,* and so on.

In the "The benefit is . . ." column, jot down the benefits each attribute brings into your life. For example, on the "Think" page you might write *I feel protected, I feel respected, I feel safe, I feel like I have options,* and so forth.

Your page labeled "Think," then, might look something like this:

Positive Attributes	I like this because . . .	The benefit is . . .
Creative	I have original ideas	I feel like I have options
Solution oriented	I find answers to problems	I feel like I can take care of myself
Kind to myself	I support and love myself	I feel respected
Conscious	I am aware	I feel safe and protected
Clear	I can think straight	I stay in control in challenging situations
Able to assess	I can understand	I can make choices and take actions based on the big picture

Step Two

Following the same process above with fresh sheets of paper, ask friends, family members, and even colleagues to contribute their answers about your good qualities. (You may disagree with some of their answers. Regardless, allow yourself to hear the good that others witness in you, add them to the list, and then fill in your responses in the other columns.)

Step Three

Look over all the lists and notice which items mean the most to you. Use a highlighter to identify them. For each item, brainstorm ways you can more deeply embody it, bring it to the forefront of who you are, and further incorporate it in your life.

Step Four

For the next four weeks, choose one element to work with per week. Preferably, this will mean experimenting with each of the four categories over the course of one month. Every day do something that lets you be aware of or utilize the skill, trait, quality, or characteristic you've chosen to focus on.

Step Five

Now that you're warmed up, identify one element in each category that you can practice every day for the next thirty days. Alternatively, you can cycle through the elements, choosing a different one from each category each day. The aim is to develop daily habits in *each of the four categories.*

Step Six

Studies show that even the smallest, most simple reward can be enough (and sometimes even more powerful than a big reward) to help you stay motivated and focused on follow-through. Create a wish list of forty items to use as reward options for each day that you follow through on Step Five of this exercise. Offer yourself a range of rewards, from something as simple as giving yourself a hug to something as extravagant as a weekend getaway. Each day that you embody at least one element *in each of the four categories,* choose a reward from the list.

#10 The Problem: You've gone off track.

What is essential to developing a post-trauma identity is reconnection
across dimensions. This means reconnecting with the words to
make meaning of trauma, reconnecting with a viable self that can
live beyond survival. It means facing the feelings born of trauma. It
means bonding with others despite trauma. It means learning from
the past, living in the moment, and believing in the future.

—*Suzanne B. Phillips, PsyD*

Any of the preceding nine problems (or other scenarios you unexpectedly encounter) can create situations that cause your post-trauma identity discovery process to go off track. Sometimes you'll be immediately
aware of a negative shift; other times you may look back a week or month
later and recognize that you're going in another, less identity-evolving
direction. Once you recognize that you've gone astray, heading back in
the right direction takes a few swift and deliberate actions.

THE SOLUTION: BE AWARE AND PROACTIVE

Diligently managing your transformation helps you stay on track. As
you'll see in the following exercises, your own internal cues coupled with
your conscious and mindful knowledge are the keys to holding yourself on course and following through the full construction of your post-
trauma identity, plus life beyond.

Staying on Track During Identity Transformation

Your body and mind offer fantastic feedback mechanisms. If you feel
good about the work you're doing (even when the work feels uncomfortable), your body and mind will provide positive thoughts, emotions, and
physical sensations, letting you know that you believe in the value of the
work, the choices you're making, and the actions you're taking. If you
feel bad about any of those things (including the feeling that what you're

doing is utterly wrong for who and where you are in your process), then it's a clue you're off track; measures must be taken to put you back on a more appropriate and genuine course.

Remember, transformation always includes times when you feel worse than you'd like to feel; that's part of the transformation process. This doesn't indicate that your identity construction is off course. Instead, it indicates that you're dealing with significant material. At this time your self-care course may need to be better defined as you move through this naturally difficult process of acknowledgment.

The difference between knowing when your work is off track and perceiving that the work is uncomfortable is this: In an on-track process, any uncomfortable emotions and responses are fluid. You may feel down, but within a reasonable amount of time you find a way, either through your own actions or the support of others, to resiliently bring yourself back up. When you're off track, you continue in an uncontrollable, downward direction without interruption.

Pause, take a step back, reflect, assess. Remember that every bad behavior (even those that take you way off course) begins with a good intention. Often the motivating intention is to feel better, safer, or more in control. When you find yourself straying off course, pause, take a step back, reflect, assess, and ascertain what went wrong. Make some time to sit still and run the movie of your life backward in your head:

1. Starting from the moment you're in now, run the film backward to *just before* things went wrong.
2. Freeze that frame.
3. Play it slowly forward, looking for cues, clues, and details that represent how things began to go off track.
4. What did you do, not do, experience, feel, see, think, hear, or believe that interrupted your on-track flow?
5. What needs to be done today to correct those things and get you back on course? Who or what will help you do this?

Staying On Track After Your Transformation Has Been Achieved

Imagine you broke your leg and have worn a cast for a number of weeks. When the bone heals and the cast is removed, you won't expect to run a marathon the next weekend. You know that the recovery process will require extra time and that your muscles will need to reacclimate and limber up before you can trust yourself to comfortably stand, walk, jog, and run on that leg.

It's exactly the same scenario with healing from trauma and constructing your post-trauma identity. When you finally feel strong and free, your life will open up in a multitude of ways. Regardless of what wonderful things you experience, *your process has not ended.* During that upcoming first year, it will be important to keep yourself moving forward with well-paced, stable, and on-track purpose that continues to define and develop who you are. You will be faced with making new choices and taking definitive actions to restore your life and discover your new self-definition. Many of the challenges you faced in healing also exist in the world beyond. You may:

- experience a lack of control
- feel overwhelmed by possibilities
- encounter fear about how to inhabit your new self and who to be
- receive feedback from others who don't know how to relate to the new you
- stall or find yourself stuck and unable to move forward
- face an increase in self-criticism and doubt
- sense an urge to move too fast to make up for lost time
- notice that your actions and activities lack balance
- discover you don't know how to live in this new self and new life

Experiencing any of this doesn't mean you've lost the ground you gained. It simply means you're navigating a new and unfamiliar space that needs to be learned. When you recognize these or any other impediments to staying on track, receive them as messages to stop everything and do a full check-in. What needs to be done to strengthen who you are in this new moment? When you identify a problem and its origin:

- *Make appropriate choices.* As in your transformation, life afterward gains its strength from your conscious decisions. In every moment, assess what you want, why you want it, and how you will get it. Dedicate yourself to choices that are in alignment with your desires and values. The more you focus on choices that put you on track to getting what you want, the more on track you will remain. In this first phase of being your real, connected self, it may be wise to refrain from making huge decisions. Who you are will rapidly change and define itself over the next twelve months. Allowing yourself the freedom to observe those changes and decide which direction they will *later* lead will afford greater opportunity for your true self to evolve at the quickest and yet most natural pace.

- *Take proactive action.* You learned in trauma recovery that sitting around and waiting for change to magically occur brings zero results. The same goes for your life afterward. In order to have and be what you want, you will need to take many actions. Remember to chunk them down into the smallest achievable tasks so that you can build up to the larger success of keeping yourself on track.

- *Celebrate and savor your success.* Make a point of enjoying the moments of your large and small successes. Plan a special event with friends, do something nice for yourself, smile for one long moment. However it feels right to you, acknowledge and really allow yourself to soak in the feelings of what you accomplish. You deserve to feel proud of what you have achieved every single time. Indulging in these moments reinforces your beliefs, thoughts, ideas, and good feelings in ways that create more opportunities for you to continue in this direction.

The Take-Aways

In order to be connected with self, it is important to remain authentic and congruent, real and consistent, and to be grateful daily for what one is, has, and will be to self and others.

—*Mary Beth Williams, PhD*

You have been through difficult things. You have had to reach down inside of yourself, deeper than you've ever been, and find the strength, courage, and confidence to pull yourself out of trauma and its aftereffects into a place where hope, belief, choice, and action activate enormous changes in who you are, how you live, and how you engage, see, and experience yourself, others, and the world at large. This has been a tough journey. The road ahead, too, will contain pit stops, blind curves, and challenges that repeatedly ask, "How badly do you want to make these changes?" Every time you pick yourself back up from a fall, every time you pull yourself back on track, every time you commit—again—to your vision of what you desire for yourself and your life—in every moment that you make the choice to withstand the pressure and press full steam ahead—you restore another piece of yourself that trauma tried to strip away.

I'd like to tell you that when you finish your recovery work and have chiseled out a beautiful post-trauma identity, it will be smooth sailing for the rest of your life. Of course, you already know life is never that easy, nor does it offer guarantees. But here's the guarantee I will give you: The tools you master and the qualities you develop in the post-trauma identity and recovery processes will serve you for the rest of your life. Many of the things you do to heal have direct application outside the world of trauma. Your ability to define who you are, regulate your emotions, control and direct your stress response, choose how to connect with your past, decide how to engage with your present, imagine what you desire for your future—all of these activities form the basis of human life on this planet. After trauma you needed to relearn these skills; after recovery you will continue to use them with more force, acumen, focus, and success than ever before. While trauma may have made you feel *less than,* moving through and then out of recovery restores a transformative sense of *more than* fullness.

I'll share with you what my mother often told me when I struggled toward a much-wanted result: "You're doing just fine." Whenever I heard this from her, I had the feeling I was doing my best, and in every moment that's all I could ask of myself. That's all you can ask of yourself, too.

You hold within you the keys to the life you wish to lead and the person you most deeply want to be. Becoming that person is a process based on fully embracing the new self you have created, plus constructing a professional and personal life from the core self you have defined and continue to evaluate. Staying true to your vision of your best self and life will be your ultimate challenge every day. You have lost a significant amount of time. You can look back and lament that—and lose more time. Or, you can devote the rest of your life to making every moment part of your quest to live the life you were meant to be living as the person you most feel you want to be. Always remember: Your approach to and perspective of the life of your new self defines your experience. Develop those elements mindfully, creatively, and with a sense of well-earned fearlessness.

In every moment you have enormous healing potential. Your mission is learning to access it. Dig deep. You can do this. I believe in you!

Trauma Then and Now

On September 9, 2013, deep in the midst of writing this book, I was admitted to the emergency room of a hospital in West Palm Beach, Florida. I don't actually remember going to the hospital. For a few days I'd been experiencing flulike symptoms. In anticipation of a doctor's appointment, I had taken a shower that induced unstoppable shivering. My mother arrived to drive me to the appointment; I wrapped myself in scarves and heavy sweaters and headed out into the eighty-five-degree sunshine. The last thing I remember is getting into the car. In the next few minutes, my blood pressure dropped so low I had zero cognitive function.

When I came to in the emergency room, I was in a hospital gown, lying on a gurney hooked up to monitoring machines. Two IVs pumped copious amounts of fluid in an attempt to increase my blood pressure. When that didn't work, the doctor prescribed medication and the nurse tilted the gurney upside down, forcing more blood to reach my brain. When they asked, I knew my first name. I understood I was in the hospital, but that was all. I had no idea what day or month or year it was. I didn't know who the president was. When asked to describe what was happening in a picture on the nurse's cell phone, I could neither understand the scene nor find the words to express that. Mutely I looked at the nurse hoping he could divine what I was thinking: "Can't talk." When the neurologist visited for an ER assessment, I did the same, as I did when my physician tried to explain what they thought was happening: some kind of infection. Not only could I not respond; I couldn't follow a train of thought or understand simple English. My mother, father, and brother absorbed words and their implications while I lay on the gurney, fearful, powerless, and suddenly disconnected from the language and comprehension skills that had defined me throughout my childhood and professional career.

Over the next five tumultuous hours I was poked, prodded, tested, x-rayed, catheterized, examined, and CAT-scanned and had a port inserted in my right clavicle. All normal procedures for a team trying to discover how to treat me. All potentially triggering for a woman whose original trauma was a medical emergency in which a small infection turned into a possibly lethal allergy for which no doctor knew the cure. There was, however, one major difference between the mysterious illnesses of September 1981 and September 2013: In the interim I had done a lot of hard recovery work to sever the emotional weld of trauma, rewire my brain, and release myself from the past. I would have to depend on the solidity of those changes to help me through now.

By 2013, several years had passed since I had completed my trauma and PTSD recovery. In the beginning, I had often wondered what many survivors wonder: Will all the work stick? When symptoms leave, do they stay away? If another trauma occurs, will the aftereffects—or even PTSD—come back? I'd been in subsequent triggering situations and was relieved to find that not only did I remain calm and in control, but there were zero side effects afterward. None of those experiences, however, were as extreme as the one in which I was now involved.

I lay on the gurney in full survival mode. Without full cognitive function, I had zero control over my body or mind. My body spastically flailed around in a spontaneous effort to escape. Involuntarily I shouted, "No!" to every medical person who had the unfortunate job of coming near me. I struggled against every touch, every procedure, so that I had to be restrained by orderlies while doctors and nurses followed protocol to save me. It was determined that I was in septic shock, a seriously life-threatening condition. In response to the presence of a bacterial infection, the body produces an overwhelming immune response that releases chemicals which create enormous inflammation in the body, putting all of the body's major organs and systems at risk.

The biggest challenge for me came during a simple procedure for transferring me from the gurney to the CAT scan bed. By then my blood pressure had risen to a still very low but more stable number. I had regained enough of my cognitive faculties to have small and simple conversations. Things were seeming to calm down when I was wheeled into the CAT scan lab, where three orderlies wrapped me in a sheet and attempted to move me from gurney to the CAT scanner. This process triggered a visceral flashback to my original trauma and induced a panic attack that had me gulping for air. I screamed at the orderlies and begged them to stop the transfer. They stilled their actions when my mother came to stand by the gurney, saying to me repeatedly, "Michele! You're okay. It's two thousand thirteen. You're okay. Do your mantra." My father appeared on my other side, coaching, "Breathe, Michele. Breathe."

As they had been during my first trauma, my parents were instrumental during this one. As she had during a pivotal moment back in 1981, my mother locked eyes with me now and challenged me to reclaim control. Again, I did as she said. I went inside, focused my concentration, and searched for my strength, repeating, "I can do this" over and over.

This time around, I had more than a mantra and my parents to help me through: I had all the knowledge contained in Chapter 2 of this book. While I lay on the gurney with my body convulsing, a part of me separated from the situation and observed. This calm, informed self reminded me about the power of the breath and how it can reset your physiology in two minutes of measured breathing. It reminded me about the ninety-second rule and how your mind can change your emotions through a process of redirecting attention. It also reminded me about how many neural pathways I had worked so hard to rewire for calm and how they were available to me in that moment. I could engage all of these things, this self counseled, in a response to override my body's survival mode.

I took a deep breath. "Give me two minutes," I told the orderlies. "I can do this."

Silently and quizzically they stepped away from the gurney. Leaning back against the wall in the dimly lit CAT scan room, they exchanged looks with each other and the technicians behind the window in the lab. I closed my eyes, focused on my breath, repeated my mantra, and visualized my body relaxing from the tense cords of my neck all the way down to my scrunched-up toes. I visualized this stronger self beside me. I focused on the center of my chest, where I imagined that all my courage was stored. Little by little I felt my body settle as I reclaimed control. It took five minutes, and then I opened my eyes and with a quiet tranquility announced, "I'm ready." Easily and without incident, I was wrapped in the sheet and transferred to the CAT scanner.

In all, I was in the ICU for four days and the hospital for another four after that. On the exact date I had been released from the hospital in 1981, I was released in 2013, and went home to begin the process of healing from major trauma, again. By then I had regained my memory of our political leader, plus other little details that go with daily life. Still, I faced a slow recovery. My brain had suffered a serious trauma from the lack of blood flow. I had trouble with language. I couldn't remember basic words and couldn't follow the flow of ideas in a conversation. My brain would go blank as I waited for the next word in the sentence I was trying to construct, or I would completely forget what I was saying midparagraph. I couldn't read. When I tried to look at a page, my mind simply could not focus, synthesize, or understand the letters. I couldn't remember all the science about trauma I had worked so hard to understand, or even the keynote speech I had given many times and was scheduled to give again one month later. The specialists we consulted assured me my full brain function would be regained, but it would take patience.

Healing from trauma the second time around was dramatically different from the first time. Whereas in 1981 I had felt frightened, fearful, lost, confused, and disconnected, in 2013 I felt confident, calm, connected, and self-directed. Yes, there were moments and ideas that caused me pause. Healing from trauma isn't supposed to stop us from thinking, feeling, responding, and reflecting. We are human; we can and should always take note of experience and its meaning. The benefit of a successful recovery and the strengths it develops is that we engage those processes more quickly and healthily the next time we need them. For example: I came to the realization that if I had attempted to drive myself to the doctor on September 9—and lost cognition as I did—I could have killed someone else on the road, and most definitely myself, as the crash would have prevented me from getting the immediate medical attention I needed. In 1981, such a thought would have sent me into a downward dark spiral for days. In 2013, sitting in a hospital room letting the feelings come over me, I acknowledged the disturbing thought, observed it, and let it go along the flow of all the other thoughts I had that day. My overwhelming emotion was one of elation: I had survived! I almost felt giddy.

As a preventive measure, I literally went from the hospital to my hypnotherapist's office. Since she was the practitioner who had most helped me overcome PTSD, I called on her to jump-start the process of healing this new trauma by helping me release and clear what I had experienced so that both my body and mind would be given the chance to let go of the traumatic energy as quickly as possible. With her help and the other tools I'd developed, I smoothly transitioned out of trauma and into healing mode. Except for a few nightmares in the hospital, I experienced zero side effects from this extremely traumatic experience.

It took six full months for me to truly feel like myself. Within one month I could both read and write, although it would take more time for me to do this with the fluidity and speed I was used to. Within four months I could speak without pausing to reach for words or losing the purpose of a conversation. By six months after the incident, my full brain power and energy had been restored. As I look back on it all now, I see the answers to many questions that I and other survivors face:

- How does trauma change us?
- Can those changes be reversed?
- What do we learn from trauma and recovery?
- How do we use what we learn in our daily lives?
- Is what we learn available to us in later traumatic situations?
- Is it possible to be stronger after healing from trauma?
- Can we survive other traumas more effectively and efficiently?

The overall answer is yes, trauma changes us, and many times, given the opportunity, we have the potential to change again, even for the better.

We look at trauma as a bad thing, which it is. Still, while we would never choose to experience it, there are good things that come out of our tragedies. Trauma can make us stronger, even more able to survive because of what it teaches us about survival. It can develop in us more clarity and efficacy in facing life's challenges because it teaches us things about ourselves we might otherwise never have discovered. I love knowing that while in 1981 I lay completely passive in the hospital bed, in 2013 I was swinging and shouting to protect myself. I love knowing that while in 1981 I gave in to trauma and let it warp my mind, in 2013 I quickly claimed control and guided myself to safety, both during the trauma and afterward. We don't always have such clear-cut or sensational comparisons, and we don't need to. Noticing the small instances of how you've grown—how you make more deliberate choices, take more empowered actions, and consciously apply what you've learned—will let you see where you have succeeded, where you can improve, and how you can use your traumatic experiences to develop an even more life-affirming, life-choosing, and life-desiring approach to your world.

There will always be questions about who you are, could be, and will be. Whether you have future traumas or not, you absolutely can use the past to strengthen your present and propel you into the future with a sense of calm, confidence, and control. Achieving those things will be challenging, as it should be. If it were easy, you wouldn't learn half as much or gain an iota of the strength that will serve you so well in the future. Nor would you gain the ultimate gift of trauma and recovery: discovering how much you can depend on yourself to activate your full power and become the whole You you can be.

Suggested Resources

SUGGESTED READING

The following pages list books that have either been meaningful to me in my own recovery or that I respect as a healing professional. Because there are so many terrific books in the trauma sphere this is not intended to be an exhaustive list. Rather, it's a jumping off point to starting your own list and introducing you to perspectives, stories, ideas and philosophies that might support your transformation process.

LEARNING THE FACTS ABOUT TRAUMA

Herman, Judith. *Trauma and Recovery: The Aftermath of Violence – from Domestic Abuse to Political Terror.* New York: Basic Books, Reprint edition. 1997.

Karr-Morse, Robin. *Scared Sick: The Role of Childhood Trauma in Adult Disease.* New York: Basic Books, 2012.

Naparstek, Bellaruth and Robert Scaer. *Invisible Heroes: Survivors of Trauma and How They Heal.* New York: Bantam, 2005.

Porges, Stephen W. *The Polyvagal Theory: Neurophysiological Foundations of Emotions, Attachment, Communication, and Self-Regulation.* New York: W. W. Norton, 2011.

Rothschild, Babette. *The Body Remembers: The Psychophysiology of Trauma and Trauma Treatment.* New York: W. W. Norton, 2000.

Scaer, Robert. *8 Keys to Brain-Body Balance.* New York: W. W. Norton, 2012.

Scaer, Robert. *The Body Bears the Burden: Trauma, Dissociation, and Disease.* New York: Routledge, 2014.

Scaer, Robert. *The Trauma Spectrum: Hidden Wounds and Human Resiliency.* New York: W. W. Norton, 2005.

HEALING FROM TRAUMA

Amen, Daniel. *Change Your Brain, Change Your Life: The Breakthrough Program for Conquering Anxiety, Depression, Obsessiveness, Anger, and Impulsiveness.* Goshen: Harmony, 1999.

Bass, Ellen and Laura Davis. *The Courage to Heal – Third Edition – Revised and Expanded: A Guide for Women Survivors of Child Sexual Abuse.* New York: Collins Living, 1994.

Brown, Richard P. and Patricia L. Gerbarg. *The Healing Power of the Breath: Simple Techniques to Reduce Stress and Anxiety, Enhance Concentration, and Balance Your Emotions.* Boston: Shambhala, 2012

Cori, Jasmin Lee. *Healing from Trauma: A Survivor's Guide to Understanding Your Symptoms and Reclaiming Your Life.* Jackson: Da Capo Press, 2008.

Doidge, Norman E. *The Brain That Changes Itself.* New York: Penguin Books, 2007.

Hanson, Rick. *Buddha's Brain: The Practical Neuroscience of Happiness, Love, and Wisdom.* Oakland: New Harbinger Publications, 2009.

Hanson, Rick. *Hardwiring Happiness: The New Brain Science of Contentment, Calm, and Confidence.* Goshen: Harmony, 2013.

Lemle Beckner, Victoria and John B. Arden. *Conquering Post Traumatic Stress Disorder: The Newest Techniques for Overcoming Symptoms, Regaining Hope, and Getting Your Life Back.* Minneapolis: Fair Winds Press, 2008.

Levine, Peter A. *In an Unspoken Voice: How the Body Releases Trauma and Restores Goodness.* Berkeley: North Atlantic Books, 2010.

Levine, Peter A. *Waking the Tiger: Healing Trauma.* Berkeley: North Atlantic Books, 1997.

Rosenbloom, Dena and Mary Beth Williams. *Life After Trauma, Second Edition: A Workbook for Healing.* New York: The Guilford Press, 2010.

Rothschild, Babette. *8 Keys to Safe Trauma Recovery: Take-Charge Strategies to Empower Your Healing.* New York: W. W. Norton, 2010.

Salzer, Alicia. *Back to Life.* New York: William Morrow, 2005.

Schiraldi, Glenn. *The Post-Traumatic Stress Disorder Sourcebook: A Guide to Healing, Recovery and Growth.* New York: McGraw-Hill, 2009.

Shapiro, Francine. *Getting Past Your Past: Take Control of Your Life With Self-Help Techniques From EMDR Therapy.* New York: Rodale, 2013.

Siegel, Bernie S. and Cynthia J. Hurn. *The Art of Healing: Uncovering Your Inner Wisdom and Potential for Self-Healing.* Novato: New World Library, 2013.

Siegel, Daniel J. *Mindsight: The New Science of Personal Transformation.* New York: Bantam, 2010.

Wehrenberg, Margaret. *The 10 Best Ever Anxiety Management Techniques.* New York: W. W. Norton, 2008.

Williams, Mary Beth and Soili Poijula. *The PTSD Workbook: Simple, Effective Techniques for Overcoming Traumatic Stress Symptoms.* Oakland: New Harbinger Publications, Second Edition, 2013.

CREATING YOUR NEW LIFE

Beck, Martha. *Finding Your Way in a Wild New World: Reclaim Your True Nature to Create the Life You Want.* New York: Atria, Second Edition, 2013.

Canfield, Jack and Janet Switzer. *The Success Principles: How to Get from Where You Are to Where You Want to Be.* New York: William Morrow Paperbacks, 2006.

Day, Laura. *Welcome to Your Crisis: How to Use the Power of Crisis to Create the Life You Want.* New York: Little Brown and Company, 2007.

Dyer, Wayne W. *Excuses Begone!* Carlsbad: Hay House, 2011.

Dyer, Wayne W. *The Power of Intention: Learning to Co-Create Your World Your Way.* Carlsbad: Hay House, 2005.

Hay, Louise and Cheryl Richardson. *You Can Create An Exceptional Life.* Carlsbad: Hay House, 2013.

Myss, Caroline. *Sacred Contracts: Awakening Your Divine Potential.* Goshen: Harmony, 2003.

Tolle, Eckhart. *The Power of Now.* Novato: New World Library, 1st Edition, 2004.

SURVIVORS' HEALING STORIES

Hingson, Michael (with Susy Flory). *Thunder Dog: The True Story of A Blind Man, His Guide Dog and the Triumph of Trust.* New York: Thomas Nelson, 2011.

Nakazawa, Donna. *The Last Best Cure: My Quest to Awaken the Healing Part of My Brain and Get Back My Body, My Joy, and My Life.* New York: Hudson Street Press, 2013.

Otis, Carré and Hugo Schwyzer. *Beauty, Disrupted.* New York: It Books, 2012.

Rosenthal, Michele. *Before the World Intruded: Conquering the Past and Creating the Future.* Palm Beach Gardens: Your Life After Trauma, 2012.

Ross, Tracy. *The Source of All Things.* New York: Free Press, 2011.

Salamone, Nancy. *Nancy's Story: A Victory Over Violence.* [Kindle only.]

Sanford, Matthew. *Waking: A Memoir of Trauma and Transcendence.* New York: Rodale, 2008.

Venable Raine, Nancy. *After Silence: Rape and My Journey Back.* New York: Broadway Books, 1999.

Warner, Priscilla. *Learning to Breathe: My Yearlong Quest to Bring Calm to My Life.* New York: Atria, Second Edition, 2012.

BOOKS SUGGESTED BY SURVIVORS

I asked my radio audience and blog readers what their favorite healing books are. These are the titles they recommend:

Bersell, Michelle. *F.E.E.L.: Feel Every Emotion as Love.* Living Source, 2012.

Brach, Tara. *Radical Acceptance: Embracing Your Life With the Heart of a Buddha.* New York: Bantam, 2004.

Brach, Tara. *True Refuge: Finding Peace and Freedom in Your Own Awakened Heart.* New York: Bantam, 2013.

Bradshaw, John. *Healing the Shame That Binds You.* Deerfield Beach: HCI, 2005.

Bradshaw, John. *Homecoming: Reclaiming and Championing Your Inner Child.* New York: Bantam, 1992.

Chodron, Pema. *When Things Fall Apart: Heart Advice for Difficult Times.* Boston: Shambhala, 2000.

Cohen, Barry M., Esther Giller, and Lynn W. (eds.). *Multiple Personality Disorder From the Inside Out.* Brooklandville: Sidran Press, 1991.

Crisman, William H. *The Opposite of Everything Is True: Reflections on Denial in Alcoholic Families.* New York: William Morrow & Co., 1991.

Emerson, David and Elizabeth Hopper. *Overcoming Trauma Through Yoga: Reclaiming Your Body.* Berkeley: North Atlantic Books, 2011.

Frankl, Viktor. *Man's Search for Meaning.* Boston: Beacon Press, 2006.

Hay, Louise. *You Can Heal Your Life.* Carlsbad: Hay House, 1984.

Hiatt, Juanima. *The Invisible Storm.* CreateSpace Independent Publishing Platform, 2012.

Kabat-Zinn, Jon. *Full Catastrophe Living: Using the Wisdom of Your Body and Mind to Face Stress, Pain, and Illness.* New York: Bantam, Rev Upd Edition, 2013.

Lee, Deborah (with Sophie James). *The Compassionate-Mind Guide to Recovering from Trauma and PTSD: Using Compassion-Focused Therapy to Overcome Flashbacks, Shame, Guilt, and Fear.* Oakland: New Harbinger Publications, 2013.

Lew, Mike, and Richard Hoffman. *Leaping Upon the Mountains: Men Proclaiming Victory Over Sexual Child Abuse.* Berkeley: North Atlantic Books, 2000.

Matsakis, Aphrodite. *I Can't Get Over It: A Handbook for Trauma Survivors.* Oakland: New Harbinger Publications; 2 edition, 1996.

McLaren, Karla. *Language of Emotions: What Your Feelings Are Trying to Tell You.* Louisville: Sounds True, Inc., 2010.

Mines, Stephanie. *We Are All In Shock: How Overwhelming Experiences Shatter You . . . And What You Can Do About It.* Pompton Plains: New Page Books, 2003.

O'Conner, Richard. *Undoing Depression: What Therapy Doesn't Teach You and*

Medication Can't Give You. New York: Little Brown and Company; 1ˢᵗ Edition, 2010.

Peck, M. Scott. *The Road Less Traveled: A New Psychology of Love, Traditional Values and Spiritual Growth.* New York: Touchstone, 1988.

Pelzer, Dave. *Help Yourself: Finding Hope, Courage, and Happiness.* New York: Plume Books; 1ˢᵗ Edition, 2001.

Pressfield, Steven. *The War of Art: Break Through the Blocks and Win Your Inner Creative Battles.* Black Irish Entertainment, LLC, 2012.

Rinpoche, Yongey Mingyur. *The Joy of Living: Unlocking the Secret and Science of Happiness.* Goshen: Harmony; Reprint Edition, 2008.

Salmansohn, Karen. *The Bounce Back Book: How to Thrive in the Face of Adversity, Setbacks, and Losses.* New York: Workman Publishing Company; 1ˢᵗ edition, 2008.

Schiffmann, Erich. *Yoga: The Spirit and Practice of Moving Into Stillness.* New York: Pocket Books; 1ˢᵗ edition, 1996.

Singer, Michael A. *The Untethered Soul: The Journey Beyond Yourself.* Oakland: New Harbinger Publications/Noetic Books; 1ˢᵗ edition, 2007.

Terkeurst, Laura. *Unglued: Making Wise Choices in the Midst of Raw Emotions.* New York: Zondervan, 2012.

Thurman, Robert. *Freeing the Body, Freeing the Mind: Writings on the Connections Between Yoga and Buddhism.* Boston: Shambhala, 2010.

Walker, Pete. *Complex PTSD: From Surviving to Thriving: A Guide and Map for Recovering From Childhood Trauma.* CreateSpace Independent Publishing Platform, 2013.

Walker, Pete. *The Tao of Fully Feeling: Harvesting Forgiveness out of Blame.* Lafayette: Azure Coyote Publishing, 1995.

Williams, Mark. *The Mindful Way Through Depression: Freeing Yourself From Chronic Unhappiness.* New York: The Guilford Press, 2007.

EXPERT INTERVIEWS

On my radio show, originally called, *Your Life After Trauma,* I have interviewed many of the experts and some of the survivors mentioned throughout this book and on the suggested reading list. The complimentary archives and podcasts are available on my website: ChangeYouChoose.com/archives. Interviews that may interest you include:

Beck, Martha. *Releasing the Past Through Engaging in the Present.*
Berceli, David. *Tension and Trauma Releasing Exercises.*
Emerson, David and Elizabeth Hopper. *PTSD and Yoga: Ideas for Success.*
Gerbarg, Patricia. *Using Your Breath to Heal.*

Hanson, Rick. *Hardwiring Happiness*.

Hill, Andrew. *The Healing Power of Neuroscience*.

Hingson, Michael. *Surviving 9/11: A Blind Man and His Guide Dog*.

Karr-Morse, Robin. *Childhood Trauma and Adult Disease*.

Levine, Peter. *How the Body Holds Trauma*.

Naparstek, Belleruth. *How We Heal*.

Ross, Tracy. *How to Find Words After Trauma*.

Rothschild, Babette. *Hope for Trauma Recovery*.

Sanford, Matthew. *Trauma, Identity and the Mind/Body Connection*.

Scaer, Robert. *8 Keys to Brain-Body Balance*.

Siegel, Bernie. *The Art of Healing*.

Siegel, Dan. *Integration in Trauma Recovery*.

Siegel, Ron. *An Introduction to Mindfulness*.

Shapiro, Francine. *How to Overcome Fear + EMDR Therapy*.

Warner, Priscilla. *How To Find Your Healing Path*.

Williams, Mary Beth and Dena Rosenbloom. *How to Apply Coping Techniques that Work*.

Wehrenberg, Margaret. *Wrangling Anxiety: How To Tips You Can Use Today*.

Yehuda, Rachel. *How Trauma Affects the Brain*.

ADDITIONAL RESOURCES

When you're focused on dealing with symptoms and striving toward transformation, it can be hard to take time out to develop recorded programs and worksheets to support your interaction with the exercises in this book. I completely understand that. I remember being too physically tired, mentally exhausted, and emotionally spent to have to work on the smaller, administrative details of recovery.

To make things as fluid as possible, I've developed some free resources for you. Simply visit **YourLifeAfterTraumaBook.com** to download support materials, including MP3s for some of the imagery exercises plus PDF files for collecting data, carrying out self-assessments, and completing other processes.

A QUICK GUIDE TO TWENTY STRESS REDUCTION PRACTICES

When you're on the go and dealing with unexpected stimuli, you don't always have time to take a comprehensive inventory of the techniques available to help you maintain balance and control. This list, culled from everything you learned in these chapters, gives you a cheat sheet for those moments you need some internal support but can't remember what to do. Tear out the sheet, laminate it, and carry it with you for specific direction anytime, anywhere.

1. **Change Your Physiology in Two Minutes**: Inhale through your nose; exhale through your lips as if they were wrapped around a straw.
2. **Breathwork**: Inhale (4 counts) + hold (4 counts) + exhale (6 counts) + hold (2 counts). Repeat cycle eight to ten times.
3. **Naturally Produce Oxytocin**: Give yourself a long, comforting hug (try for two minutes).
4. **Ninety-Second Rule**: The chemicals connected to any emotion naturally subside in ninety seconds *if you shift your attention to a different thought.* Count to ninety, sing, imagine your most favorite place, laugh, call a friend, or do any other activity that distracts your focus and allows your mind's chemicals to reset.
5. **Interrupt Negative Responses**: Follow these five steps: (1) Pause. (2) Step back. (3) Ask (empowering questions). (4) Assess (your choices). (5) Act (on a decision).
6. **Relabel and Redirect**: Observe, identify, and name your behavior or response; engage in a replacement activity.
7. **Meditation**: Choose any of the options to train your brain: focused attention, open monitoring, automatic self-transcending.
8. **Mindfulness**: Remember to be present, acknowledge and allow what you feel and experience, and suspend judgment.
9. **Take in the Good**: Consciously experience a good feeling by absorbing it into your body and letting it expand for twenty to thirty seconds.
10. **Practice Gratitude**: Seek things to be grateful for; take a moment to reflect on and embrace the feeling of gratitude and what about you allows you to connect with it.
11. **Wheel of Awareness**: Imagine yourself as the peaceful hub of a wheel while the spokes attend to your thoughts and feelings.
12. **Power Position**: Sit on the edge of your seat, feet a foot apart, palms down on your thighs, hips rolled forward, shoulders back and down.
13. **Progressive Relaxation**: Starting with the top of your head, focus your attention on each body part, deliberately relaxing it as you move down to your toes.
14. **Refocus Your Intention**: Fill in the blanks with what you want, why it's important to you, and what you will gain by having it: "I want _____ because _____ so that _____."
15. **Shift to "I Can Handle It!" Thinking**: Replace fear by giving yourself three reasons you will be able to handle approaching the thing you're afraid of.
16. **Fact-Versus-Fiction Thinking**: Ask yourself the following questions: *How true is this thought? How do I know it's true (what's the proof)? Would everyone else believe this is true? What are other possible interpretations of this moment?*
17. **Clarify Your Thinking**: Dismantle assumptions, interpretations, limiting beliefs, and the negative commentary of your inner voice by identifying how to be present in the moment and find alternative details, narratives, and responses that lead to empowered actions.
18. **Slow Down**: Find a way to reduce the speed of your thoughts, emotions, reactions, and physical actions.
19. **Recalibrate Balance**: Identify where you're skewing more one way than another and choose an action to create a new balance in your experience.
20. **The Sedona Method**: Become very present with the uncomfortable feeling. Ask yourself: (1) *Can I welcome this feeling as best I can?* (2) *Could I let this feeling go?* (3) *Would I let this feeling go?* (4) *When?* When you feel ready, answer, "Now". Repeat the sequence until you feel completely emptied of the feeling.

APPENDIX B

SELF-COACHING PRACTICES CHEAT SHEET

Over years of work with many clients, I've distilled an effective self-coaching process down to a ten-step cheat sheet you can use anywhere, anytime, any day to shift yourself out of feeling stuck and into a fluid plan that moves you forward.

When you feel anxious, sad, depressed, frustrated, or anything else uncomfortable, get yourself focused and back on track by following this process:

1. Identify the problem.
2. Explore the problem's impact on your life (become very clear on the issues it creates).
3. Define what life would look like if the problem were resolved.
4. Examine why resolving this problem is important.
5. Pinpoint what needs to be done to resolve the problem.
6. Break down the resolution into small, manageable tasks or steps.
7. Set up a sequence and strategy for how the steps will be taken (and who might help).
8. Commit to a timeline.
9. Develop a plan for accountability.
10. Check in with yourself about progress, challenges, and successes.

While you're working through these steps, ask yourself empowering questions (i.e., questions that are open-ended, meaning you can't simply answer yes or no). Begin questions with words like:

- when (e.g., When can I take this step?)
- how (e.g., How will I get this done?)
- what (e.g., In what way is this problem impacting my life?)
- who (e.g., Who can help me with this?)
- where (e.g., Where do I want to focus my actions?)
- why (be careful with this one; why isn't always useful unless it's applied to your desire for something in the future)

Avoid questions that begin with *do, can, will, could,* or *might.*

Index